Know That You Are Lucky

Know That You Are Lucky

a memoir by **KATHAN BROWN**

CROWN POINT PRESS
SAN FRANCISCO, CA

Editor: Judith Dunham
Designer: Laura Lovett / By Design
Production: Sasha Baguskas / Crown Point Press
Front-matter photography: Laurie Frankel

Printed in China through Colorcraft Ltd, Hong Kong

Distributed by: Small Press Distribution
1341 Seventh Street
Berkeley, CA 94710

Available from: www.crownpoint.com or www.amazon.com

TABLE OF CONTENTS

Vienna in the winter of 1956.

1.

INTRODUCTION

HOLD ON LIGHTLY

I spent most of the summer of 1956 in a painting class in the town of Salzburg, Austria. Our teacher was the great, but aging, expressionist painter Oskar Kokoschka. For the fall/winter term, I went on to London to study at the Central School of Arts and Crafts.

That was the year of Hungary's heroic revolt against the Soviets; we in the West watched newsreels of tanks plowing into unarmed crowds. The Central School's Christmas holiday occurred as refugees poured into Austria, and I responded to a plea from a friend and took the train to Vienna, which was cold and bleak. Exhausted, nearly silent people moved from a long line into a crowded room where I and other volunteers fit them with warm clothes that had been airfreighted from the United States. The clothes were donated by Americans eager to do what they could. Now, whenever I see a hard candy with the wrapper twisted at both ends, my mind's eye pulls up two overlapping memories.

Kokoschka, when he especially liked something about a student's work, would hand the painter a candy, individually wrapped, the ends twisted. This happened rarely enough that it caused the recipient great joy. In Vienna, later, I saw a similar joy, slow spreading and tinged with disbelief, on the face of a boy of eleven or twelve when he reached into the pocket of a coat and pulled out a handful of candies in paper wrappers with twisted ends. The boy was shivering and clinging to his father, with whom, I was told, he had crossed over the border through gunfire. Those two memories symbolically interlock the art world and the real world for me, sweet and sharp. The year 1956 set the

Markus Raetz, *Flourish*, 2001.
Photogravure printed in black
and red on gampi paper chine
collé, 21½ × 18¼ inches.

course for the rest of my life. After my experiences in Austria, I went back to art school in London and became engaged with the hands-on, time-consuming processes of making and printing etchings.

The etching illustrated here (you will find it in color in plate 1) is titled *Flourish;* it is by Markus Raetz, an artist who lives in Berne, Switzerland. Raetz has created a shadow of a hand holding a little swirling shape lightly, with confidence and style. Raetz, who is primarily a sculptor, was born in 1941 in a small town near Berne. He worked as an assistant to a local artist during school vacations, took teacher training, and as a young man was a high school teacher. He had very little formal art education, but he knew, he says, from the age of ten that he would be an artist. "My father liked to draw. He saw that maybe I would do something he had wanted to do." In 2012 Markus Raetz is Switzerland's primary living artist; he has had exhibitions in many of the world's leading museums, and in 1988 he represented Switzerland in the Venice Bienniale.

Flourish is one of five etchings Markus made in a two-week period working hands-on with printers at Crown Point Press, my small business in San Francisco. When he walked into our studio on September 24, 2001, the first thing he asked for was some wire. He twisted an odd shape. Then he asked if we could find a copy of Laurence Sterne's 1759 novel, *Tristram Shandy*. We got the book and found the image in it. *Shandy* is an old word meaning "half-crazy," and *Tristram Shandy* is full of fragments of language and other anomalies, including a few blank pages and a few odd drawings; the book has influenced many modern writers, including James Joyce. The drawing in it that Markus copied in wire illustrates the arc of a walking stick and is next to these words: "'Whilst a man is free!' cried the corporal, giving a flourish with his stick thus. ... My uncle Toby looked earnestly towards his cottage and his bowling green."

Markus had flown to San Francisco from the East Coast a few days after September 11, 2001. When the twin towers went down, he had been in Amherst installing an exhibition; he shared the shock we all felt. Reading *Tristram Shandy* in our studio, the printers and I thought the twisted-wire shape was about *our* freedom—our cottages and our bowling greens—and I still hold that feeling in my mind. But in the end, events that influence the making of a work of art don't have much effect on how people see it. I have

been lucky enough to be in on the beginning of many artworks, to see them being made, and then to see their meanings grow and change. Markus's *Flourish* holds a tenuous balance, a balance of the sort I would like to maintain as I, myself, move through time.

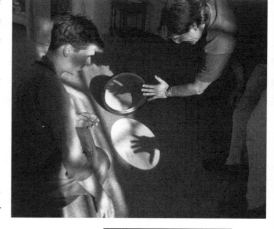

In illustrations on these pages, you can see Markus turning the wire shape into an etching. He begins by doing tests, recording the shadow of his hand in a light-sensitive ground. Next, he is sitting under a skylight with a flat copper plate in front of

Markus (right) with printer Lothar Osterburg.

him. The plate, under protective cardboard, is coated with light-sensitive material. Markus holds the twisted wire and moves his hand under the light to find the right shadow pattern. He settles on what he wants.

The printer removes a protective cover from the plate. Markus must hold completely still for several seconds while sunlight coming through the

Marcus exposing the
photogravure plate
to the sun.

skylight closes the ground around the shadow of his hand. This is the crux
of it, the body of the work. It is precisely timed. The artist is not guessing.
Because of the tests he has done, he knows, or thinks he knows, where he is
going. He concentrates. Nothing can disturb him. He is seeing only the work
in front of him.

The timer bell rings, Markus shakes out his hand, and a printer carries the plate into another room, where tools, materials, and trays of liquids
wait. Markus follows. Now, he needs help. He has come to something unfamiliar, indeterminate; he is not sure how to do it, and he can't do it alone.
But he is not turning his project over to someone else. He and the printers
work together until they reach a stasis. Then Markus begins adjustments. He
makes unambiguous judgments. Print the piece of wire, the flourish, in red.
No, a darker red. Can we get rid of that little smudge? He is fine-tuning now.

Unexpectedly, he is finished. Like a newborn, the art is slinging its arms
and legs about—the artist-maker is conscious of its gawkiness. But he beams a
shy smile; he loves it. It is a living thing: it will grow as it is exposed to people's
perceptions of it. His enjoyment of the moment is clear.

The title of this book is about luck; its themes are art and business. I
am going to tell you true stories about those subjects and other aspects of
life. I'll also give you concrete information about my particular small art business, Crown Point Press, which passed the fifty-year mark in 2012. For half a
century, as the world has been remaking itself, my co-workers and I have been
engaged in a simple, basic activity: printing by hand and publishing in limited editions what are called "original" or "fine art" prints—terms most easily

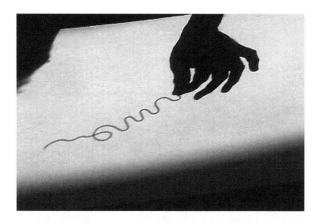

explained by saying they do not mean reproductive prints. Just as an identical twin is not a copy of his brother, the prints in a fine art edition are not copies of one another. They all come from the same matrix, which, at Crown Point Press, is usually a copper plate holding an image created by an artist working in our studio using the old, slow process of etching.

I am going to talk about creativity; the subtitles of my chapters are lessons I've learned from some of the most creative people on earth. In gathering my memories around lessons learned from artists, I'm creating an artifice that, I hope, lets me organize looking backward into a way of looking forward. All the way along, one way or another, I know that I've been lucky. Here's what happened.

Clarissa Bradford Brown, circa 1937.

2.

THE FAMILY STORY

GO AS FAR AS YOU CAN SEE

"Go as far as you can see. When you get there, you can see further" was a saying of my mother's. She was born in 1908. Her father, a small-town banker, had one of the first Model Ts, and she and her sisters drove it by themselves one day, overturned it into a field, righted it with the help of a farmer and his horse, and returned it without their parents ever discovering the adventure.

My mother's address in boarding school, she often laughed, was Clarissa Bradford, Bradford Academy, Bradford, Massachusetts. When the crash of 1929 came, she was enrolled at the Chicago Art Institute. In 1930, with no more money from home, she went to New York.

After spending her last dime defiantly on coffee and pie, and wondering where she would sleep that night, she walked into a settlement house, where she was given room and board in exchange for working with the neighborhood kids. She was still there and the world was still stuck in the Great Depression four years later when she met my father, Elwood Stanley Brown, called Stanley. He had dropped out of boarding school at Phillips Exeter and had no possibility of going to college. When he met my mother, he had a job as a stock clerk, but he thought of himself as a photographer. He took this picture of her on a New Year's Eve sometime after I was born, in 1935, in New York City.

Our family moved to Daytona Beach, Florida, when I was five years old. The portrait on the next page is of my father's mother, Louise Powis Young. The photo is stamped on the back "Your Portrait Studio," my father's business, and since it is tinted and undated, I may have done the tinting; over the years,

Louise Powis Brown Young, circa 1945.

I think from the time I was eight or nine, I helped my father by painting transparent colors onto studio photos. We had a darkroom in the house, and as I got older my father taught me to develop film and to make photographs—how to print them and how to frame them in the camera.

My father could hardly see without his glasses, so he couldn't join the army when World War Two began. Instead, he concentrated on his photography business. What money he made came mostly from shooting weddings. Our house always had art hanging in it, photos by my father, watercolors by my mother, and children's art by my brother and me. Out back, we had another little building where my mother had a nursery school; I came home after school to help. Often a child or two would stay nights and weekends with us.

When I was sixteen I got a Saturday job as a clerk in the town dime store. My brother, in his teenage years, spent his weekends in our driveway underneath cars he fixed for word-of-mouth customers. Everyone in the family worked what seemed to be all the time, but there was no regular income. We would begin each meal with the food in serving dishes. Once you put something on your plate, you'd have to eat it. Anything left on the serving plates appeared at the next meal, or in soup. I still often make soup, and cleaning my plate at every meal is a habit I cannot shake.

Daytona Beach was about an hour's drive down the coast from the unincorporated area where my grandmother and her husband, Owen D. Young, lived. Louise Powis Brown Young had married her first husband, Elwood S. Brown, my grandfather, when she was twenty-three and moved with him to Manila, the Philippines, where he was "physical director" of the YMCA. She admired the embroidery the women there did and designed some embroidered silk lingerie that local people made for her. Her mother took samples to department stores in New York, and Louise's small business began. She developed a workroom/factory and purchased the silk in China.

On a slow boat to China, my grandmother met Owen D. Young, who at the time was chief counsel to the General Electric Company; he was later the company's chairman. Mr. Young was a confidant of at least two presidents, was sent to negotiate European treaties on behalf of the United States on two occasions, and was frequently in the news in the 1920s. He and Louise corresponded for years, and met occasionally in Asia or New York.

My grandmother's lingerie business made her a millionaire by the time she was thirty-five in 1922. That year her husband addressed the International Olympic Committee for the third time, advocating "regional games," an idea he called "play for all." His work in organizing games around the world led to the inclusion in the Olympic Games of some nations, especially Asian ones, that would not have been there otherwise. Elwood S. Brown died of a heart attack in 1924, and Louise moved with her two teenage children to New York, where she set up a showroom featuring Chinese rugs, Philippine embroidery, and hand-built furniture, much of which she had designed. The enterprise didn't survive the Depression.

In 1937 (I was two years old), my grandmother married Owen D. Young, whose wife had recently died. He retained his family home in Van Hornesville, New York, where his children also owned (second) homes, and bought for Louise a parcel of Florida scrubland once owned by a family named Washington. They called the property Washington Oaks and constructed a modest rustic house—you had to walk outside, along an open veranda, to

Grandmother Louise's factory in the Philippines.

get to the bedrooms. They lived with no electricity until—after a visit from a
General Electric colleague—the Florida electric grid was extended to reach
that portion of the coast. The property became a state park after both Owen
and Louise died, and, as I write, it is in danger of being closed, along with
many other parks across the nation.

On Sundays, about once a month from September through May when
Louise and Owen were in Florida, my father drove us in our wood-sided
station wagon to Washington Oaks,
about an hour away. On the facing page is an image from a book of
photoetchings called *Album* that I
made in 1972, using photographs of
my father's. Back in the forties, when
we were children, my brother and
I chased each other on paths lined
with flowers, crossed little pools on
split-log bridges, and swam in the big
warm spring-fed pool that smelled of
sulfur. We rowed a flat-bottomed boat
on the river and once slid right over a
sleeping alligator. Washington Oaks
extended from the river to the ocean
across a narrow strip of land with a
road running through it. On the other
side of the road, which we sometimes
sneaked across, was the orange grove,
then the wild part (there were snakes),
and eventually the ocean, always
rough, with its long flat coquina rocks made up of tiny shells.

With my step-grandfather,
Owen D. Young, 1947.

Grandfather Young sometimes sold oranges by the roadside. Once,
when I was helping him, I overheard two customers arguing: "You're crazy.
Of course it's not Owen D. Young." I didn't tell them that it was. I wondered
how the man knew. Sometimes we would listen to newscasts on an enormous
radio, and Grandfather would say something about world events. I don't
remember what he said, but I think my long-standing interest in politics is a
residue of my childhood.

In 2004 the University Press of Florida published the letters of Marjorie Kinnan Rawlings, a writer who came to dinner at Washington Oaks on some Sundays. I read that Mr. Young (that is what she called him) had told her "he had learned the secret of contentment." She countered: "No man is done with his job until he's put away in the ground." His reaction surprised her: "He lifted his eyebrows and banged his pipe and dropped hot coals on Louise's rug, and I felt very fresh and impudent." That was in 1950.

Remembering my childhood: a photoetching from *Album*, 1972.

Before reading Rawlings's letters, I had been engrossed in a book by Liaquat Ahamed called *Lords of Finance*. I learned that in February 1929 Germany was in danger of default on its debt, and delegates from European countries and the United States met in Paris for "yet one more summit devoted to reparations." Owen D. Young was chairman. Ahamed wrote of "his perfect diplomatic skills" and his experience as a key member of the first reparations committee, convened in 1922.

Negotiations at what was later called the Young Conference were intense and frustrating (some delegates walked out), but finally Young brought the participating nations to what was generally seen as a workable agreement. The great but then out-of-favor economist John Maynard Keynes dissented. "The Young plan will not prove practicable for even a short period," he wrote, "and I should not be surprised to see some sort of crisis in 1930."

Crisis came on October 29, 1929, with the great stock market crash. Germany's dominoes continued to fall into World War Two. Of course, Germany was not the only cause of the crash, and it is now clear that the politics of reparations were impossible. But when I read Rawlings's letters, I wondered about Grandfather Young's undisclosed "secret of contentment" and I shivered at realizing the heavy weight he carried.

The title of an essay by John Cage came into my mind: "Diary: How to Improve the World (You Will Only Make Matters Worse)." I thought about the larger focus of Grandfather Young's life, in which he helped place General Electric in a position to become our nation's largest corporation. Did that improve the world? Certainly the Radio Corporation of America did—Young is credited with creating it in 1919 at the request of our government in order to keep the airwaves, essential to the new technology of radio, in American control. And what about my other grandfather, Elwood S. Brown, who did something comparatively small, by helping set up inclusive premises for the Olympic Games?

Probably neither Elwood S. Brown nor Owen D. Young would be remembered today if it weren't for Google. I didn't know, before Googling him, that Elwood S. received a Légion d'Honneur award from France and the Distinguished Service Medal from the United States. I didn't know, before Googling him, that in 1929 Owen D. had been named Man of the Year by *Time* magazine. When I Googled Marjorie Kinnan Rawlings, I was surprised to find that several of her books are still in print. She gave me a copy of *The Yearling*, autographed to me, and in 1946, when I was eleven, I saw the movie *The Yearling*, starring Gregory Peck and Jane Wyman. Rawlings was also a famous cook—you can buy her cookbook on Amazon—but she never cooked when she ate dinner with us.

I always helped Grandmother Louise in the kitchen. My grandmother didn't explain; I copied what she did and did what she said: "chop this" or "don't let that pot boil over." Mainly it was "wash that." She didn't allow dirty dishes or pans to pile up around us. Now, when people remark how orderly the Crown Point studio is, I sometimes think of my grandmother's kitchen.

The house at Washington Oaks was elegantly plain; rustic furniture from the Philippines coexisted with Chinese lamps and scrolls. Louise designed everything, gardened, started a community-weaving center, and took up pottery in her older years. I still have on my desk a pottery bowl she gave me when I was a young adult. She said it wasn't so good, but it was the best bowl she had made.

Other people called me Kathy when I was young, but I was always Kathan to my grandmother. It is a name that she had suggested, a Welsh surname on the Powis side of her family. When I set out for college, she advised me always to introduce myself as Kathan, so that the girlish name would not follow me to the new place. Only salesmen call me Kathy now. My brother was the last holdout. He died in an auto accident about two dozen years ago. He had become an engineer and was one of many at Cape Canaveral who "sat at the console" (as he put it) during the first American manned space flight in 1961.

After my brother and I had both left home, my mother moved to a nearby university town and earned a degree in education. My father stayed the rest of his life in our house. He died of cancer (too much smoking and drinking) while still in his fifties. After finishing her studies, my mother got a government job teaching elementary school on army bases overseas. She lived, always in town (off the military base), in Morocco, Ethiopia, Crete, Holland, Turkey, and Sardinia before she retired. She was eighty-nine when she died, and she spent her last twenty-four years in the San Francisco Bay Area close to me.

The lives my mother and my father might have lived were short-circuited by the Depression. But my mother was like the Model T: rolling it over into a field didn't put a dent in it.

With my mother, Clarissa (Clare), 1993.

John Cage working on a score for a print, 1980.

3.

JOHN CAGE

No Dawdling

John Cage was born in 1912 in Los Angeles, four years later than my mother. His father, John Milton Cage Sr., was an inventor; in the year of his son's birth he set a world record by staying underwater for twenty-four hours in a submarine of his own design. Among his many other inventions, including improvements to the internal combustion engine, the elder Cage developed a crystal radio for home use. As a girl in Florida, I spent many hours wearing huge earphones listening to a crystal radio that my father built for me from a kit.

The younger John Cage began piano lessons at the age of nine, was valedictorian of his high school class, and entered Pomona College at the age of sixteen. Two years later he dropped out, hitchhiked to Houston, and from there made his way by ship to France. His parents supported him in painting, composing music, and traveling in Europe until they lost their house in the Depression. John returned to Los Angeles, worked as a gardener and a dishwasher, and practiced daily on a piano housed in the printing shop of a friend. Later he studied with several important new music composers and eventually with Arnold Schoenberg, who took him as a student on condition that he give up painting and "devote his life to music."

Cage was sixty-five years old in 1977 when I invited him to come to California from his home in New York to make etchings at Crown Point Press. In reply to my invitation, he told me of the promise he had made to Schoenberg. Then he added another story. He had once received an invitation from a friend to walk with her in the Himalayas, and he had not accepted. "I have always regretted this," he concluded. Because of that regret, beginning

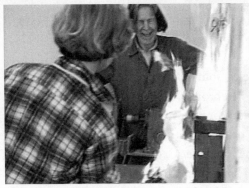

From the number one favorite video:
Cage "printing" *Eninka*, 1986.

in January 1978, he worked with us almost every year, fifteen times before his death fifteen years later.

The number one favorite video that I have shot of artists in our studio is of Cage working in 1986 on the series called *Eninka*. John is slowly and deliberately walking toward the press, which is flanked by two printers. He is carrying an armload of loosely balled-up newspapers, which he deposits on the press bed and calmly lights on fire. The printers jump back; then at a signal from John they lay a sheet of thin paper over the fire, pull down the press blankets, and smother the flames by frantically turning the press handle.

John is laughing. But he becomes solemn when the printers pull back the press blankets to see burned fragments on the bed. The situation looks hopeless, but slowly the printers separate the printing paper fragments from those made of newspaper, and—with John watching energetically—float them in a bath of water to straighten them. There are more steps, and eventually the burned paper takes on a coherent form, mounted on another sheet. John is now gazing at a stopwatch, timing how long an iron ring is heated before a printer uses it to brand the print. Finally, he is laughing again. The print, *Eninka*, is illustrated later in this chapter.

Crown Point's fiftieth year is a hundred years after John Cage was born. We celebrated our twentieth and his seventieth in 1982 with an exhibition of his work in our gallery in Oakland, and at the opening he read his just-completed mesostic poem "Composition in Retrospect." It was published for the first time in the show's catalog, and the reading was broadcast that night by KPFA, a local public radio station.

"Act in accord with obstacles," one stanza says, "using them to find or define the process you're about to be involved in, the questions you'll ask. If you don't have enough time to accomplish what you have in mind, consider the work finished." In the mesostic form, a key word runs vertically through the center of the poem. You can see in the illustration here that in the text I just quoted, the word *circumstances* plainly appears. John created scores for both his music and his works of visual art by asking questions about the obstacles, available time, and circumstances connected to the particular work.

John generally spent two weeks with us each year, and although some projects continued from year to year, he designed many others to be completed in a two-week period. He often used fire for those works and sometimes centered them on drawing around stones in honor of the stone garden at Ryoan-ji, a Zen temple in Kyoto, Japan. When planning for a project of short duration, he made scores that were relatively simple.

In printing with fire, John would specify in a score the number of newspaper sheets and the length of time the sheets should burn before covering them with printing paper and running them

aCt
In
accoRd
with obstaCles
Using
theM
to find or define the proceSs
you're abouT to be involved in
the questions you'll Ask
if you doN't have enough time
to aCcomplish
what you havE in mind
conSider the work finished

through the press. There was always at least one more step so other marks could appear, but overall, the artworks that involved burning and/or drawing around stones are quite simple. These are John's best-known works of visual art, but they are narrow slices of his total production. I don't believe either the simple or the complicated slices are better or more beautiful. But they are different. "I always go to extremes," he would say.

At the other extreme from the fire prints are the series titled *Changes and Disappearances* (plate 2), *On the Surface*, and *Dereau* (plate 3). *Changes and Disappearances*, for example, took three years (four visits) to complete. We would stop when it was time for him to leave, and when he came back we would pick up where we had left off. "Oh, it's going to be horrendous," he exclaimed, laughing, when a printer pointed out that a single print could have up to two hundred colors. We laughed with him. When I think of John, I

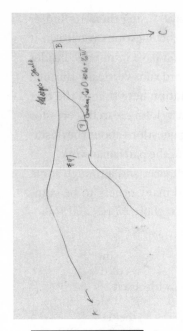
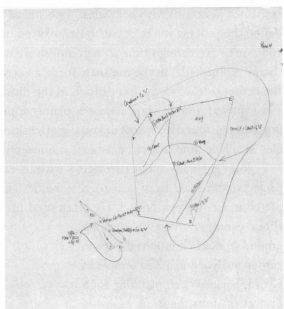

Maps for *Changes and Disappearances #16.*

often think of a saying by Montaigne: "The most manifest sign of wisdom is continual cheerfulness."

Each of the thirty-five *Changes and Disappearances* images contains combinations from a pool of small shaped plates. Normally, an artist makes the plates, changing them and proofing as he or she goes, and then the printers print the final prints, the edition. All edition prints are normally the same. But in *Changes and Disappearances*, John added new lines, mixed new colors, and changed plate positions as the prints were being made. He didn't do this capriciously. For each print he created a "score" and a set of "maps" that together gave instructions for making and printing the work, including individual colors for each line and individual positions for each plate. We dropped the idea of an edition and called the prints a series.

If you know nothing else about John Cage, you probably know of his music composition nicknamed "Silence." It was first performed in 1952 by a pianist sitting quietly at a piano before a concert-hall audience and not performing as expected. Some members of the audience coughed, whispered,

The score for #16.

shifted in their seats, or left the hall, while others listened, hearing sounds that they would not normally notice. Cage's title for this work, *4'33"*, describes its duration: four minutes thirty-three seconds. He wrote out a score that the pianist followed using a stopwatch. At the end of each of the work's first two movements, the pianist closed and then reopened the keyboard cover; he closed it finally at the end of the third movement, then stood and bowed.

The members of the audience who coughed and whispered, not taking the work seriously, were dawdling. But others paid attention to whatever sounds occurred and quietly noticed the passage of time. You can't dawdle if you are aware of duration. You can't dawdle if you are paying attention. As a famous Yogi Berra saying puts it, "You have to be careful if you don't know where you're going because you might not get there."

I think John would have said it is fine not to know where you are going so long as you pay attention on the way. But, because of his scores, he did know where he was going, at least in general, unless the performers dawdled, misunderstanding him. Influenced by Zen, he tried to give up judgments, but he complained to his friends when performers performed inattentively and was unstinting in his praise of skillful execution.

The score for *4'33"* is simple. At the other extreme are the *Freeman Etudes*, which Cage composed for the violinist Paul Zukofsky around the time (the late 1970s) that he was working on *Changes and Disappearances* with us. He described the *Freeman Etudes* as "the possibility of doing the impossible." Zukofsky, he told us, in a frustrated moment had cried out, "I cannot go on.

John Cage, *Changes and Disappearances #16*, 1979–82. One in a series of 35 color etchings with photoetching, engraving, and drypoint in two impressions each, 11 × 22 inches.

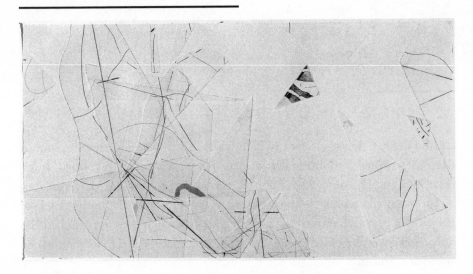

Look at my wrists!" But nevertheless he did perform the piece, "beautifully," John said, nodding with pleasure.

Cage used the same general approach both in music and in art. In making the complex scores for *Changes and Disappearances*, for example, he started by asking as many questions as he could think of about the circumstances of the work. Then he did a number of tests to see what the answers would look like. After that, usually he would try to improve his skill level. He would practice with each tool until he could use it fluidly.

Here are some of the questions John asked in making *Changes and Disappearances*: "How many colors are available? How many mixtures is it practical to make? How many different tools are there? How many types of lines: straight, curved, etc.? Are there ways to make lines besides drawing them?" In answer to the last question, he cut plates so their edges made lines, and he dropped string on plates and traced over it for a different line character. He also added thick lines copied photographically from drawings done by Henry David Thoreau in his journals. John leaned toward complexity; his

John Cage, *Eninka #42*, 1986.
Smoked paper monotype
with branding on gampi
paper chine collé,
24½ × 18½ inches.

colors, for example, were always mixtures—he said he wanted them "to look like they went to graduate school."

Once he had settled on his questions, he used what he called "chance operations" in order to make his score. In the years I knew him, he usually did that using a computer printout based on tables in the Chinese *Book of Changes*, the *I Ching*. He told Robin White, who interviewed him for our Crown Point publication *View*, "Most people don't realize I use chance as a discipline. They think I use it—I don't know—as a way of making choices. But my choices consist in choosing which questions to ask."

The scores for *Changes and Disappearances* are more complicated than the prints themselves, and from our point of view, following them was difficult and required undivided attention. The studio was full of concentration. Cage did not like background music, and there was very little talking. An unmonitored alarm going off in the building across the street for an hour or so drove us crazy and didn't seem to bother him. But when someone downstairs practiced the piano, playing one piece haltingly over and over, John was beside himself.

We got together and elected printer Lilah Toland as "most diplomatic" among us, and she went down and explained the situation. "A famous composer is working upstairs. Have you heard of John Cage?" Fortunately, he had. "Would you like to meet him?" Yes, he would. "He will be leaving at the end of next week. Could you possibly hold your practicing until then?" Yes, he could.

When we would break, John cooked food for everybody. He laughed— we all laughed—and he told stories. One of his stories was about going door to door in Santa Monica in 1932 (he was twenty) offering lessons in art and music for twenty-five cents a lesson. We asked if he had customers, and he assured us that he did. He told us about driving a bus in early 1940 with his percussion orchestra through rainy Oregon, everyone sleeping in the leaky bus for want of money. That story came to mind because Doris Denison, who had been a member of that orchestra, visited him at the press. We felt incorporated into his life. He laughed at the end of every story and so did we.

One story was about a party hostess in New York who, given wild mushrooms by a guest, fed some to her dog before serving them at dinner. After everyone had eaten, the butler came in and whispered, "Madam, the dog is dead." She rushed everyone out to have their stomachs pumped, and afterward found that the dog had been run over by a car. John laughed more than the rest of us at that story. He was a mushroom expert, a founder of the New York Mycological Society, and famous for his mushroom-hunting expeditions.

We weren't dawdling. Dawdling is procrastinating, delaying, frittering

At Crown Point with John, 1982.

away time. Almost everyone has had the experience of solving a previously intractable problem while in the shower or doing something else not connected to the problem—the answer is just suddenly in your head. That kind of insight is probably related to something called the "middle way" between sustained intense focus and meditation. It is the way we normally go about our lives if we pay attention to whatever we are doing at any particular time. John told me that though he studied Zen philosophy, he never became seriously involved in "sitting cross-legged." His mentor, Daisetz T. Suzuki, had assured him, he said, that work was equally valuable.

In creating the *Changes and Disappearances* prints, working with Cage present and following his scores to the letter, we felt we were close to meditating. This situation was more demanding than the printing we ordinarily do, but it was not different in kind. After you reach a certain level of competency, many activities—including cooking, playing music, and gardening—are meditative. The activity, a step beyond paying attention, refreshes the mind. Cage's work is about doing something, seeing something, or hearing something in full measure, relaxed yet attentive, temporarily putting aside everything else.

Edward Rothstein, a critic, wrote in the *New York Times* about a month after Cage died in 1992 that "Cage didn't want liberation from law: he was actually always seeking to submit himself to it. The only requirement seemed to be that the law be meaningless." Cage often said that he wanted to "imitate nature in her manner of operation," and since nature operates in a meaningless way, Rothstein's comment is correct. However, I believe it is also correct to say that Cage ended up with something meaningful.

In the same time frame that Rothstein's article appeared, the *New York Times* also printed a more friendly one by Bernard Holland. "The Enlightenment said the mind would soon make sense of most things," Holland wrote. "The succeeding age of scientific discovery and industry said machines could be invented to take care of the rest. John Cage's art announces the failure of both philosophies. It suggests that we shall never really know what is going on in the universe, much less control it. It asks the ear to bend to uncertainty, to negotiate with chance, not defiantly but with wit, grace and invention."

Most of our great thinkers of the past four hundred years, including the founding fathers of our country, have been guided by the philosophy of the Enlightenment, the Age of Reason. If you don't mind oversimplifying, you can think of the Enlightenment using a phrase from the seventeenth-century French philosopher René Descartes: "I think, therefore I am." A taxi driver, back in the days when taxi drivers had no earpieces and overheard conversations, broke into one of mine with this: "René Descartes walked into a bar. 'Would you like a drink?' the bartender asked. 'I think not,' Descartes replied, and disappeared."

In 2010, an article in *Artforum* magazine by Ina Blom, a Norwegian art history professor, stirred up my thoughts about Cage and Descartes. Blom wrote that Cage "made it possible for artists . . . to start seeing artworks in terms of codes, diagrams, and the productivity of forces rather than the play of forms."

A "productivity of forces" might require something different from what we think of as thinking, a middle way, not precisely rational but at the same time not abandoning the mind. When you look at Cage's art, you cannot talk about "push-pull" or "developing forms in space" or "figure-ground." And pure feeling, the opposite approach, doesn't fit—Cage said that he found self-expression in art and music "trivial and lacking in urgency."

"Left to itself, art would have to be something very simple," Cage said. "It would be sufficient for it to be beautiful. But when it's useful it should spill out of just being beautiful and move over to other aspects of life so that when we're not with the art it has nevertheless influenced our actions or our responses to the environment." Cage's urgent pursuit was to hear sounds as sounds, see lines as lines, and "wake up to the very life we're living, which is so excellent." I try to do this; I really do. But sometimes I think that the door that Cage cracked open is now flapping at its hinge.

John Cage began using notation to create art that calls attention to embodied forces at least as early as the 1950s. Now, in our time, the world is full of notation with concrete meanings available only to initiates. We had, in 2008, a horrendous financial collapse caused by codes that even many of the professionals using them didn't fully understand. We are swimming—maybe close to drowning—in a "productivity of forces" that leaves traditional productivity (the employment of people) behind and is so strong that ordinary reason (at least in politics) is hard to hold on to. This is life, not art, but the best artists encapsulate life in ways we hardly can recognize when we are in the thick of it.

Could the philosophy of the Enlightenment, with its reverence for science and rational truth, disappear? If so, could it be replaced by something beneficial to society? Or are we already backtracking toward the Middle Ages, a time of extreme differences between rich and poor, a time when religion, superstition, and hearsay held sway over reason and allowed a few lords in their castles to dominate those who worked hard, danced in the streets on feast days, and joined their masters in burning malcontents at the stake? In the summer of 2011, with our country on the interminable edge of recession, I heard a congressman say on television that he aimed to "vilify" the president of the United States "so he will be a one-term president." He used the word *vilify* twice in the interview.

"How to improve the world," Cage wrote. "You will only make matters worse." I asked him if he voted, and he said, "I wouldn't dream of it." But, speaking for myself, I am wondering, If we don't try to improve the world, at least by voting for officeholders who will work cooperatively and respect an institution like the presidency, how can we survive?

Here's something else I heard on television, on a panel including Jennifer Granholm, former governor of Michigan. The group was talking about a debate among presidential candidates. "It's a lot of fun," Granholm said. "We get out the popcorn, and I'm tweeting, you're tweeting." I visualized it. Short comments zinging through the air at the moment something is happening among people separately watching an event and engaging in a conversation about it.

"I think it's time for us to turn everything into art," John Cage said in the interview Crown Point published in *View*. "In other words, to take care of it and to change it from being just a mess into being something that facilitates our living.

Could world improvement be accomplished through individual acts of paying attention, through choosing the right questions to ask? Could whole populations become resistant to dawdling? Could our culture's newfound fascination with codes, forces, and diagrams work to the advantage of everyone? "Oh my!" John Cage would say, and laugh.

In 1959 when I first came to the San Francisco Bay Area. The Golden Gate Bridge is in the background.

4.

THE FIFTIES AND SIXTIES

Do It Right

My grandmother paid for my education at Antioch College in Ohio. Every student spent half of every year working in a real job—that is why I chose Antioch. Because of the job program it took five years, rather than the normal four, to complete a B.A.

I worked in a children's museum in Worcester, Massachusetts, and in my second job period I was a child-care worker in a migrant camp for bean pickers in Pennsylvania. I spent one period on campus as a teaching assistant in the English department, and the craft of disciplined editing I learned has served me well since then. In my final year in the job program, I was the sole employee of the nature museum on the edge of the college's substantial woodlands, Glen Helen. There was a small budget, and I could run the place as I pleased. That experience was useful to me later on, but at the time I chose it mainly to stay on campus.

I had lived the previous year in London and returned reluctantly, but once I was back I appreciated Antioch's atmosphere of inquiry and collegiality and didn't want to leave the campus for part of my final year. Just recently, in 2011, I read a summary of a study of higher education today. Although students often receive excellent specialized training, the authors said that in graduates of many colleges "gains in critical thinking, complex reasoning, and written communication are either exceedingly small or empirically nonexistent." I thought, Where would I be now if I hadn't made gains like that at Antioch?

My year in London was at the Central School of Arts and Crafts. There was no "junior year abroad" program back in the fifties, but you could live abroad and pay overseas tuition for less than the cost of a year at Antioch, and Antioch allowed us to transfer out for a year with a guarantee that it would apply the overseas credits toward our degrees when we came back. We had to make the arrangements ourselves.

I mentioned to my painting instructor that I wanted to go to London. I had in mind something connected to English literature. "I can get you into the Central School of Arts and Crafts," he said.

"But I'm not an art major," I replied.

"You should be," he said. So I ended up in art school.

At the London Central School I became enamored with etching and its old slow ways, and at the same time I enmeshed myself in a world of new art completely surprising to me. In 1956 I learned about (and copied) the French *tachiste* painters who ennobled touch and worked similarly to the abstract expressionists in New York. In the second year I spent at Central, 1958–59, I saw at the Whitechapel Gallery an exhibition of Jackson Pollock's drip paintings, which stunned me, and in that same year learned about Jasper Johns's 1955 painting of a flag—it was a big jump to try to grasp one after the other. The jump was possible because one of my teachers at Central, sculptor William Turnbull, in 1956 let his students in on the idea that art is a branch of philosophy, a way of figuring out how to approach the world.

When my first year in London was up, I wanted to stay on and forget my degree. But my grandmother promised that if I came home and graduated, she would stake me at $100 a month to use as I liked for another year after that. Her stipend, combined with savings from job earnings, provided for my second year at the Central School.

There, I met the man who was to become my (now ex-) husband, Jeryl Parker. He had come to London from California and went home shortly before I did. When my year was nearly up, I bought a plane ticket to San Francisco. I had just enough cash left for a good-bye vacation in Edinburgh with school friends. We stayed in a rooming house long used by students. In the backyard of the house was a pile of rusting metal and wooden spokes. "Isn't that an etching press?" I asked the landlady.

"Yes," she replied. "You're the first person to notice it in years. Some students from the Edinburgh College of Art left it here to save it from being melted down for scrap during the war. I'd like to get rid of it. Why don't you take it?"

The press from Scotland.

I did take it. I turned in my plane ticket and, at less cost, found a freighter going from Glasgow to San Francisco through the Panama Canal. There were a few passenger berths, and any amount of baggage was free. The trip took two months, but I had plenty of time.

It was 1959. In San Francisco I quickly got a job with an insurance company as a typist—in high school all the girls took typing in case we should ever need a job, and I've always been glad to have that skill. We set up the press in the studio of John Ihle, a friend of Jeryl's. Dennis Beall, a friend of his, joined us, and four of us worked in the studio—printmaking friends.

In 1962 Jeryl and I—by this time married and with a son, Kevin Powis Parker, almost a year old—rented a storefront for an etching studio in Richmond, an industrial town across the bay from San Francisco. We lived in a three-room apartment in the back. Jeryl had a teaching job at the California College of Arts and Crafts in Oakland, and I ran the shop.

Unbeknown to us, we were in what economic historian Robert Skidelsky calls "the special economic performance of the golden age from 1951 to 1973," a good time for young people entering the commercial world. Skidelsky is the biographer of John Maynard Keynes, whose ideas at that time were temporarily superseding those of Adam Smith. Skidelsky, in *Keynes: The Return of the Master*, says that classical economics, which Smith represents, is analogous to Newtonian physics with its faith in the balancing force of gravity. Skidelsky explains that Smith believed "full-employment 'equilibrium' was to be conceived of as a 'normal' condition to which the economy tended to return after a 'shock.'" Then he quotes Keynes's most quoted remark: "This *long run* is a misleading guide to affairs. In the long run we are all dead." Keynesian theory

In Crown Point's first studio in Richmond, 1962–63. Jeryl Parker is in the photo at left.

focuses on abating uncertainty. Skidelsky's short, simple explanation of it is "When confidence is high, the economy thrives; when it is low, it sickens."

I think I know the exact moment when confidence began to wane in the United States. If you are a person of my generation, you can answer this question: What were you doing on the afternoon of November 22, 1963, when President John F. Kennedy was assassinated in Dallas, Texas?

I was printing, my hands full of ink, listening to the radio as I usually did in the studio. An announcer's voice intoning about the motorcade's progress suddenly turned frantic, stifling sobs, haltingly describing shots he had heard coming from "the grassy knoll" near where he was standing. Later, when official reports said there was only one shooter, Lee Harvey Oswald, who was in the School Book Depository building across the street from the knoll, I couldn't believe them. In 2012 I went on YouTube and looked at a contemporaneous video close-up that showed Secret Service agents on the back bumper of the president's car being ordered away from their posts seconds before the shots. This all happened almost fifty years ago and still is not settled. It was the beginning of the climate of the mistrust of

government that fuels the uncertainty we live in today.

In 1962, in Richmond, Jeryl and I first called our new etching workshop Crown Point Intaglio. *Intaglio* is an Italian word meaning printing from an image that is below the surface. We quickly realized how few people knew or cared about the meaning of that word, however, and changed the name to Crown Point Press.

I had the idea to use the name "Crown Point" after seeing a photo of the Crown Point gold mine in California. It showed a rickety railroad trestle at the mine, with two engines precariously placed on it and a small group of people standing proudly, dwarfed by what they had made. I thought of the impossible achievement of the trestle, not so much that it served a gold mine—I wasn't naive enough to think printmaking could be that.

We modeled Crown Point after a printmaking workshop Jeryl and I had attended in London on Charlotte Street. It was founded and run by a friend, originally from Sweden, named Birgit Skiöld. Birgit named it simply the Print Workshop; we mostly called it Charlotte Street. It was a hangout for artists who paid a small hourly fee to be there. We all worked intensely. We all loved

The Crown Point
mine that inspired
the press's name.

presses and tools and materials like tar and wax.

Some of my workshop people in Richmond, and later Berkeley, were printmakers who needed a place to use a press, and others were artist friends whom I talked into trying this medium. One of our activities was a Live Model Group; we met to draw on metal plates from a model. One day in 1963 I got a telephone call from Richard Diebenkorn asking if he could join the group.

Diebenkorn, already the San Francisco Bay Area's most respected living artist, was meeting weekly with a drawing group, but he wanted to try ours as well. A graduate student he was advising had given him some zinc plates and a drypoint needle, and he had become interested in that kind of drawing. "You think you're doing something," he said, "and the metal says, 'Oh, no you don't.'" That was what he was looking for, a material he could use to change what he would normally do, what he was used to doing.

I tried to teach him to print, without success, and eventually printed for him. He wanted only one print of each image, and another if he changed it, to see what he had done. He liked not being able to see with any clarity what he was drawing on a plate. He took plates home and drew things and people. If he was having trouble with a painting, he sometimes would copy it onto a plate to see what it looked like reversed and stripped to its essentials.

At that time, Diebenkorn, like the other artists who came to the workshop, would pay me by the hour for using the space and for my time if I printed for him, and also he paid for his materials. In a single evening model session, without worrying about the expense, he would use both sides of maybe half a dozen zinc plates, but he shied away from rag paper. He wanted me to print on newsprint, and I would tell him newsprint would soon turn to dust.

Finally I realized he was not making anything to last, or to sell, or even to make it, exactly. He was just doing it, and when he knew that he was doing it right, that everything was falling into place, he would keep on going. He wouldn't risk derailing a period of right momentum by feeling his materials were precious. He was frugal (using the backsides of plates sometimes caused trouble). But, nevertheless, to keep things going, if things were going right, he had to think of the metal plates as if they were newsprint. It was an important lesson for me. "We should be doing something, not making something," he said. Doing something, and doing it right as best I could, became a maxim for me.

In 1964 my grandmother, at the end of her life, sent me $5,000 to be used, she specified, as a down payment on a house. I got the check in the mail, and put Kevin, who was nearly four, into his stroller and walked down the street to a real estate office, where we spent the afternoon looking at a big book of photographs of houses.

I bought the house we picked that day from the photographs. The agent drove us to see it, and I don't remember looking at any others, although I must have done that. I knew from the start this one was right. Kevin liked it because it had a small yard with big trees and a homemade fishpond with a little plaster elf house next to it. I liked it because it had an aboveground basement for the workshop and it was located on the edge of downtown Berkeley. People looking for the workshop could easily find the house, I could buy it with $5,000 down, and it didn't need remodeling. I could see right away where to put the press and every piece of furniture I owned.

Only a few years later, as we entered the seventies, inflation was raging—by 1974 mortgage rates were

Richard Diebenkorn, *#19* from *41 Etchings Drypoints*, 1963. Drypoint, 7¾ × 6½ inches.

at 9 percent. My mortgage was at 6 percent; I had bought the house at a good time. Jeryl had to pose as co-purchaser since he had a salary and was a man (masculinity mattered to the bank). He did that and signed the deed back to me. He helped me move in and set up the studio, but he didn't move in himself. We had grown apart, and he wanted to live with someone else.

At that point, I thought I was in good shape financially—I was so happy to have the house. Nothing that I was doing paid regularly (this is still true), but Crown Point Press had regular workshop participants, and I printed editions for an artist friend, Beth Van Hoesen, whose prints sold so well that she could provide fairly steady work. And because I was in Berkeley, I was able to run a class in my studio that was sponsored by the University of California Extension Program.

Kevin was usually with me in the studio, but he also spent time with his father and enjoyed day-care programs. I was signed up with a temporary agency as a typist, and whenever I needed cash, I worked for a few days or weeks at a bank or insurance company. I remember very well the typing pool at the Bank of America: rows of women at small desks, each with a typewriter and Dictaphone, facing a woman at a large desk who, it seemed to me, did nothing but watch us. To go to the restroom, you asked her permission. It never occurred to me to look for a regular job.

A gallery in San Francisco showed, and sometimes sold, my own prints, and a specialized print gallery in New York (Associated American Artists) made some sales and helped me obtain three commissioned editions in that period: one for a hotel and two others for a print club called the International Graphic Arts Society. In 1964, before moving from Richmond to Berkeley, I produced a bound book titled *The Ocean's Warning to the Skin Diver* that contained my etchings as illustrations for poems by a friend from Antioch, Judson Jerome. This was a large *livre d'artiste* of the type I'd seen in the British Museum print room in my student days.

Now, I do some of my reading on a Kindle, and though I continue to love books, I see *livres d'artistes* as specialized indulgences. They are generally unwieldy, hard to hold, hard to read, and too big for a bookshelf. Now, I think the best place for a beautiful print is not in a book but on the wall. You can't beat an original print for everyday art companionship: it's there when you want it but doesn't dominate everything in the room. A good original print is strong enough to hold its space no matter what else is nearby. And you don't

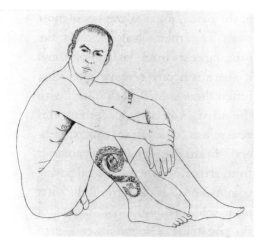

Beth Van Hoesen, *Tattoo*, from *The Nude Man*, 1965, a book of 25 etchings, 6 × 7 inches.

have to worry about accidental harm because it is framed under glass.

But back then I was in love with the antiquated form of the handmade book. In 1965 I printed and published three *livres d'artistes* by artists other than myself. Looking back, I can't figure out how I managed to find enough time for that, but the books exist with the date printed in them.

The first book, after mine, was by Richard Diebenkorn. I asked him if Crown Point Press could publish prints from the plates he had been making. Publishing is different from printing in that the publisher pays all the costs and takes on the job of selling the work. The publisher commonly gives the artist half the finished works and keeps the other half to sell for the press—this is what I did when I first began to publish. The more professional long-term arrangement, however, is for the publisher to retain all the works in the edition and pay the artist a commission on each sale. The artist, the publisher, and the printer all keep proofs, which are recorded on a documentation sheet. At Crown Point we normally make ten artists' proofs regardless of edition size. These we split 50-50 between the artist and the press.

I arrived at the idea of a 30 percent artist commission by thinking of it as a major cost and adding 20 percent for our time and materials. This parallels splitting the edition prints themselves 50-50, and it also matches what I think is the standard system for markups in the commercial world. The hardware store charges roughly twice as much for the hammer as it pays for it. Art galleries normally give artists (who are also the manufacturers) 50 percent of each sale.

Occasionally, at an artist's request, we still split editions, but overall we've been paying commissions at 30 percent of sales since 1977. The commission structure is the same for all our artists. The publishers I worked with

Richard Diebenkorn, *#16* from
41 Etchings Drypoints, 1964.
Drypoint, 13¼ × 9¾ inches.

in the 1970s, so far as I know, in most cases paid themselves back for the printing costs from the first sales, and if there was any revenue after that (often there wasn't), they split it with the artist as it came in. I think this system was copied from book publishers. I heard many complaints about it from artists, so when I started paying commissions, I paid from the first print sold, taking the risk, myself, of the possibility of not selling enough to pay the costs. I'm not sure, but I think my system is the one most print publishers use now.

The Diebenkorn book was my first publishing venture, so I hadn't figured out a formula for paying commissions (and, in fact, couldn't have managed to pay them). The edition size was twenty-five; Diebenkorn gave his half to his dealer, I believe. I could sell only a few of mine then (the individual prints were $100 each). But I did sell them later (some particular images for as much as $10,000 each), and overall it worked out fine.

For his book, Diebenkorn chose forty-one images (fewer than half the number he had made by that time). To accommodate my desire for a book, he put them in an order that visually worked for him. We left half of each edition unbound so that individual prints could be framed and/or sold; this was a model I followed with future books whenever the artist didn't envision the work only as a book. Diebenkorn called his book *41 Etchings Drypoints*. Soon after I finished the printing, in 1966, he moved to Los Angeles.

Beth Van Hoesen, who had been with Crown Point from the beginning, had the idea to draw all her men friends naked. The man shown in this chapter from Van Hoesen's book, *The Nude Man*, is Dennis Beall, one of the printmaking friends who shared my press when I first came to California from London. He had been in the navy; that's where the tattoo came from. Tattoos back then were rare except in the underworld. And in the art world of 1965, a picture book of naked men was shocking to a lot of people.

The third book I published that year was by Wayne Thiebaud. It contains seventeen small, traditionally drawn etchings in black and white: a banana split, a cherry stand, a gumball dispenser, a piece of pie. Betty Jean, Wayne's wife, titled the book *Delights*. This was a satisfying project in every way except one: I yielded to the advice of Thiebaud's New York painting dealer and made an edition of one hundred. It was simply too much printing for me, and it took twenty years or more for the market to absorb that many prints. Nevertheless, it was a lesson learned.

Wayne Thiebaud, *Gum Machine*, from *Delights*, a book of 17 etchings, 1964. Hard ground etching, 4 × 4 inches.

Thiebaud was the first artist I published out of the blue, without earlier contact through my workshops. In 1964 I had seen an exhibition of paintings of pies, cakes, and other edibles at Art Unlimited, the gallery in San Francisco where I showed. Thiebaud exhibited that same work later in New York with laudatory reviews in the *New York Times*, *Art News*, and other magazines. But the *San Francisco Chronicle*'s critic had hated the Art Unlimited show. I loved it, and I called Thiebaud and asked him if I could publish some prints of his.

Wayne Thiebaud working in the Hawthorne Street studio, San Francisco, 2011.

5.

WAYNE THIEBAUD

Do It Well

I have often told the story of Wayne Thiebaud's first day at Crown Point Press in 1964. He asked me to prepare a number of small plates with traditional hard ground, and after I had done that he arranged them in a row in front of him on the worktable. Then he got out a stack of snapshots of his paintings and made another row; each plate had a photo behind it. With an etching needle, he slowly and attentively began copying the images onto the plates. I went upstairs to my kitchen to fix lunch, sandwiches, with an avocado half and a beer each.

I was high-minded about printmaking. I think this was partly because as a nascent publisher I was discovering that many people thought of printmaking as "reproductive" and therefore second-class, and partly because I was steeped in the notion of bringing the image out of the materials. For whatever reasons, before he could even take a bite of the food I had prepared, I started lecturing Wayne about copying himself. Remembering that moment, I am grateful that he is a patient and forgiving man.

He listened respectfully without saying anything, and then took one of the small plates and drew the lunch. He neatened up the sandwiches in the picture and added a garnish. Then, as we ate, he talked.

He said that he was trying to find out what was important in making a picture. A piece of pie, he said, could call to mind Mom's apple pie, or pie in the sky, or it could be a triangular shape on a round one. Does the tool matter—a brush or an etching needle? If he slathers paint like frosting on a picture of a cake, is that cheating? Can he bring off the same image without paint?

Wayne in 1964 working in my basement studio, Berkeley.

In 2002 with Wayne and printers (from left) Dena Schuckit, Rachel Fuller, and Catherine Brooks, San Francisco.

He accepted my invitation to make etchings in order to try to find the answers to these questions, he said. "When you change anything," he added, "you change everything."

Fast-forward forty-seven years to 2011. Things have changed, but not everything. Emily York, who was not even alive when Wayne told me about pie in the sky, is doing the printing, and Valerie Wade, in her twenty-third year at Crown Point, is gracefully managing ongoing activities, large and small. And I am still here, age seventy-six. Thiebaud is working on a group of small plates, just as he was doing long ago, and he is sitting at exactly the same table, a library table I bought at a sale from the University of California, Berkeley, in 1964 when I moved Crown Point into the basement of my newly purchased house. The table has traveled from Berkeley to downtown Oakland, then across the bay to a light-filled loft in San Francisco that we lost in an earthquake in 1989. Now, it is here in the Crown Point Press permanent space across the street from the San Francisco Museum of Modern Art. And sitting at it is Wayne Thiebaud at the age of ninety-one.

Wayne Thiebaud was born in Mesa, Arizona, in 1920 to a Mormon family; with his family, he spent part of his early childhood on a ranch in Utah, but he grew up mainly in Long Beach, California. In high school he worked on the stage crew in the drama department, learning to understand a simplified,

dramatic approach to stage lighting. He has said this early experience affected his later paintings. Another early influence was an uncle who was an amateur cartoonist.

Thiebaud was only sixteen when he got a job at Walt Disney Studios as an "in-betweener" drawing the hundreds of frames between the beginning and ending frames of a character's movement. In the Air Force in World War Two, he was assigned duty as an artist and cartoonist in the Motion Picture Unit. After the war, he returned to the Los Angeles area, where he worked in commercial art, and ended up in Sacramento, California, where he earned college degrees in fine art and began teaching at Sacramento City College. He still lives in Sacramento.

Wayne has done sixteen print projects at Crown Point since our first one, and some have included large colorful prints. Take a look in the color section in the back of this book at *Park Place* (plate 4). The color tones come from using aquatint, an etching process invented in the seventeenth century to simulate watercolor. Notice that this image is the same as one printed here in black and white. We published three versions, all printed from the same six plates: the color version in plate 4; *Black and White Park Place*, shown on the next page; and a version called *Park Place Variation*, which has one plate printed in red and the others in transparent black. Being able to change everything simply by changing the

Wayne Thiebaud, *Black and White Park Place*, 1995. Hard ground etching with drypoint, spit bite aquatint, and aquatint, 29¼ × 20½ inches.

color is one of the special values of printmaking. And, by the way, the three print editions are structurally very similar to a Thiebaud painting titled *Park Place*.

Park Place, in all its variations, shows a city downhill street with a tall building pressed tightly into a hillside landscape. There is, as Wayne has said about his cityscapes in general, "the loss of the convenience or comfort of standing and looking at things," yet this is the feeling of a city, a "surrender to the joy of a city . . . the craziness of putting such a big building on such a little piece of earth."

Wayne told me that once when he had set up his easel on a San Francisco street, a man stopped to watch and asked if he had been to art school. "I had to admit that I hadn't," Wayne replied.

"You could spend just a short time in one of those places," the man said, "and get that perspective thing worked out."

Wayne made his *Park Place* prints in 1995. Also on these pages you'll find pictures of two of his 2011 small black and white prints. Compare them with *Park Place*. The small prints were done sixteen years later. The subject matter is different, and the means much more limited, but "everything" hasn't changed. If it had, there would be no chance of remarking, as some of us sometimes do, that a row of cakes in a bakery or a rolling hill in Northern California "looks like a Thiebaud."

Wayne is partial to limited means, and since a project at Crown Point usually includes several images, we have many black and white ones on our list of his works. We also have many prints, including *Park Place*, in which he has used drypoint, the process that dominates the 2011 prints.

Drypoint lines are carved out of a copper plate by hand with a sharp tool, not etched with acid. As the artist pulls the tool through the metal, a burr is thrown up at the side of the line, creating a rich soft character that changes depending on the angle of the tool and the force of the artist's pull. Drypoint is physical; it takes strength and steadiness. And it is also unpredictable. Sometimes the metal grabs the tool and makes it do something you couldn't imagine. This is both the most straightforward and the

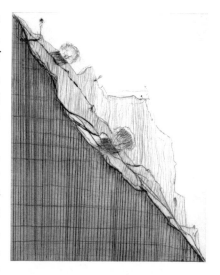

Two drypoints by Wayne Thiebaud, 2011. *Diagonal Ridge* (above), 8 × 6½ inches, and *Sierra Cloud*, 6½ × 8 inches.

most demanding way to make a print. There is not a whiff of the technological about it.

At a public conversation at the National Gallery in Washington, D.C., at the time of an exhibition held there to mark Crown Point's thirty-fifth anniversary, Wayne remembered his first project with me. "It was in the basement. Kathan and I and her son Kevin, and a wonderful Dalmatian dog, along with a cat, were the principal inhabitants. We just really worked. When lunchtime came she would go upstairs and fix us lunch. The workshop was very basic, perfectly adequate, not fancy, not overly developed. She took the most important aspects of doing etchings and worked with quite simple means. It's the opposite concept to that of a technocrat who lets you know you are involved in technology and seems to be wondering in what way the results measure up to that technology."

Looking back at the prints from that time, I don't think my technology was very good. I see lots of little specks, called foul biting; the aquatint tones are coarse compared with those we do now; all kinds of flaws come to mind. I was always good at printing—that's my personal technical contribution, formalizing printing in such a way that anyone can learn to do it well. But Crown Point's other advances in making beautiful prints have come from our printers over the years.

In our fifty years, thirty printers have completed a three-year apprenticeship to become Crown Point Press master printers, and most of them have remained in this field. Fifteen have started and successfully maintained their own printmaking shops, usually after long-term work with us. Some others, after leaving us, have worked in other shops or taught in universities or colleges. Two left to raise families, one to start and run a gallery. My point here includes everyone trained in our studio and even those who went into nonart fields. I think our life-work successes are at least partly due to learning from our artists how to maintain a strange kind of satisfaction in whatever we are doing. Maybe we could call it intrigue.

Wayne is a dedicated teacher, continuing to give classes at the University of California, Davis, long after his supposed retirement. In 1972 he said this to a group of students: "Don't worry about creativity and emotion and individualism. You've all got your driver's licenses already. You're already individuals. You're already creative. All you have to worry about is being good at something."

When I visited the exhibition "The Steins Collect" at the San Francisco Museum of Modern Art in 2011, I remembered that remark. The exhibition showed notebooks detailing Matisse's instruction in a school started by Sarah Stein, the wife of Gertrude Stein's brother Leo. Gertrude, apparently, joked about this, calling Matisse *"chere maître"* (dear master), or C.M. for short. The more unruly Picasso would never be pinned down to teaching.

According to Jack Flam in *Matisse and Picasso: The Story of Their Rivalry and Friendship*, the two artists were also fundamentally different in that

Picasso believed that "pictorial disharmony and the destruction of the human image would best capture the spirit of the new century," while "Matisse would never become reconciled to the idea of radically linking destruction with creation and violence with modernity."

Maybe as our new century progresses we can find ways to use displacement instead of destruction as our template. Could the divisiveness now dominant in our public lives become something more generous? There is not much sign of it now—certainly not in govern-

Wayne Thiebaud, *Lemon Meringue*, from *Delights*, a book of 17 etchings, 1964. Hard ground etching, 4 × 4 inches.

ment—but Wayne's approach sets an example to us as individuals. He has said that he uses in his painting "a tremendous amount of adoption, adaptation, and change." He says he "essentializes" his subject matter, reducing it as a sauce is reduced in cooking.

"How do you figure out how to transpose visual images from one kind of sensibility or media to another?" he asked rhetorically in the National Gallery panel discussion. "A painted image has a certain character, depending on the technology of the paint. The question is, When you translate it into something smaller, in black and white, and printed, what do you do, and what's the intrigue, why do it? Well, I think the intrigue is in the relationship between one kind of thing and another; what the differences are, the distinctions."

Recognizing distinctions, finding the intrigue, that's what leads to doing things well.

The Oakland building where Crown Point moved in 1971. The studio was on the third floor. City Hall is behind.

6.

Put One Foot in Front of the Other

One morning in 1971 I was standing at my kitchen sink looking out the window. A taxi pulled up in front of the house, and a pleasant-looking man got out. "Where can he be going?" I thought. He stood on the sidewalk looking up at the house for a moment, then opened our gate, walked up the steps, and rang the doorbell.

When I opened the door, my two big dogs raced out, pushing him against the railing, which he grabbed to save himself from falling. "Is this the Crown Point Press?" he inquired politely, straightening himself. When I managed to say that it was, he said that his name was Sol LeWitt and Bob Feldman of Parasol Press had sent him here to make etchings.

I still cannot figure out why I didn't expect Sol that day. I know that Feldman had spoken with me on the telephone about him—I had written down Saul LeWitt (Bob probably spelled the last name but not the first). I thought I would go to the library to find out something about him. But so far as I can remember, the conversation with Bob was inconclusive and took place only a few days before Sol showed up. "There must be printers in New York who can do this," I had said on the phone.

I imagine that someone in New York could have done it, but the dominant way of printing etchings in the United States back then was an "expressive" variant of the traditional approach that I'd been taught at the Central School in London. I had learned to begin with a cloth tarlatan pad (a "rag") and finish the wipe with the palm of the hand. This is the French approach. The variant American method generally involves wiping plates only with the rag, although

Hand wiping (top). With Kevin in the basement studio, 1965 (bottom).

some printers finish with a flat paper sheet. Using the palm of the hand for the finish wipe produces prints with more overall contrast and more precise tonal variation than rag wiping alone or rag and paper in combination.

Because a printer trained in the French method does not think of the wiping as expressive, all the prints from the same plate are consistent in the way they look; everything in the plate shows. In the French method, the artist makes plates and the printer prints them straightforwardly; another printer trained the same way would produce essentially the same result, even though each print is individually printed by hand. In the American style of printing, however, the printer generally leaves more ink or less in certain parts of the plate in order to express a character or quality he believes the artist wants; and since this character is not necessarily in the plate, there are usually differences from print to print in an edition. I think one reason Feldman liked my style of printing, the French style, was its consistency.

I had met Bob Feldman through Wayne Thiebaud. Bob owns Parasol Press, a New York print publisher without a print shop of its own. He was a friend of Alan Stone, whose gallery had given Thiebaud his first show in New York, and Parasol Press had contracted with Thiebaud to publish a portfolio of his prints. Bob had in mind big color lithographs and silk-screen prints. He had seen the etchings from *Delights* and they confirmed to him what he (and lots of other people) had assumed about etching: small, black and white, linear—not what he wanted. But Wayne had assured him I could do colorful work in reasonable size—he had watched it being done in our workshop—and Bob agreed that Wayne could work at Crown Point to make two of the prints for the set.

The two we made, *Triangle Thins* and *Big Suckers* (plate 5), are dated 1971. Crown Point did nearly all Parasol Press's printing for the next five years, and etchings have continued to dominate Parasol publications during Parasol's long life. Bob "semi-retired" and moved from New York to Portland in 2004, but he still keeps his office in New York.

When I answered the door for Sol LeWitt on that sunny morning in 1971, the same year I was finishing Thiebaud's *Triangle Thins* and *Big Suckers*, I had no idea that my business had changed, and things would never be the same again.

Until then, all the artists I had worked with were from the San Francisco Bay Area. I did everything myself with occasional help from a student, a friend, or a workshop person. The studio was mostly populated with work-shoppers doing their own work, and I was teaching two classes, one in my Crown Point basement studio for the University of California's extension program and the other at the San Francisco Art Institute.

When Kevin was not in school, he was digging forts in our front yard with neighbor boys or hanging out in the studio. He had become a good etch-ing printer and was interested in photography (we had a darkroom in the house). Also, from an early age, he enjoyed visiting the Schuberth bookbind-ery, where Hans Schuberth and his small staff were binding by hand the *livres d'artistes* that I was publishing. When Kevin was still in elementary school, Schuberth sold us a small bookbinding press. Kevin installed it in our base-ment and started restoring old books for pocket money. When he was thirteen, in 1974, he did the bookbinding for a small-edition project for Crown Point, the first of many he would do for us.

I was publishing books with prints in them because

Wayne signing
Big Suckers, 1971.

I liked doing them, even though they were, in fact, practically unsellable as books. I did sell, at $100 each, some individual Diebenkorn and Thiebaud prints from the portfolios, but it was clear very early that the book idea wasn't going to pay for itself. Nevertheless, after my big push in 1965 when I produced books by Diebenkorn, Beth Van Hoesen, and Thiebaud, I averaged one book a year. Between 1965 and 1970, I printed and published two books by Fred Martin, *Beulah Land* and *Log of the Sun Ship*, both symbol-filled narratives of California, and three by Bruce Conner, collectively titled *The Dennis Hopper One-Man Show*. Conner (who died in 2008) was a sculptor who worked mainly with found objects and also spliced film to make influential, surreal short films. He wanted to make prints from collages of old engravings.

For Bruce Conner's project, I used Kodak materials that were made for manufacturing circuit boards in order to produce photographic images on etching plates. By 1974, I had improved that technique and used it for photographs in a book called *A Scratch on the Negative,* by Jim Melchert. The book starts with an image of baseball players, and a section of the image is gradually enlarged to focus on a scratch.

I had started working with photoetching in the late sixties when I made the first plates for *Album*, a book in which I remember the Washington Oaks of my childhood. I didn't publish it until 1972—there wasn't much time for my own work. But I followed it with *Sardinia* in 1975, and by that time my use of photographs in etching was more accomplished.

I carried the photoetching idea as far as it would go in *Paradise* (plate 7), the last book of my own in which I used etchings. Some of the photoetchings are in color, the plates created with a homemade version (filters in our enlarger) of commercial printing's four-color separation process. I began work

Jim Melchert, from the book *A Scratch on the Negative*, 1974. Photoetching, 6 × 10½ inches.

WITH THE OTHER. AS THE LAMP'S FLAME FLICKERED, SHE SAW, STANDING ANGUISHED AND ASTONISHED BEFORE HER, EROS, THE GOD OF LOVE.
HAVING CRIED ALL AFTERNOON, PSYCHE THOUGHT NOW SHE WOULD DIE OF CRYING, AND HER SOBS SHOOK HER BODY AS EROS KNELT BESIDE HER ASKING WHY SHE WOULD WANT TO KILL HIM. FINALLY SHE WAS ABLE TO TELL HIM WHAT HER SISTERS HAD SAID. HE CRIED THEN, TOO, AND HE TOLD PSYCHE THAT SHE WAS CARRYING HIS CHILD, AND THAT IF THIS HAD NOT HAPPENED THEY WOULD HAVE BEEN ABLE TO MOVE OUT OF THE MOUNTAIN AND LIVE WITH THE GODS AFTER THE CHILD WAS BORN. BUT AS IT WAS NOW, EROS HAD TO KEEP

Bruce Conner, from the book *Dennis Hopper One Man Show, Volume 1,* 1971–73. Photoetching, 13¼ × 9 inches.

Kathan Brown, from the book *Sardinia,* 1975. Photoetching, 13¼ × 10½ inches.

on *Paradise* in 1978 and published it in 1982. By that time Kevin was twenty-one. He is credited in the *Paradise* book with making the plates and doing the bookbinding. I had hoped that he eventually would take over Crown Point, but by 1982 he was already running his own small business, which is bookbinding related. It occupies him fully in 2011, his fiftieth year. But I am getting ahead of my story.

Before Sol LeWitt came to Crown Point Press in 1971, I was running a business, but it was mainly for myself and my friends so we could work in etching. And I was simply doing one thing and then the next thing that seemed to be in front of me to do. I'm not sure if I even thought my book publishing was, exactly, a business. Since 1966, I had been teaching at the San Francisco Art Institute. Also, I was running a workshop, and I thought of myself as an artist-printmaker, part of a lively printmaking community in the San Francisco Bay Area. There were two organizations, the California Society of Etchers for etching and the Bay Printmakers for lithography. They later merged to become the California Society of Printmakers, which is still very active.

Lithography and etching, both used for hand printmaking, are fundamentally different. Etching, along with gravure (its photographic version), is an intaglio process. That means there are incisions in the plate, and in the finished print the ink is embedded in the paper. Lithography is a planographic process. The plate is uniformly flat, and ink sits on top of the paper. Lithography, invented at the end of the eighteenth century, was the first new printing process since etching and engraving had appeared in the mid-fifteenth century. (Woodcut was much earlier.) Now, digital inkjet printing has come along, but it has not yet superseded lithography for printing books, magazines, and newspapers. Commercial lithography is streamlined from the process artist-lithographers use. Etching has no commercial use in our present-day world; it lingers in memory with an Irving Berlin song: "on the Avenue, Fifth Avenue, the photographers will snap us and you'll find that you're in the rotogravure."

In the 1960s artist-printmakers, both lithographers and etchers, dominated the print world all across the country; many taught in art schools and universities. Artists who made plates but didn't learn printing skills rarely got involved with the medium. Fifty years later, artist-printmakers are still active; they are the ones who fill our Crown Point workshops with great enthusiasm. But the number of artists who rely on professional printers to print their prints has enormously increased. I think this is healthy for our craft, and I am pleased that Crown Point Press helped bring it about in the United States. But we didn't start the trend. The prime movers were the lithography workshops that came on the scene somewhat earlier.

In 1963, soon after I had set up my etching workshop in the Richmond storefront, I made a trip to Los Angeles to call on June Wayne and tour the Tamarind Lithography Workshop that she had founded in 1960 with a grant from the Ford Foundation. Tamarind's mission was, to quote its website today, "'rescuing' the dying art of lithography," and June Wayne (with continuously renewed grants from Ford) certainly enlarged lithography's scope in the United States. She ran Tamarind in Los Angeles for ten years. After that, in 1970, it became part of the University of New Mexico, and other dedicated people (Marge Devon is now director) continued the work.

June Wayne, who died in 2011, was an artist, not a printer. As an artist, she had made prints in France, at a traditional lithography shop. The master printer I met in Los Angeles was French and had worked with Picasso at

Mourlot, the most famous Paris lithography atelier. I thought that Tamarind was extending the traditions of French workshops, but I didn't think it was exactly "rescuing" the medium—the artist-printmakers I associated with included lithographers.

Wayne invited artists—some with printmaking knowledge, some without—to make lithographs at Tamarind. They worked with a master printer who was assisted by young men whom he was training to become lithography printers. After the trainees had earned the title Tamarind Master Printer (which took two years), many of them founded lithography workshops of their own. The first woman Tamarind master printer was Judith Solodkin, who entered the program in 1972 after it moved to New Mexico. Solodkin still owns and runs Solo Impression in New York.

June Wayne welcomed me on my visit in the early sixties and was encouraging about my etching workshop. When I met her, however, I didn't think Tamarind offered a business model. I still don't, but a decade later, after I started to work for Bob Feldman's Parasol Press, I slipped into something like June Wayne's system of a master printer, assisted by other printers, working with an artist. But at Crown Point, as soon as I had more than one printer trained to the "master" level, I didn't run the shop with one person continuously in charge. Our printers take turns leading projects, and we credit the master printer in charge of each project in documentations and with a blind stamp in the margin (or a rubber stamp on the reverse) of each print.

Tamarind set an example in the printmaking world in many ways. It encouraged printers to be openhanded about techniques and materials (this was not part of the French tradition). At Crown Point we have always spared time to help other printmakers solve problems, and when we have had the resources, we have published instructional material for etching, as Tamarind does for lithography.

The idea of using a stamp on each print identifying both the press and the printer comes from Tamarind. And, following Tamarind's example, I give our trained etching printers the title Crown Point Master Printer, echoing the Tamarind Master Printer formality. I think the word *master* implies a high level of training, and if that word is used, the source of the training should be included. The phrase *master printer* doesn't mean much without identifying the organization that issued the title.

An element of Tamarind's legacy that I've resisted is routinely using the word *collaboration* to describe the relationship between printers and artists. I think the art is the artist's. A printer supplies needed skills, but the crucial element, the art, is a fragment of an artist's lifework and is generally outside the printer's scope. Sometimes an artist does collaborate with another artist or a co-creator in another field (possibly a printer), but when that happens both parties contribute content (different from technical knowledge) and the content of the art reflects both minds. Full-blown collaborations seem to be most successful when they come from long-term relationships (husband and wife, for example). Our printers are trained to think of themselves as teachers and facilitators, not collaborators.

Tamarind offers rudimentary business training as part of its master printer program, and many of its master printers over the years have started businesses and run them successfully. But Tamarind has always been a non-profit corporation, and attempting to be "self supporting" through print sales, as nonprofit workshops usually do, is not the same as being in business. The pioneer in hand printmaking as a business in the United States is Universal Limited Art Editions, ULAE, founded on Long Island by Russian immigrant Tatyana Grosman in 1957.

Grosman, like June Wayne, was not a printer. ULAE started out using silk-screen printing to reproduce artworks. A curator at the Museum of Modern Art advised Grosman to make original prints instead of reproductions, and by 1960 Jasper Johns and Robert Rauschenberg, the most important artists of the time, were working with her first master printer, Robert Blackburn, an African-American WPA artist and expert lithographer who had started the Printmaking Workshop in New York in 1948. He kept his workshop going during his tenure at ULAE, which lasted from 1957 until 1963. The Robert Blackburn Printmaking Workshop is still alive, renamed to include Blackburn's name after he died in 2003.

ULAE was a lithography shop until 1967, when it began publishing etchings alongside its lithographs. Its present owner/director, printer Bill Goldston, has been there since 1969. In 1976 Grosman turned over much of the running of the business to him; she advised him until her death in 1982. Johns, Rauschenberg, and other important New York artists of their generation produced many great prints that ULAE published—Johns, though he has had a printer on his personal staff for many years, still regularly publishes through ULAE. In 1982 Goldston, according to the ULAE website, began its current program publishing younger artists who are mainly involved in "painterly" work.

Rauschenberg first, and then Johns, also worked at Gemini G.E.L., beginning in 1967, when Rauschenberg made *Booster,* a life-size X-ray of himself printed with silk screen and lithography. "We're a support system, not a co-creator," said Sidney Felsen, one of Gemini's founders, voicing a sentiment I share. However, the founding printer-partner, Kenneth Tyler, who came out of Tamarind, freely used the word *collaborator* throughout his long and technically innovative career.

Tyler had entered the Tamarind program in 1963 right out of art school and in 1965 founded Gemini Ltd. in Los Angeles with his wife, Kay. At the end of 1965 the business became Gemini G.E.L. (Graphic Editions Limited), and Tyler became partners with Felsen, an accountant, and Elyse and Stanley Grinstein, collectors very much engaged with the lively art scene in 1960s Los Angeles that centered on the Ferus Gallery and included a dash of Hollywood glamour. Ferus showed the most inventive artists in Los Angeles, and many of them, Ed Ruscha for example, have worked at Gemini in lithography beginning in the early days. Gemini's early days coincided with the Ferus Gallery's first shows of New York artists, and when they traveled to Los Angeles for exhibitions, they sometimes made prints at Gemini.

Artforum magazine started in San Francisco but moved in 1965 to Los Angeles. It rented space upstairs from Ferus and contributed to a scene into which the out-of-town artists comfortably blended. "The so-called mythical figures of the East became ordinary figures in the West," said John Coplans, *Artforum* editor. In addition to Johns and Rauschenberg, other important artists from New York and a few from Europe made prints at Gemini in the late 1960s and early 1970s, and Gemini has remained a force in the print world ever since. Kenneth Tyler moved to Bedford (and later Mt. Kisco), New York, commute distance from New York City, in 1973 and founded Tyler Graphics there. He remained an influential printer and publisher until he sold his business to the government of Singapore in 2000 and retired at the age of sixty-nine.

In the San Francisco Bay Area in 1971, Sol LeWitt, working at Crown Point Press and drawing with an etching needle in wax grounds on copper plates, made forty-seven images. There are four small ones not in sets, including *Lines in Four Directions, Superimposed in Each Quarter of the Square Progressively.* There is also a set of sixteen called *Bands of Color in Four Directions & All Combinations*

Sol LeWitt, *Lines in Four Directions, Superimposed in Each Quarter of the Square Progressively,* 1971. Hard ground etching, 11 × 11 inches. Published by Parasol Press.

(plate 6), a black and white set based on squares, and a color set called *Scribbles.* "I'm making drawings on walls in pencil, and they don't show up much," Sol told me after I etched the first plate and the lines came out clear and strong. He redrew the image, and after that I etched the plates delicately.

Because the image on an etching plate is embedded in it, printing involves pressing ink into the marks and lines and then wiping the surface clean without disturbing the ink that is below the surface. A little too much pressure on the tarletan "rag" or with the hand "wipes out" a delicate line, but not enough pressure leaves a film on the background. Many of Sol's prints were in color, and color ink tinges grayish green through oxidation if wiped actively against a copper plate; only the lightest touch can keep the color clean. A couple of images were solid yellow, the worst color for oxidation. Steel facing the plates after etching them would have solved the oxidation problem, but that wasn't something I could do back then.

My wiping difficulties, combined with the sheer number of prints, made Sol LeWitt's first project the most difficult one I ever printed. But I found the etchings surprisingly touching in their modesty and forthrightness; the longer I looked at them, the more beautiful they became. I looked at them too long, however. Business had been good for Bob Feldman. He telephoned me: "I need those prints. There's nothing in the drawer."

Brice Marden, *20 (a)* from *Ten Days*, 1971, a portfolio of eight aquatints with hard ground etching, 15 × 20 inches. Published by Parasol Press.

A weight lifted from me when, months after Sol had returned to New York, I stacked what I thought was the last batch of his prints into blotters to dry. The next day I discovered that a workshop person had disturbed the stack, and the ink on some of the prints was smeared. I had to do those few over, but eventually everything was on its way.

Later that year, when I moved Crown Point Press into a commercial loft space in Oakland, I stopped offering workshops. It was a difficult decision because the workshoppers were mainly friends and because I had started the press with the idea of workshops. It was clear, however, that Parasol would be keeping me busy and I had to create a professional shop. After that, the workshops were dormant for seventeen years. But in 1990, the year that followed Crown Point's move into our present spacious space, we picked them up again and have held them every summer (and some weekends) since then, twenty-one years (and continuing) at this writing.

Looking back, I see that I was quick to make the decision to work for Parasol, and to move the press and hire a staff. Brice Marden was the first artist to work in the Crown Point studio at 1555 San Pablo Avenue in Oakland, and his project is dated 1971, the same year as LeWitt's.

The building held several artists' studios; I learned after we moved there that the one I had rented was briefly Diebenkorn's, just before he moved to

Los Angeles. We were upstairs over a hat store; if we went on the roof behind us, we could look through a skylight into the hat factory behind the store. Our studio had a long row of windows facing San Pablo Avenue, a downtown street in the city center. City Hall is on San Pablo just a block away from where we were, and in the neighborhood we also had two department stores and a decent hotel (all of which are now closed).

Brice Marden went downstairs on the first day and bought a hat, which he wore while he was working. We had booked him into the hotel, the Leamington, and he walked to work past two buildings faced with ceramic tile, a disused Deco theater with blue and silver tiles, and the I. Magnin department store, with elegant walls of green tile. There are a lot of tile buildings in Oakland, including the Paramount Theater, then newly restored. They are a hallmark of the city. Brice loved them. "How's the I. Magnin building?" he asked me in New York when I saw him after the project.

Brice called his project *Ten Days*, the amount of time he spent with us. He made five prints, medium sized, black and white, tactile, some of them heavy with ink. He used mostly aquatint tones in simple rectangles. "I paint nature," he said later in our Crown Point interview series. "I mean, I refer to nature. I accept nature as a reality. It's what the painting's about." Much later, Brice (very much a New Yorker) told a curator at the Tate Gallery in London that those first prints at Crown Point had to do with looking out over the Oakland cityscape. "What was impressive was that there was lots of sky and it was very open, but still it was a city." On a later visit, he made a group called *Tiles*.

With printer Pat Branstead in Oakland, 1971.

The hat factory downstairs from the studio, 1971 (left). Brice Marden working (right).

Patricia Branstead is listed as the printer for Marden's *Ten Days*. This is the first project at Crown Point that I did not print primarily by myself. Pat had been a student of mine at the San Francisco Art Institute and had been working for me in the basement from time to time. She is the first master printer on our Crown Point list after myself. She has brilliant red hair that formed a great cloud around her head in those hippie days. Many years later she left Crown Point to start Aeropress in New York and became a sought-after printer there.

The rest of my first staff also was mined from my Art Institute students. Gwen Gugell was a printer and Deward Drollinger a jack-of-all-trades. "Dewey never looks like he's doing anything," Chuck Close said, remarking on our odd California ways, and then added, "but at the end of the day, everything is done."

For our Chuck Close project in 1972, I had to buy a larger press; Feldman loaned me the money on easy terms. My first contact with Chuck was a telephone call; he asked if he could do a mezzotint. Mezzotint is a little-used process that starts with a plate roughened so that it prints solid black. The artist burnishes the ink-holding tooth in the plate so the image appears in shades of gray. It's very time-consuming and skill dependent. I explained that, but Chuck stuck to his idea. I asked him how large he wanted to work.

"I paint very large," he said, "but maybe I could go down to about three by four feet."

"Most mezzotints are in the range of three by four inches," I said. I

thought he hadn't understood what I was talking about, but after Pat and I went to Los Angeles to see an exhibition of Chuck's paintings, I realized I was the one who hadn't understood. The paintings were enormous detailed portrait heads in black and shades of gray, painted with an airbrush. Every pore showed. Size was the astonishing, essential thing; except for the size, the paintings resembled mezzotints.

Normally the overall basic texture on a mezzotint plate is a network of dots put in by rocking a many-pointed tool repeatedly over the entire plate. However, this would have been impossible for a plate of forty-five by thirty-six inches, which is what we settled on. Instead, I used my photoetching techniques to etch the plate overall with a very fine dot screen. This worked (after some trial and error) to create the black background on small-scale tests, and Chuck began by using the small plates to practice burnishing an image.

When we scrubbed our first big copper plate prior to coating it with emulsion, everyone was excited. The plate was gleaming and huge; it took two people to handle it. But right away we ran into trouble. We attempted to dry it by blowing air from a compressor, as we had done with the small ones. But before half the plate was dry the other half started turning gray green from oxidation. Clearly the whole surface had to be dried almost instantaneously. We

Chuck Close burnishing the plate for *Keith*, 1972 (opposite left). *Keith*, 1972. Mezzotint, 45 × 36 inches (opposite right). Chuck with Bob Feldman, 1972 (left).

devised a system with squeegees. Chuck pushed the largest one down the center, since he was the tallest. Gwen, Pat, and Dewey worked on the edges, and I stood over it all with the air hose running down stray droplets. All this with the noise of the compressor chugging, and everyone falling over everyone else in our haste to evaporate the water beads before they left their little green marks. "The Marx Brothers clean a plate," someone commented when it was over.

The plate was successfully cleaned, but the processes of coating, exposing, and etching it were yet to be worked out. Days passed as we solved one problem after another, usually failing before succeeding. Then, when we were sure we had everything in place, we failed again by a fluke. We all sat silently in a cloud of despair, and finally, one by one, people went home. Gwen and I were left. "Well," I said, "at least the next one has to be perfect. There's nothing else that could possibly go wrong."

"Wouldn't it be nice," Gwen mused, "if when Chuck comes in tomorrow he had a plate that he could work on?"

"You mean do it now? We can't, just the two of us."

"If we could get one more person for the squeegeeing, I think we could do it ourselves."

I called Pat and Dewey but neither answered. I called a couple of friends, but no luck. So I went home and got Kevin, gave him a squeegee, and the three of us did it. By 11:30 the plate was ready to be etched, and Kevin (then ten) was asleep on the couch.

I got in early the next morning, and when Chuck arrived the plate was almost ready. He was ecstatic. "No more scrubbing, no more squeegeeing, no more chemicals, no more lugging that thing around wet and dripping," he exulted. As I printed, the excitement was back to the level of our very first big plate. This time, it turned out fine. All we had done at that point, however, was to create a plate that printed solid black. About ten o'clock that day Chuck started work, scraping and burnishing the plate's texture to create an image. It was Friday of the third week.

He finished the print five weeks later. His biggest complaint was that he couldn't see what he was doing; he needed a lot of proofs, at least at first. Each time the plate went through the press, it received more than a thousand pounds of pressure per square inch, and copper is a soft material. I wasn't worried about the blacks (the part he hadn't worked) wearing out because those dots were close together and etched in, but repeated printing would surely diminish the areas he had burnished. I calculated that if he kept proofing at his initial rate, we would have made several hundred proofs before the plate was finished, and most likely there would be nothing left of the mouth, where he had begun.

By the time he had worked his way up to the nostrils, however, he got the hang of burnishing and started going faster with less need for proofing. The mouth area in the finished print is lighter than the rest. It may be because he overdid the burnishing at first, and it may be because of the proofing. Probably it was a combination. Chuck didn't seem to care much, one way or the other, that the mouth printed lighter; "it shows the process," he said. He was more concerned about the grid lines in the finished print.

The way Chuck works is to copy a photograph by squaring it off and scaling it up using a grid of squares on the canvas, or in this case on the copper plate. In his canvases, he was used to painting out the grid as he went along, but the grid lines he drew on the plate were generally stronger than the texture that created the mezzotint surface. As he scraped and burnished the plate, the grid remained in many areas. It was clear right from the beginning that all the grid lines weren't going away, so Chuck accepted that. In the end he liked it. Most of his paintings since then have allowed the grid to show.

The simple fact that *Keith* exists is almost unbelievable to print scholars because of its size and the precision of Chuck's scraping and burnishing. Just as he did in his airbrushed paintings, he copied by hand the photographic image as exactly as possible. At a glance the print almost seems to be a photograph.

A radical next step for a painter working so precisely would be to accept a photograph itself as a work of art. It is a step Chuck contemplated back in the 1970s and has acted upon over subsequent years by creating and selling actual photographs using daguerreotype, Polaroid photography, and holograms, and, since 1996, by publishing with Adamson Editions in Washington, D.C. straight-out photographs as ink-jet prints.

While he was burnishing and scraping the big *Keith* plate, Chuck asked us to try to produce a photograph of his friend John in color photoetching the same size as *Keith*. Youth and inexperience led me, with my printers, to attempt that impossible task in 1972. We failed, but we got something promising. A few years later, we succeeded in the technique with *Paradise* (plate 7), but its plates are minuscule in size compared with what we attempted with *John*.

Take a mental leap forward with me now to 2012. Over the intervening years Crown Point Press switched from photoetching to an older and better technique for etching photographs: photogravure. In photoetching everything in a plate is etched to the same depth, while in photogravure the image has varying depths, and consequently holds ink with more richness and subtlety. I asked Chuck if we could test our experiments in developing color-separated photogravure by using a photograph of his, and the self-portrait in plate 8 is the result. To me it is a thrilling technical breakthrough. To Chuck, as he said to me, "being technically amazing doesn't make it a work of art." So, we are not printing an edition. But I am glad to be able to show it to you.

Putting one foot in front of the other involves starting somewhere and keeping moving, even if taking a step back is necessary once in a while along the way.

Pat Steir in 1981.

7.

PAT STEIR AND AGNES MARTIN

No Pretensions

On a winter afternoon in 1972, I was talking with Bob Feldman in his New York office when a big-boned woman with short gray-streaked hair walked in, and Bob introduced me to Agnes Martin. I had heard the Agnes Martin legend and, like all the artists I knew, admired her paintings: horizontal stripes, wavering lines, or grids in soft pure colors. The paintings had been in exhibitions, but Martin herself had been absent from New York for the previous five years.

Agnes Martin had moved to New Mexico and built a house with her own hands. Then she built a studio. Just as she was ready to begin painting again, she had received a letter from Bob Feldman inviting her to make prints. He suggested etchings—he was going to send her to Crown Point—but she had a particular problem she wanted to solve. She wanted the printer to straighten out her lines, which she said she could never paint straight enough. She had seen some silk-screen prints she liked, and that was the medium she wanted to use.

When I met her, she had already made thirty drawings in squares all the same size using grids, lines, and bands in light gray ink. These were maquettes for the print portfolio eventually titled *On a Clear Day*. Feldman had sent them to Edition Domberger in Stuttgart, Germany, a respected silk-screen printer, which had made proofs, straightening out her lines, and sent them to Bob. Agnes was

Agnes Martin, circa 1972.

in New York on the way to Stuttgart to finalize the color and the paper, neither of which was right. Bob planned to fly with her and leave her there if necessary. He would have to return after just a day, he told me.

I said he should stay as long as she did. I was pretty sure one day wouldn't be enough, and I thought that after being in New Mexico for five years without much company she would need support in Germany. Bob said I was right and asked me to go along. That was how Feldman did things. I hadn't even known he was working with Agnes Martin until I happened to visit on the day she arrived, and all of a sudden I was on the telephone getting my passport sent express from home.

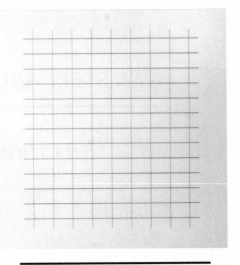

Agnes Martin, *On a Clear Day*, 1973.
One of 30 screenprints, 12 × 12 inches.
Published by Parasol Press.

In the years Agnes had been in New Mexico, she told me, she was able to have conversations only occasionally with old friends who searched her out in the desert. She was disappointed to learn later that at least one couple returned to New York without finding her. Those were the days before cell phones, but even if her searching friends had had such things, Agnes had no phone. When she wrote to me, later, she printed the words *no phone* beneath her return address.

In the desert, when she wanted to talk, she said, she talked to a lizard that stayed unafraid at her building site. She built the house truly by herself, only occasionally hiring a teenage boy from a nearby farm when she needed to set beams or do some other work that required two people. Not having had anyone to talk to for five years, she talked a lot to me in Germany. I started to think she could read my mind, because when it would wander, I thought she would alter the conversation to start talking about what I had been thinking about.

It was snowing in Stuttgart, and I was not dressed warmly enough. I can still visualize a country path we walked every day in the snow to get to the shop. The people at Domberger spoke English and were wonderful to us.

Their method of operation was to trace artists' drawings and cut them into film that they adhered on screens printed semi-automatically by a machine tended by people. There was no artist's studio, but the director loaned Agnes his office so she could pin up proofs and look quietly at them. The only place to pin them was the back of the door, which occasionally opened, but it worked out all right.

The paper was the tricky part, but we ended up with a sheet that took the ink in the right way; adjusting the exact shade of gray was reasonably fast once Agnes had settled on the paper. We were there about a week. As we were leaving, both of us thanked everyone at the shop profusely, and Agnes, shaking hands, saying good-bye, added reflectively, quietly, "You are all such wonderful people. I can't understand how you could have done those things to the Jews." I said something different very quickly, hoping they hadn't heard or understood the English. They didn't act as though they had.

I, myself, have been told that "sometimes your mouth speaks without your brain's involvement." I think it happened in Agnes's case because of spending a lot of time alone. It happens to me mostly when I'm heeding the subtitle of this chapter: no pretensions. Pretensions are the skins of second-guessing, and shedding them is not always advisable. But hasn't nearly every thinking person (including every thinking German) at one time or another asked Agnes's question, if only in his or her own mind? I showed an early draft of this chapter to Pat Steir and asked if she thought I should include Agnes's question. "What the Germans did is so monstrous," I said. "I don't believe it could ever happen again."

"We could do something like it," she replied. "A lot of money right now is pouring into trying to develop a massive cult mentality here."

When I began this chapter, I had intended to focus it wholly on Pat Steir, a mainstay of our Crown Point artist group and a long-term friend and influence on me. But when I began thinking about Pat, Agnes Martin came into my mind, and I started there. Pat often says in interviews that Agnes Martin, John Cage, and Sol LeWitt, all of whom she knew, are her three major influences.

Pat Steir was born in 1938 in Newark, New Jersey, with the name Iris Patricia Sukoneck. Her father's parents were Jewish immigrants from Russia. Their children became lawyers and accountants, she says, except her father, who went to art school and ended up with a business designing window

Pat working on a self-portrait series, 1987.

displays and neon signs. Her mother's parents were Sephardic Jews from Egypt. Pat married young and took her husband's surname.

Pat received a B.F.A. from the Pratt Institute in 1962, the same year I started Crown Point Press. She had quick success in art, being included in an exhibition that year at the High Museum in Atlanta and, soon after, 1964, in a show called "Drawings" at the Museum of Modern Art in New York. She was barely out of school when, in 1964, she had a one-person show at a respected gallery in New York. Then, in 1966 she got a job as an art director for the book publisher Harper & Row. She arranged flexible hours, was able to continue painting, and became an active member of the New York art scene.

Until the mid-1970s, Pat contributed to the feminist art movement by being on the editorial board of the journal *Heresies*. She says she did not make feminist art, but in her art she was trying to escape isolation. "I wanted to be seen simply as an artist, I wanted to be a contender, an equal," she said in a 2011 interview with the *Brooklyn Rail*, a youthful free newspaper for art and culture. "I think my existence and survival in art, along with other women of my generation, has political implications beyond the personal."

Pat met Agnes Martin a year before I did. In 1971 art critic Douglas Crimp, a friend of Pat's, had rounded up some Martin paintings for an exhibition at the gallery of the School of Visual Arts in New York. The show was reviewed favorably, and Crimp received an invitation from Martin to visit her in New Mexico. He took Pat along, and for the next thirty-three years she continued to visit Martin frequently, her last visit being a few weeks before Martin died at the age of ninety-two in 2004.

I met Pat in 1975. Sol LeWitt was doing a project at Crown Point for Parasol, his third, I think. Feldman's artists stayed at the hotel in Oakland, the Leamington, except Sol, who stayed in our guest room. Since he had worked with us when Crown Point was in our basement, my son, Kevin, and I saw him as different from everyone else.

One day near the end of the project, Sol said to me, "I'm expecting someone. I hope it's OK if she joins me for a couple of days." This is Pat's version of the story: Sol was working on a wall drawing at a museum in Los Angeles. She was temporarily teaching there. Sol invited her to go to Italy with him, with a stop in Berkeley on the way. The school term was just ending. She packed her bags and, as he instructed, showed up at our house. She didn't at first know why Sol was there, but when she saw what we were doing with etching, she told me later, she started trying to figure out how she could work with us.

Two years after that, in 1977, Pat arrived at Crown Point Press to make a print to be given by a museum to its contributors. Pat and I had liked each other right away, and though I was still working mainly for Parasol Press, I was glad to have an opportunity to take that small job. Fortunately for me, it didn't turn out to be small. "I did many prints," Pat remembered in a 1991 interview, "and I was on the telephone calling other print publishers, trying to get somebody to publish the other prints, and Kathan told me she would publish them."

Actually, it wasn't so many, only seven: one fairly large, one small, and five even smaller and bound into a book. They are restrained in color, mostly a kind of golden umber, and beautiful. All Steir's work has a tactile beauty slightly at odds with the restraint of her contemporaries. The following year

Pat Steir, *Self After Rembrandt #1,* 1987. Hard ground etching with drypoint, 11 × 11 inches.

Pat Steir, *Drawing Lesson, Part 1, Line*, 1978. From a portfolio of seven sugar lift and spit bite aquatints with drypoint, printed in brown, each 11¾ × 11¾ inches.

she came back to do many more prints, also published by Crown Point Press. These included a dozen in burnt umber, some of them accented with bright primary colors, in a series called *Drawing Lesson*. In the years since 1977, we have published more than a hundred prints by Pat Steir. She is the artist with the largest number on our list.

Although Pat's art has always seemed to me to be romantic and sensual, she makes clear in every interview that she does not think of it as expressionistic. "The self is like a bug," she said in 1988. "Every time you slap it, it moves to another place." In an interview for the Crown Point publication, *View*, in 1978, she told Robin White that making art is "a desire to transcend the limits of a single human being. The urge for art, for me, is the urge for language. I start with a mark, and the mark is a universal desire to speak or communicate."

In that period, a lot of ideas floating around New York were derived from the French philosophers of deconstruction, who wrote of language, signs, symbols, codes, and the impossibility of finding Truth. Pat often has incorporated words into her prints, and she has done paintings and prints, including self-portrait prints, that deconstruct work by great artists of the past. *When I Think of Venice*, 1980 (plate 10), shows geometric figures and different kinds of marks and, like most of Pat's work in the seventies and eighties, refers to what I think of as her intellectual side. In her recent work, Pat seems to escape intellect, but, in fact, intellect is part of her nature. At one point in her life, she was even an editor for a magazine called *Semiotext(e)*.

You wouldn't think of the word *intellectual* if you watched her in the studio, though. She clunked around in high-heeled shoes ("I'm short," she said, "and I'm used to them") and posed for photos, sometimes making faces. Then, in later years, she started throwing paint at her plates. The printers put plastic sheets up strategically, but we still have a few drips and splats on our walls.

But what about Pat's influence from John Cage, and how does that fit with her involvement with Agnes Martin? She met Cage in 1980, through me, but before meeting him she had studied music and been engaged with his ideas. After that, she saw him sometimes in New York. Agnes, on the other hand, resisted Cage. Here is a quote from an undated letter I got from her, probably in 1980:

> *Between you and me, Kathan, John Cage is still negative because although he has surrendered self direction to chance that does not make art work. He does not believe in inspiration, beauty, truth, reality but only chance. With chance one still must choose to act and he is back to intellect. Inspiration is possible when you say to yourself "I do not know what to do" and the answer comes to you. It is a command. If you ask for it you have to do it. It is the cause of effective action in this world and it is the path of life. Cage and others like him who move according to intellect are not on the path.*

Of all the words on Agnes's list, the only one I think John didn't believe in is *truth* (at least not in eternal or universal Truth). I'm not sure what he would say about *inspiration*, but he did receive it from nature and also from thinkers he admired—Henry David Thoreau, for example. I am sure John believed in beauty. "Isn't it beautiful? Isn't it marvelous?" is one of his expressions that I frequently joyfully quote. And he believed in reality. It was his primary material, and chance was a means of accessing it.

Consider Martin's sentence "With chance one still must choose to act and he is back to intellect." It is true. Not only did John choose to act, but he chose the circumstances within which he would act. He set up parameters of action, then within those parameters cultivated a chance-directed plan. Except within

Pat Steir, *Long Vertical Falls #1*, 1991. Soap ground and spit bite aquatints, 45 × 23 inches.

tightly specified situations, he did not tolerate an "anything goes" attitude.

Did John Cage want to escape intellect? He created scores that offered escape and opened unthought-of possibilities, then accepted whatever results he obtained from following the scores. But the scores, themselves, came from his mind. Agnes's escape from intellect through inspiration was of the purest kind, not intellectually constrained. If it were generalized, I would be wary of her word *command*. "If you ask for it you have to do it" is a refrain too often employed in the real world with tragic consequences. In Agnes's world, however, setting aside intellect meant appreciating the forces of nature.

"I really think it's great to be alive," Pat told me in a 1981 interview, at the beginning of the Reagan years. "No matter what. I hope that if I'm in a coma they do every operation they can to keep me alive, in case I'm thinking or something. I would live any way at all just to be alive. But it is a pessimistic time. I wish it were an optimistic time, but the final way to see art is as a political mirror, and . . . the new art is about the imminent end of the world."

At this moment, in 2012, I find it difficult to remember the "pessimistic time" when I interviewed Pat. In 1981 a financial boom was in the making, but also a dramatic crash. After Reagan's term and that of George H. W. Bush, Bill Clinton, a Democrat, was elected president, and he wiped out an enormous national debt and created a surplus. That surplus was destroyed during the following Republican administration of George W. Bush, who hosted in 2008 another financial crash, bigger than Reagan's, and left office with the national debt unbelievably high. In 2012 we have not recovered from that crash. We hear television talkers daily bemoaning "uncertainty" about "regulations" on business, and I wonder why the talkers think unregulated financial markets won't again crash the stock market.

Every once in a while a commentator—economist Paul Krugman, for example—says we would have been in a true depression, rather than the recession we experienced, if costly financial manipulation by both Bush and his successor, Democrat Barack Obama, had not happened. Krugman thinks the government should have spent more, and should spend again now, and at the same time the Republicans in Congress are ranting against spending and trying to cut social programs. End-of-the-world speculations are coming from both ends of the political spectrum. Their roots are partly in the continuing unemployment crisis (with Europe suffering something similar, maybe worse) and partly in voguish medieval-like thinking: computer fantasy games abound and "social conservatives" assume a religious obligation to legislate moral activity for people other than themselves.

At the end of the sixties, I was thinking about the "imminent end of the world" because of the Cold War and the thermonuclear threat, a threat that lasted about twenty years because of Soviet hostility and has reappeared after 2001 as a peril of terrorism. In the early eighties, Crown Point published the work of a young Italian artist, Francesco Clemente, who had been living in India. One of his images, *Not St. Girolamo*, shows a peaceful Japanese garden in the midst of a quiet sexual scene involving a man and two lions, the whole supported by a tortured figure frantically holding up pillars while the world caves in around him. "I'm not sure everything is under control," Francesco said in *View*. "I'm afraid of the opposite. It's like there is a huge evil thing coming. Not something that has to do with ideas, but really just bad people who overcome the good people."

"The young people," Pat said in my 1981 interview with her, "are not doing something kitschy—that was possible. They're doing work with heavy emotional significance and doing it quite coolly." What Pat and I did not know then is that thirty years later kitsch would be dominating the art world. Contrast Francesco Clemente's statement with remarks made in 2008 by three younger artists. Jeff Koons said, regarding his forty-foot-high topiary of a puppy: "I wanted the piece to deal with the human condition, and this condition in relation to God. I wanted it to be a contemporary Sacred Heart of Jesus." Damien Hirst said, speaking about his paintings of colored spots: "They are what they are, perfectly dumb paintings which feel absolutely right." And Matthew Barney said, about a scene in a film he produced: "Metabolic changes related to the digestive process, from glucose to sucrose, to petroleum jelly, tapioca, meringue, and then poundcake, a complex carbohydrate." All were reported by Calvin Tomkins, the dean of art writers, in the *New Yorker.*

In our 1981 published discussion, Pat and I talked about Andy Warhol, the forerunner of the new kitsch artists. Pat called Warhol "in a very real way the artist of our time because he took everything and made it his own. If you look at a picture of Marilyn Monroe, you think of Warhol. If you eat Campbell soup, you think of Warhol. If you see a picture of Chairman Mao—everything is Warhol!" I argued that Warhol wouldn't last. I was wrong about that, but I wonder how people a hundred years from now, looking at a Warhol painting in a museum, will make sense of our time.

Oh my! (As John Cage would say.) We are far afield from the question of how Pat Steir is influenced in her art by both Agnes Martin and John Cage. But if you believe, as I do, that Cage, Martin, and Steir will continue to be remembered in the future, it might be useful to see them in comparison to Koons, Hirst, and Barney, who came along a generation later and also, it appears, are destined to be remembered.

Thinking about Pat's remark that "the final way to see art is as a political mirror," I notice that the art of Koons, Hirst, and Barney is made in ways that parallel the structure of business and government today: it is constructed remotely, by artisans in factorylike situations, and is impossible to separate from its connection with money. A "spot painting" by Damien Hirst sold at auction in 2011 for just over a million dollars, and on January 12, 2012, the "complete spot paintings," 331 of them, went on exhibition concurrently at eleven branches of the Gagosian Gallery in New York and around the world. This kind of art, in addition to being about money, indulges personal obsessions that John Cage (I think) would have thought of as "trivial and lacking in urgency." Asked about his spot paintings when he was being interviewed on television, Hirst said flatly, "I like color," and nothing more. I thought his answer typified an attitude also visible in the political mirror of our time.

I called Pat and asked her how Agnes Martin influenced her. "Agnes

Pat with her husband, Joost Elffers, 1988.

worked the way a bird sings," she said. "The bird doesn't think, 'I'm making a beautiful song. I'm making a song that's about this or that.' You remember," she went on, "how I used to wear those wedgie heels? On my first visit, with Douglas Crimp, Agnes took us on a hike out in the desert. 'You can't walk in those,' she said. And she gave me her shoes. The whole time I was thinking, 'I'm walking in Agnes Martin's shoes.'"

"And what about Cage?" I asked. We reminisced about the last few days of 1984 when, after a project of Steir's at Crown Point, she and I and my husband, Tom Marioni, and her husband, Joost Elffers (they had just married), drove down the coast to see Hearst Castle. We spent New Year's Eve at a barn dance that we stumbled on in a small town, Pat and Joost making up steps and everyone laughing with the out-of-towners. On the way home, we picked up John in Santa Cruz, where he had been visiting a friend, and he started work at Crown Point on January 5 (he began almost every new year with us).

Although we normally focus our attention on only one artist at a time, Pat worked in the studio with John Cage for a day. "John was free and buoyant and unbelievable," she remembers. "He was a big thing flapping around— playful and funny and serious and hardworking. He opened a whole new

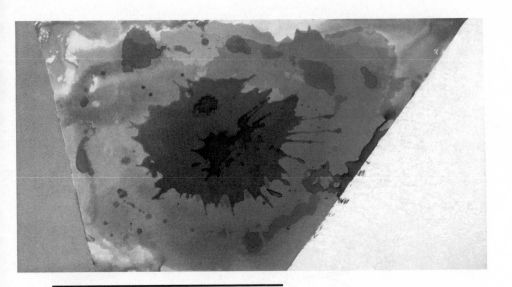

Pat Steir, *Alphabet: Grisaille,* 2007. Color spit bite
aquatint with aquatint, 23½ × 44½ inches.

world." I asked about his influence on her. "For my work now, I have set up
a little system that involves chance," she said. "Chance is like a partner, an
amusing partner: we'll make something and see what happens."

In a review in the May 2011 *Art News,* Barbara Pollack describes Pat's
system this way: "a method of making a kind of art that, free of constraints,
is liberating to experience. It is impossible to look at these magnificent new
paintings without imagining the strength and tenacity of this artist, who
every day climbs a ladder thirteen feet in the air, taking risks and relinquish-
ing control."

The system, Pat has explained, is one of choosing paint colors and dilu-
tions, and then pouring these from the top of the canvas. "I can't believe a
seventy-year-old lady climbs up on a ladder and does that work," a young person visiting the show was heard to say. I think both Pat and I learned from
John Cage not to worry whether or not you can manage to do what you are
doing. You might be "a big thing flapping around," but in the next moment
your engagement with the task at hand takes over and you find you are doing
it seriously and with aplomb.

If Agnes Martin escaped the intellectual through inspiration and John

Cage escaped it, temporarily, through chance, what about Pat Steir? Meditation? "Meditation, maybe, OK," she said. "First the meditation, then the leap. But don't forget about Sol."

In any exploration of the art of our time, it is impossible to forget about Sol LeWitt. But I will save my thoughts about him for later and only remark here that systems were to him what chance was to Cage and inspiration was to Martin. LeWitt and Cage are closer to one another than it would at first appear; both differ fundamentally from Agnes Martin, the third of Steir's influences, in attitude toward the mind. "I hope you have given up on the magazines," Agnes wrote me in an undated letter.

> *The intellectual domination of the art field is a worry. I was invited to have a retrospective at the Whitney but when I refused to have a catalogue they withdrew the invitation. They think that what they have to say about my work and life is more important than showing the work. The intellectual in art work is even more hair raising. We have literally hundreds of thousands of artists in this country illustrating ideas. We could have an art renaissance if this were not so.*

Oh, dear. I wish the Whitney Museum of American Art hadn't waited until 1992 for an Agnes Martin exhibition (with a catalog), but I can't agree with Agnes that the world would be better off if artists were not working with ideas, and I think Pat agrees with me. An influence from Agnes Martin helps Pat Steir show, in all her work, that it's great to be alive, no matter what. But at the same time, like John Cage and Sol LeWitt, she holds ideas in high regard.

Speaking for myself, I was especially keen on ideas in the late seventies when Agnes wrote me that letter because, by then, I had become close to the work and life of Tom Marioni. At the breakfast table today I asked him if he tries to escape the intellect in his work. "Certainly not," he said. "I consider my art to be involved with serious ongoing intellectual activity."

Tom Marioni in the Crown Point studio, 1994.

8.

TOM MARIONI

KNOW WHERE YOU ARE AND WHAT IS GOING ON

Tom Marioni grew up in Cincinnati, the second oldest of four boys. His mother was born in Syracuse, New York, into a family of twelve children. Her father worked in a factory, and her mother had a dairy. She had started by selling milk from her parlor and eventually owned a bottling plant and trucks that delivered milk to homes. Both of Tom's mother's parents had emigrated from Italy. On the other side, Tom's grandfather had been an ice-cream man in Italy. Tom's father immigrated at the age of 21, not speaking any English, and eventually became a doctor. He put himself through medical school by making ice cream. "I come from a dairy family," Tom says.

Tom went to Catholic schools, was an altar boy, studied music, and played the violin in a youth orchestra. He had visited San Francisco on a family vacation when he was young, and the day after he graduated from the Cincinnati Art Academy he took a train out here. That was in 1959, the same year I arrived in San Francisco on a freighter with my etching press. But we did not meet until 1974. That year, Lucy Lippard, an art writer from New York, visited me. She said that Tom Marioni was doing "the most interesting work being done out here." Crown Point published a print of his before 1974 had ended.

I had been working mainly for Parasol Press but was doing Crown Point projects whenever I could. I had just completed *A Scratch on the Negative*, by Jim Melchert, and I met Tom at a party at Melchert's house soon after Lippard's visit. I found him soft-spoken and somewhat shy. He was living in his studio, recently separated from his wife (he has three sons, the oldest about the age of

Tom drawing on a big copper plate at the Robinsons', 1974.

my son). His manners, I thought, were courtly. Someone at the party kidded him about being a famous beer drinker, and he said he might be a "famous" beer drinker but he was "not a big beer drinker." This went over my head.

When I invited Tom to make a print, he suggested a beer label, and I told him our printing process wasn't suitable. Eventually I came around to the label, but back then he quickly switched gears. Could he make a print outside, in a garden? He had a commission from art supporters David and Mary Robinson, who lived in Sausalito. (Mary still lives there, but David died in 2008.) They had asked for a performance piece in their garden. It was not the way I was used to making prints, but we did that. The print is titled *The Sun's Reception.*

The Robinsons invited friends, many of them artists, and served a wonderful lunch on a beautiful day. We used a big copper etching plate, our biggest, and Tom set it up by the swimming pool with a microphone attached to its underside and speakers behind it, then used a sanding disk on an electric drill to draw a spinning oval traced around the reflection of the sun in the copper.

This took less than a minute, and then Tom spent another half hour or so polishing the center of the oval, broadcasting quiet sounds. More sounds came from a friend stirring water in the copper base of a kettledrum, a beautiful object also fitted with a microphone. The next day, I printed the plate in pale blue, the color that comes to your eye as the afterimage of the sun. We made an edition of six and sold the print with a little book of photoetchings from the afternoon at the Robinsons'. My son, Kevin, age thirteen at the time, took most of the photos, and he bound the book, his first bookbinding project for Crown Point. More were to come.

After that early print of Tom's, we published in 1977 another drawing-based work, *Landing,* essentially a portfolio of small images. Back then, Tom was the leader of a jazz group in which he was the drummer, and he has made drawings by drumming with wire drum brushes on sandpaper for long periods until residue from the wire builds up an image that resembles a bird. The *Landing* images are related to his drum brush drawings and are a part of a series of works that Tom calls "out-of-body."

Tom has done "out-of-body" works throughout his career, sometimes with an audience, sometimes not. After traveling to Japan in the early 1980s, he began to make circle drawings (extending the *enso* tradition) by using his arm as a compass. He has made "flying" drawings alone and "with friends" by running and jumping with a pencil. He made our print, *Flying with Friends* (plate 9), at a Crown Point Christmas party in 2000. Everyone ran and jumped holding a sharp tool that marked the printing plates. Tom performed the earliest of his "out of body" works, *Drawing a Line as Far as I Can Reach,* 1972, at the De Marco Gallery in Edinburgh, Scotland, with a microphone behind his drawing paper. In the same year

he did an action piece called *Body Feedback,* at the Whitechapel Gallery in London, in which he struck a sheet of paper hanging on a wall. A microphone on a stand was facing the paper, and Tom moved his body between the microphone and the sheet to control the feedback sound.

All the drawings and prints I've described followed a work called *One Second Sculpture* that Tom created in 1969. It was both a drawing and a sculpture, and also ephemeral, documented in a photograph. He threw into the air "an instrument made from a metal tape measure that flies

Tom Marioni, *A Rose...*, 2008. Color drypoint with flat bite etching, 30¾ × 32 inches.

open like a spring in one second, making a loud sound. The object leaves the hand as a circle, makes a drawing in space, and falls to the ground as a straight line." When I asked Tom about *One Second Sculpture*, he said it "is probably the smartest work I ever did because it is a measurement of both space and time and also incorporates sound as a material."

Tom's sound and action works follow a coherent path—enough, you might think, for a career. But, wait, there's more! Since conceptual artists are, as Tom often says, "free to work in any medium," they are hard to pigeonhole.

Tom's most influential work is different from what I have described. It is what he speaks of as his "large-scale social artwork," the Museum of Conceptual Art, MOCA, now closed, and its continuing corollary, a salon I will call by one of its names, *Café Society*. (There have been several name changes over forty years.) In its earliest version, performed in 1970 at the Oakland Museum of California, it was *The Act of Drinking Beer with Friends Is the Highest Form of Art*. Now, we have reached the point of talking about why Tom Marioni is a "famous beer drinker."

Beer drinking with friends, exhibitions of art seen nowhere else at the time, a magazine, an artists' conference on an island in the Pacific—all were part of the social activity of Tom's museum. He created it as a nonprofit corporation in San Francisco in 1970 and kept it active for more than a decade.

It was a museum, by Tom's definition, because it was "concerned with restoration, interpretation, and collection." Its collection was made up of "records and residue from art actions." Tom closed MOCA in 1984 (the building was torn down by the San Francisco Redevelopment Agency in 1986), and the Berkeley Art Museum at the University of California purchased the MOCA archive.

In an exhibition titled "The Museum of Conceptual Art at the San Francisco Museum of Modern Art" in 1979, SFMOMA actually gave out free beer. It later purchased for

Tom Marioni, *Body Feedback*, Whitechapel Gallery, London, 1972.

Tom Marioni, *3rd Street*, 1995.
Photogravure with color aquatint,
6 × 8½ inches. Breens Bar was on
the street level of the Museum
of Conceptual Art.

its collection a segment of the installation including the refrigerator from MOCA ("Free Beer" is lettered on the door).

Remembering my own ignorance when I first met Tom, I am thinking that I should address a basic question: How does "conceptual art" fit within "modern art," and how does "contemporary art" jibe with those designations? The simple answer is time based: first "modern" art, and then "contemporary," and then "conceptual," an influential, fairly recent part of "contemporary."

The MOCA acronym (with the *O* in *of* capitalized) that Tom began to use in 1970 was appropriated in 1979 for the just-opened Museum of Contemporary Art in Los Angeles. Its website says it shows art created since 1940. Contemporary collections start at about that time—the middle of World War Two, when abstract expressionism in the United States and tachism in Europe began. Modern art museums go back further, usually beginning with impressionism (mid-nineteenth century) and continuing into the present. Almost all modern and contemporary museums now show at least some works of conceptual art.

Conceptual art began to gain attention with a 1969 exhibition in Berne, Switzerland, called "When Attitudes Become Form," and museums in New York and Europe have shown it since then. California museums lagged behind, and Tom's use of the word *museum* to title his large-scale artwork called attention to that. In the same vein, in 1973 when the San Francisco Museum of Modern Art had been searching for some time for a new director, Tom Marioni sent out a card announcing his own appointment to the job.

In 1970 Tom laid out a narrow mission for his museum. He described it as a "specialized sculpture action museum" and "an excuse for a party." Now, about forty years later, it's becoming clear that the moving, changing, interconnected, experiential world we live in today was predicted by early conceptual art, one form of which focused on activities (including parties) rather than on objects (including paintings).

When conceptual art, a truly international movement, sprang up in the late 1960s, there was no center from which it spread. In Europe and on each coast of the United States, it had several distinct forms. Europeans were generally materials oriented, and in England language art and land art dominated. Language art also developed in New York, along with art that used systems in various ways. Tom Marioni calls California "a body culture" and says that it took its influences from Asia and Europe and focused on actions.

Besides looking to Europe for influence, Tom and his friends drew on Northern California's long unbroken figurative tradition. Richard Diebenkorn (who had turned from abstraction to figurative art at the time), Wayne Thiebaud, and many other figurative painters were active here, and younger "funk" artists like William T. Wiley were working irreverently with figuration. Tom and the artists who showed at MOCA extended that tradition to make "body works." Tom Marioni defined conceptual art in the early 1970s as "idea-oriented situations not directed at the production of static objects."

Now, as I look back to the seventies, I realize that my association with Tom expanded my way of thinking into a much wider world than I had seen before. That wider world is clearly visible in 2012 to everyone. Well in advance of the Web's democratizing influence, Tom threw himself into a do-it-yourself-and-with-others ethos.

Tom's Museum of Conceptual Art was a big project that contained smaller ones. One smaller one is his continuing beer-with-friends salon, and an offshoot of that is the Crown Point Press publication *Café Society Beer*, 1979. It is not simply a print as a beer label; it is an actual bottle of beer with an original print for a label.

Fritz Maytag, founder and, at that time, owner of the Anchor Steam Beer Brewing Company in San Francisco, produced a beer for us with a unique formulation, and our printers helped Maytag, Marioni, and a technician bottle it in champagne bottles in an edition of one hundred. Tom designed the label to wrap around the bottle like a napkin and hand-engraved the title. The documentation sheet gives an instruction: "To complete the artwork this beer should be shared by at least two people."

Tom Marioni created the Museum of Conceptual Art because no museum in California was showing the kind of art he was interested in. He didn't bury himself in strategizing about how to get what today is called "funding." He did work within standard institutional structures and applied for, and received, some small grants, primarily from the National Endowment for the Arts. That agency created a category called "alternative art spaces" rather than give him the museum grant he applied for. (A performance space in New York, 112 Greene Street, received an "alternative art space" grant soon after.) Tom also sought and found fifteen or twenty supporting members for MOCA at $25 a year.

Tom Marioni, *Café Society Beer*, 1979. Soft ground etching mounted on a bottle of Anchor Steam beer, 5½ × 8¼ inches.

Tom's attitude has always been to do something somehow and sustain a project as long as possible with minimum support. His approach enhanced my confidence in a careful, but at the same time daring approach to Crown Point Press as a business. Tom and I independently reinforce and exhilarate each other.

I wish I had been savvy enough to visit the Museum of Conceptual Art for its early historic shows, "Sound Sculpture As," 1970, for example, probably the first sound art show anywhere, or "All Night Sculptures," 1973, nine sculptors each creating an action or an installation in a different room, or Chris Burden's one-man show in 1971, his first outside student situations. Overall, group shows were more prevalent at MOCA than one-person shows. The guiding principle was to explore concepts, and occasionally Tom put on a pure-concept show that allowed him to do that with a narrow focus.

One MOCA show of the pure-concept type was called "Chinese Youth Alternative," 1974. It consisted of debris and graffiti left in the space upstairs from MOCA when the youth organization (a front for a gang) moved out. Another, "Moroccan Experience," 1976, was five thousand square feet of wall-to-wall rugs borrowed from a shop located downstairs from Tom's space. The rugs had the spicy, earthy smell of a Middle Eastern bazaar. "I'm trying to make art as close to real life as possible without it being real life," Tom said.

Why, then, I asked, was "Moroccan Experience" not real life? These were the same rugs that had been for sale when they were in the store. "Put anything in an art context and it becomes art" was Tom's reply. This is the other side of the coin from John Cage's idea that "art should slip out of us into the world in which we live." I asked Tom if a sunset can be art. "Nature makes a sunset. People make art," he said.

"Chinese Youth Alternative" and "Moroccan Experience" were not artworks by the Chinese youths and the Moroccan shopkeeper. Although it was not mentioned in exhibition material, both shows were conceptual artworks by Tom Marioni, who placed the "found" materials into an art context and caused viewers to see them differently from how they would have seen them in the context of real life.

> *The management reserves the right to refuse service to*
>   *anyone who doesn't know where they are or what is going on.*
> *People bring their own drinks.*
> *No drinking from beer bottle except in character.*
> *Bartenders can invite up to 3 guests.*
> *Guests do not invite guests without checking with Tom.*
> *No theater people except famous movie stars.*
> *No art students except those who can pass as professionals.*
> *No art collectors except in disguise.*
> *People should sign guest book at the bar.*
> *Hours 5 to 8 PM, except on special occasions.*

This is a short list of the house rules for the Society of Independent Artists, the current version of Tom's *Café Society* salon. He has hosted the gatherings once a week since 1973. There are more rules; I left out the ones like "no popcorn, unshelled peanuts, or cake" that are mostly related to keeping the premises trouble free. The salon is normally held in Tom's studio, and the house rules apply to that location. I asked Tom to explain the ones that start with *no*. What does drinking "in character" from a beer bottle mean? "A cowboy would never drink out of a glass," he replied. Why not theater people? "Because they are too theatrical." What would be a disguise appropriate for art collectors? "That they don't announce they are art collectors."

Sometimes, *Café Society* is held in institutions rather than in Tom's studio. In 2011, for example, the Hammer Museum in Los Angeles presented it, and in the same year Tom traveled overseas to present the piece in museums in Vienna and Bristol, England, and an art center in Paris. There are conceptual artists around the world

With my future husband, 1975.

who use food, drink, and social situations as art materials, and Tom's *The Act of Drinking Beer with Friends Is the Highest Form of Art*, because of its 1970 date, is a grandfather to them.

When Tom presents his salon outside his studio, he creates a specific environment in the field institution: The beer bottles, after having been emptied, are deposited on shelves built to his specifications. He designs the bar and the lights (yellow, like California sunlight), and indicates the music to be played (jazz). Sometimes the room contains other artworks of his, an "out-of-body" drawing on a wall, for example. He has done that kind of drawing before an audience in the past, but lately his preferred performance for his salons takes another form. He tells jokes. He takes a microphone, stands up before an audience, and tells jokes.

This development was surprising to me, because I know that Tom is shy, and a person is at his most vulnerable, perhaps, in "stand-up" mode. But, thinking about it, I know that artists have to work outside their comfort zones. The best art is usually close to being out of control.

When you think about it, a lot of art being done today is under control without necessarily seeming to be. In order to recognize art, and other valuable things and ideas in the world right now, it is important to know where you are and what is going on.

With Robert Mangold and printers
Hidekatsu Takada and David Kelso, 1979.

9.

THE MIDDLE SEVENTIES

CONSTRUCT A LIFE

The subtitle I am using for this chapter, "Construct a Life," is the trickiest one on the list. I could have chosen "Construct a Style"; in fact, I almost did. But is a "style" the same as a "life"? I see in celebrity stories that the answer is no for some people, but in my own life, and in the lives of the artists I admire, essentially it is yes. Living and working are intertwined, and your style is, I think, not only the way people see you but the way you see the world. The way you see the world is reflected in the work you do.

Robert Mangold is a good example because his work is so intensely plain. He was born in 1937 and was among the artists who reacted against the excesses of abstract expressionism and withdrew from the idea of pursuing self-expression. Some artists who came of age in the 1960s withdrew also from painting, and many of Mangold's friends are sculptors, though he has always been a painter.

"To understand that time," Mangold says, "you have to remember that there was an incredible division between painting and sculpture. It was then that some people said that painting is dead." In his paintings, Mangold stepped away from process, from showing clearly how the paint is applied, and instead thought about creating what he called "flat frontality." He also began using geometric forms, but "geometric art always makes me nervous," he says. "I don't think of my work in that way. I think all my works are about things fitting or not really fitting together, with the exterior structure either dictating the terms of the interior structure or setting up a framework the interior structure plays off."

I worked with Mangold for the first time in the etching studio in 1973, and again in 1975 and 1978, each time printing for Parasol Press. Technically Mangold's work is difficult to execute because any flaw pulls the eye immediately to it and subverts his desire that no part of the work should stand out. Yet, his surfaces are not uninflected—there are often textures; lines sometimes waver, and forms are slightly askew. I enjoy being around this art because it is extreme but not excessive, and that is the kind of life I like to live.

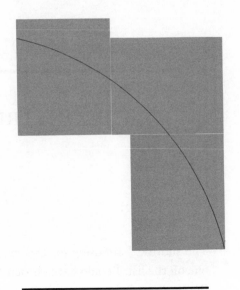

Robert Mangold, *B. Orange* from *Three Aquatints*, 1979. Color aquatint with soft ground etching, 36 × 33 inches. Published by Parasol Press.

Living and working have been intertwined for me since I was a child, and what I've found in adulthood is that living essentially means working. On television I heard Fareed Zakaria interview writer David McCullough (I read his great biography of Harry S. Truman). "Work, not ease," McCullough said, "produces the happiest time of your life." He explained that in the research he has done for biographies, reading letters, for instance, he has found, over and over, words like this: "I've never worked so hard, and I've never been so happy." Then Zakaria quoted Winston Churchill: "We haven't gone this far because we're made of sugar candy."

Malcolm Gladwell, in his book *Outliers*, says that it takes ten thousand hours (twenty hours a week for ten years) to get really good at something. He also says that, whether or not you have reached the expert level, too much introspection, too many possibilities, can paralyze action and be detrimental. I have seen this demonstrated in the studio; the most accomplished artists, I think, deliberate carefully and then move ahead without a backward look until the next period of deliberation.

Daniel Kahneman's *Thinking Fast and Slow* makes a similar point with more strings and complications and less attention to creative thinking.

Kahneman has lots of research projects to back him up in saying that if you practice particular skills for many hours, you can rely on them to guide "fast" thinking and make quick, accurate responses that involve those skills. He uses firefighting as an example: an experienced firefighter senses when the floor is about to cave in. But Kahneman's experiments lead him to advise that the mode of thinking he calls "fast" is "lazy and unreliable" in conducting most life activities, and that we should think "slow" and consider all sides when we make important decisions. I am trying to square this advice with John Cage's approach of examining all the relevant circumstances, asking questions about them, laying out a plan, and then following the plan without making judgments during the execution.

In doing that, I think of the man with an extraordinary name, Mihaly Csikszentmihalyi, who talks about the "flow" of doing something "with intense concentration on the present," so much so that you are "too involved to be concerned with failure." He points to sports as an example. Nearly everyone has experienced flow in sports or, at any rate, has watched "their" team members experience it. He says "getting into the flow" is satisfying because, once you are in it, you overcome obstacles gracefully. Obstacles enhance the possibility of flow, and eventually of creativity, which flows from "flow."

In almost every lecture or demonstration I give about Crown Point Press, I talk about "flow" in the etching studio when an artist and printers are

A Crown Point
workshop, 1999.

working together. It is an invigorating experience, each person in sync with the others, concentrating on doing something well. Csikszentmihalyi says, if I understand him correctly, that a certain amount of expertise is necessary for flow. He thinks young people should be pushed to that level. "Whereas experts in a discipline usually love what they do, this emotion is generally not available to students or young practitioners," he wrote. Thinking about my experiences, however, I have an idea that discipline practiced seriously, even if not expertly, can produce flow.

When I talk about flow, I always include artists and expert printers, but I am now ready to extend the concept—not always but often—to participants in our workshops, which are open to people of varying skill levels. Everyone seems to have the capacity to experience flow if a lead person captures it, and most of the people in close proximity have the mind-set of working skillfully—in other words, are disciplined in their approach. Each person works at his or her level, but engages with the intensity of the lead person. This is not as formal as John Cage's approach, but it is related.

Tentatively, I think I can go even further with this idea and extend the possibility of flow to include the support people at Crown Point Press: the director (who is our public face), the gallery people, the business manager, the registrar, the publications director. Again, I have seen it happen. Those with higher levels of skill lead, but interns can get on the wavelength. Everyone's not on it all the time, of course, but the possibility is there.

The cultivation of opportunities for flow can be, I think, a way of life, an attitude transferable to others, including children. My son, Kevin, who was around art-makers throughout his early life, has picked up the idea of flow and integrated it into his personality. He also was exposed at an early age to another variety of flow: travel.

I am starting to see flow as a one-foot-in-front-of-the-other kind of thing, and travel as a stripped-down version of that. You have something laid out to do and a time frame to do it in. You move along, adjusting to circumstances as they arrive, using a combination of fast and slow thinking, stewing in place sometimes but not excessively, making snap judgments sometimes but not always. When I leave the press to go traveling, I rarely call to check in. I trust the people I work with to make good decisions, and they know where I am if they need me. If I am too much in touch, it disrupts both my flow and theirs.

Kevin and I went on our first big trip together when he was five, in 1966. It was an extravagance, purely an escape, an indulgence. I made a snap judgment to use up a small inheritance from my grandmother rather than saving it. My mother was still teaching the children of overseas military troops and was living in Holland at the time. Over previous years, I had wished I could visit her in the exotic places—Morocco, Turkey, Ethiopia—where she had been living, but there hadn't been a chance of rounding up money for trips. So, when money appeared, I set out for Europe with Kevin. I still have no regrets.

We stayed for a few days in Holland with my mother, then went to Sweden to pick up our new Volvo P1800, a very pretty car—a friend called it a "girl's sports car"—part of my moment of extravagance; I shipped it home after the trip. The three of us drove to Italy, where suddenly I was unable to put the car in reverse (it never again broke down in traffic in the twenty years I drove it). We left it to be repaired and took a train and a ferry to Greece, then went on to Crete, where my mother had taught and lived, then back to Italy, picked up the car, and drove to France and Spain. I used a book on traveling in Europe with children to find sightseeing stops that Kevin liked, and though he was only five he remembers parts of the adventure. He learned to eat all kinds of food— he still eats escargot at any opportunity—and to look at art as something fun (the trick is to go into a museum and see only one show or one section).

As I promised in Chapter 6, I'm going to talk briefly about Kevin's own business. He began developing it in 1971 when he took over our home basement after I moved the press, and he had completed the first stage by 1979 when he graduated from high school. He has about seventy people working for him in 2011 (down from a hundred twenty before the crash of 2008).

At first, in the basement, Kevin was simply doing hand bookbinding— restoring old books and making portfolio cases for some Crown Point projects. But after he started high school, he built a complex machine down there, running the length of the two adjoining rooms. The machine had many linked heating elements made of copper plates, discards from Crown Point with images by Sol LeWitt and other artists. It deposited a pattern of hot glue on strips of fabric. When cooled and cut, they became binding strips that fit into a hot glue binder manufactured by Xerox.

The Xerox binder created what was called a "perfect" bind—if you remember it, you know that the pages fell out relatively quickly. Kevin invented a strip that would bind the pages so they didn't fall out. His high

Kevin with his
machine.

school astronomy club manufactured and sold the strips to support a tele-
scope they were building. They began by selling strips to a copy shop where
the Xerox binder was used by University of California, Berkeley, students to
bind term papers. Eventually a local office supply company began distributing
the strips to other shops that had Xerox binders.

Kevin was in his basement workshop day and night, every spare
moment, when he wasn't sleeping, eating, or in school. At some point after he
became a teenager, I asked him if he had a girlfriend. "Just the one in the basement," he replied. The machine in the basement required not only Kevin's
attendance, but also the presence of other teenagers, some feeding materials
into it as it chugged away and others in our front yard, cutting and packing
the strips and silk-screening a logo on cardboard boxes.

Xerox sued Kevin's fledgling business. Fortunately, the club's high
school faculty advisor, Jim Kelly, had helped Kevin patent the binding strip
and had suggested that he purchase insurance for the production operation;
the insurance, to a point, would cover the lawsuit costs. The Xerox lawyer,
confronted in court by a seventeen-year-old with a double row of high school
students behind him, offered "lenient" settlement terms: they were simply to

stop what they were doing. I said, "Well, Kevin, it looks like Xerox is going to put you out of business."

"No," he replied. "Eventually, I'm going to put them out of business, out of the binding business. Their binder is no good. I can make a better one." Kevin started college at UC Berkeley the following fall and by spring had decided to drop out and build his binding machine. To get the seed money, I took a second mortgage on our house.

In 2011 Kevin turned fifty. Xerox no longer makes a binder. The binder incorporated into one of its larger copy machines uses technology purchased from Kevin's company, Powis-Parker, Inc. Kevin's tabletop binder, the Fastback, is used by General Electric, the U.S. Navy, and many smaller businesses and copy shops for in-house binding. Powis-Parker also makes a machine that binds hardcover copies for presentation and on-demand publishing—and it manufactures an iPad case that Kevin designed. Jim Kelly, the former astronomy club advisor, has worked with Kevin at Powis-Parker for the past thirty years.

In 1975, the year Kevin started to build the big machine in the basement, Crown Point Press was preparing for change. I was still working for other publishers but beginning to realize that I was at their mercy financially. For a couple of years, until 1977, the "flow" at Crown Point was in a kind of eddy. It was a crossover time when I made some big decisions about how to proceed.

Thinking about 1975, I pulled from my bookshelf a slim catalog from that date called *Recent American Etching*. The exhibition was at the Smithsonian National Collection of Fine Arts and at Wesleyan University, and I notice that it also traveled "abroad," although the venues are not specified. The catalog essay, still brilliant after all these years, is by Richard Field, who was then curator at Wesleyan's Davison Art Center.

"No surer way to provoke controversy among art historians can be devised," Field begins his essay, "than to speak of the revival of a style or craft." And then he goes on to make a case for "a new etching revival." He doesn't think that etching was close to death immediately before his essay, but he points out:

> *Almost never during the post-war days did etching function as a vehicle for the avant-garde, as drypoint had in the teens for Cubism and Expressionism, or as etching had in the twenties and thirties for the new classicizing styles of Matisse and Picasso.*

Field sees the "excitement of avant-garde artists in the 1960s flowing into silk-screen and lithography" because of their "combinations of hand-and machine-produced imagery that capitalized on commercial processes and could paraphrase the languages of mass communications, the overt concern of Pop Art." But by the 1970s, he says, the newest artists were looking for something else. I was lucky to appear with my etching skills at that time. Field makes a set of beautiful observations about etching:

> *Not only is there the reversal of the image, the uncertain action of the acid, and the lengthy and delicate printing process, but the image itself is built up of countless layers of decisions which have been exploited and consciously incorporated into the content of the work. Perhaps the most positive feature of the new etching was its reaffirmation that the hand of the artist was an instrument of intellect rather than of emotion. Etching was cool, and cool was desired. . . . Etching's cool derives from the fact that it is the most subtle form of sculpture. The lines and tones are in fact physical textures; they stand in relief and are not illusion.*

Beyond his affirmation of the qualities of etching, Field wrote about the artists included in his show and made clear his "conviction that it was Jasper Johns's turn to etching that forced every serious artist to consider the medium's possibilities." Johns's early etchings were printed at Universal Limited Art Editions by Donn Steward, who was also the lithography printer there in the late sixties and early seventies. Steward had studied etching at the University of Iowa under Mauricio Lasansky, the chief exponent of the American (expressive) way of printing etchings, the opposite approach to the sharply focused French method I use.

In Johns's early etchings, the soft character of the printing is part of them; Johns adjusted to the printing style, and the etchings are works of art. Later, in 1976, Johns worked with the French printer Aldo Crommelynck, whose printing I would characterize as "crisp" rather than "soft," to make beautiful etchings for Samuel Beckett's *Foirades/Fizzles*, published by Petersburg Press. The differences in the two styles of printing are visible, but I don't think Johns "collaborated" with the printers. You could say, however, that he collaborated with Beckett in the Petersburg Press book (though Beckett didn't collaborate with him).

Richard Field didn't include in his exhibition or mention in the catalog the etchings Crown Point Press published by Wayne Thiebaud or Richard Diebenkorn in the early sixties (perhaps he didn't know about them). But Crown Point is well represented by work we printed for Parasol Press. In fact, Field says in his essay, "It is to Kathan Brown's uncompromising dedication to purity and to Donn Steward's sensitivity and inventiveness that much of this exhibition owes its character."

Details of the years immediately preceding 1977, the year I restarted serious publishing for Crown Point, are hazy to me now. In October 1973, I wrote my mother a letter (she saved it) saying that I had decided to move to New York. "My life here is very good," I wrote, "but that isn't really enough. I need to go somewhere else with my art and I really have a great desire to start my life over again."

I met Tom Marioni the following year. By that time I had already purchased a raw-space loft on Greene Street (between Broome and Spring), but I didn't have the money to fix it up so it was sitting idle. In 1974 our country slipped into a (fairly brief) recession accompanied by both high unemployment and high inflation. The art world was being fueled by that inflation; nevertheless it wasn't a good time for me to move. Apart from the money matters, I was worried about uprooting Kevin, and I was enjoying a developing relationship with Tom, who made it clear he wouldn't move to New York under any circumstances.

I sold the loft for less than I had paid for it and set out to "start my life over again" while staying in California. You may know this Zen story: A man hands a hot dog vendor a twenty dollar bill and says, "Make me one with everything." The vendor hands him a hot dog, but no change. "Change comes from within," he says. In 1974 I quit my teaching job at the San Francisco Art Institute.

It was around that time that I began forming a plan to separate Crown Point from Parasol Press and develop a publishing program of my own. I also decided to throw myself into another book, a personal artwork, to see if I should keep thinking of myself as an artist.

It turned out that I didn't want to "go somewhere else with my art." I stayed on the track I had been on since my first photo-based book, *Album*, in 1972. My books, infrequent as they were, had become my art. In 1976 I published an ordinary book of my own, not a *livre d'artiste*. Here are the first words in that book:

I remember quite clearly, at the age of ten, seeing newsreel photographs of Hiroshima, then hearing my grandfather talking about it. Suddenly it came over me, in physical waves of fear, that we could easily blow up the world. It could even happen by mistake. I felt (and still feel) absolutely powerless.

Voyage to the Cities of the Dawn contains my photographs and text along with excerpts from diaries (and some photos) by Kevin, age fourteen, and Tony, Tom's son, who was twelve. We took a family trip on a cruise ship to Mexico and Honduras, and then Kevin and I continued to Guatemala, which had just had a devastating earthquake, to visit friends there. On the book jacket I said I was reporting on a journey in Central America while "reflecting on life in 1976 in the United States."

One element of life in 1976 in the United States was ongoing newspaper coverage of the bank robbery trial of Patty Hearst, heiress of a newspaper dynasty, who had been abducted and, her attorney said, brainwashed by the Symbionese Liberation Army, the SLA. In my text, I threaded thoughts about cult life (Werner Erhard's EST, the SLA, the Moonies, Scientology, Hitler's Germany) with information about the Maya, who, my hosts in Guatemala explained, are still fatalistic, though perhaps less so than in the ancient times when they built the cities whose ruins we visited.

"I can understand your interest in comparing the Maya to present-day civilization," I quoted one of my shipmates as saying. "Sometimes I feel as powerless over the things that mean the most to me in my life as the Maya must have felt over their lives." I went on to say that my generation lives with that feeling, but young people "believe deep down that they can be powerful. And they can, by acting with a group—it has been proven over and over. The question and the problem is whether the group will exert the ultimate power over them."

What would be that "ultimate power"? It was demonstrated in extremity in 1978, two years after I wrote *Cities of the Dawn*, when more than nine hundred people in Jonestown, Guyana, stepped up one by one for a cyanide-laced drink and kept on stepping up even as they saw the partakers in front of them lie down and die. This is the origin of the expression "drinking the Kool-Aid," used to describe a passionately held but seriously misguided faith. It has crossed my mind, listening in 2012 to the televised "debates" of Republican candidates for president, that their partisan audiences are perilously close to

In Mexico, 1976 (left). A photo from *Voyage to the Cities of the Dawn*, 1976 (right).

the Kool-Aid: in one instance a candidate rousingly shouted, "Send Obama back to Chicago," and the crowd chanted, "Back to Kenya, back to Kenya . . . "

I paid for the printing of *Cities of the Dawn* with an artist grant I had received from the National Endowment for the Arts. Crown Point Press is a business, and it has never received (or applied for) grant money. The grant was my own, but I used the Crown Point Press name as publisher. That meant sending copies to everyone I knew and to newspapers and magazines around the country. One of them, the *Washington Review*, published a review five years later. The writer, Michael Lally, had collected several books that, he said, "refuse to fit into the simplistic and arbitrary categories created by the market-oriented managers of the publishing corporations and conglomerates." After describing my book's premise, he wrote this:

> *The journey, plus events occurring in the USA about the same time, generate some unique and sometimes profound connections between one of the original cultures of the Americas and one of the most recent. Though obviously snapshots, the photos are haunting and even moving. The commentary, though in ways already dated, remains provocative and enlightening. The perfect antidote to the usual coffee table book. This one should last.*

Claes Oldenburg, *Floating Three-Way Plug*, 1976. Color soft ground etching and spit bite aquatint, 42 × 32¼ inches. Published by Multiples, Inc.

I published *Cities of the Dawn* in 1976, before Amazon existed (it began in 1994), and I am grateful now that Amazon has made viable the kind of self-publishing that I first attempted three decades ago. Crown Point Press sells our published books and magazines, even the old ones, in our bookstore and on our websites, but to make the book business work we also need Amazon, as well as the nonprofit local organization called Small Press Distribution.

Always, however, book publishing has been a sideline to etching activity at Crown Point. *Cities of the Dawn* was something I did for myself. At the same time, I was trying to figure out what my next step would be with the press.

In the etching studio, I had an excellent group of printers. John Slivon, Doris Simmelink, Patrick Foy, and Stephen Thomas were with us in those years, and my ex-husband, Jeryl Parker, was printing at Crown Point from 1974 to 1977. Jeryl had tired of teaching and he asked to work with us. His motive, he told me, was to test whether he might want to set up his own shop. He is an extraordinary printer and problem-solver, and he managed to pull off a difficult and amazing project for Parasol, Dorothea Rockburne's *Locus* series of aquatints printed in white ink on folded paper. (A review in *Art News* of a 2011 retrospective of Rockburne's work mentions *Locus* as a highlight of the show.) Between 1975 and 1977 we produced, also for Parasol, etchings with Robert Ryman, Robert Mangold, Sylvia Plimack Mangold, and Mel Bochner (each working more than once). We also did repeat projects with Sol LeWitt, Brice Marden, and Chuck Close. I learned a lot from these great artists and loved getting to know them.

In the mid- to late seventies, besides the Parasol artists, Crown Point

With printers (from left) John Slivon, Patrick Foy,
and Stephen Thomas, 1976.

worked with a few artists sent by other publishers: Helen Frankenthaler, published by the John Berggruen Gallery, San Francisco, was one of them, and Claes Oldenburg, published by Multiples, Inc., New York, was another.

I had hired a business manager and happily turned over the business part of the operation to her. She was devoted to me, so much so that she didn't feel she should "bother" me when things went askew. She thought she would be able to right everything eventually. Consequently, one morning I appeared at the press to find the staff standing on the sidewalk and a padlock on the door. It was put there by the Internal Revenue Service. I honestly had had no idea that we were behind in paying our payroll taxes.

With my first computer, 1979.

10.

THE LATE SEVENTIES

Attempt What Is Not Certain

In 1976, when the IRS briefly shut us down at Crown Point, we were not publishing. We were printing for other publishers, and we were very busy, so it was clear that we weren't charging enough for our work. It was even clearer that I had to start seriously paying attention to the business side of things. I began to study elementary business books. I learned to make spreadsheets in which I could record and predict cash flow, expenses, and income. Although I bought my first computer, a Zenith, in 1979, I used it only for word processing. With a calculator, I assembled my spreadsheets on paper until 1982 when a Vector computer with a database program arrived. Since 1976 I have run the business side of Crown Point Press myself with help from an outside accountant and an in-house manager.

The subtitle of this chapter comes from Richard Diebenkorn. It is part of a list of notes to himself that his wife, Phyllis, shared with a few friends after he died. I am using it here because, looking back, I realize that by the time I fully understood that I had a business going, I already had laid out my life in the way an artist would. I could attempt what was not certain, but I thought the uncertainty should be made by me, not by publishers for whom I was working.

Crown Point's current publishing program officially began in 1977, and our price list begins there (the earlier works are on an archive list). That year, I started by asking Richard Diebenkorn if he would come from Los Angeles for a project. He spent a week working in Oakland with us and made a series titled *Nine Drypoints and Etchings*, black and white lines that he described as

The staff, Oakland, 1979 (from left): Hidekatsu Takada, Nancy Anello, Robin White, unidentified intern, Jan Mehn, Richard Pinegar, Lilah Toland, and Stephen Thomas.

"the bones of Ocean Park," the name of the Los Angeles district where he had his studio. Diebenkorn's son and daughter live in the Bay Area, and he and Phyllis had a place to stay, but everyone else I invited to work with us in the seventies and early eighties stayed with Tom and me in our house in Berkeley.

We had a big stove in the kitchen. Sometimes we gave parties. In one party for John Cage, John cooked mushrooms that he, along with my mother, Kevin, and me, had gathered that afternoon in the Berkeley Hills. Everyone we knew came to that party; every museum director in the Bay Area was there, and every friend Tom or I had—even now, we sometimes reminisce with old friends about it. For our other most-remembered party, I baked brownies because one of our New York artists had brought with him a big lump of sticky black material that was—as he said—full of camel dung and needed to be baked. Everyone had a great time, especially my accountant, who had never been exposed to anything like that before.

In that time period, also, I took a weekend workshop in business philosophy from Peter Drucker. He was introduced as a business "guru," and he said good-naturedly that people use the word *guru* because *charlatan* is hard to spell. He was mesmerizing. I have bought and marked up many of his books; I did so just a couple of years ago.

Everyone who has ever worked at Crown Point since 1976 will tell you Drucker's "orchestra story" if you ask. Even Crown Point Press interns know it: Our business is like an orchestra. Sometimes one of us has a solo, or a small group is playing, but each person is always conscious of the whole orchestra. When any one of us makes a decision, he or she consults everyone who might be affected by that decision. We all keep an eye on the conductor, and we are all playing from the same score.

I'm proud to say that every person who works here has a real job, as opposed to being in the "independent contractor" category that many small-business employees, especially in the art world, fall into. We've always provided fully paid health insurance, along with other benefits, including a "print credit" that helps employees own examples of what we produce. And master printers usually receive a signed proof of each editioned print on which they worked with an artist. These often have been a source of capital enabling them to move and/or to start their own businesses.

In 1977, the year that Crown Point Press embarked on our planned program of publishing, Jeryl Parker left Crown Point. In 1981 he moved to New York and started an etching print shop there; he didn't publish. With my blessing, he took over Parasol's projects and eventually did some work for Crown Point with artists who did not want to leave New York.

In 1978 we lost three master printers, Doris Simmelink, Patrick Foy, and John Slivon. John, after twelve years as a printer, dropped out of the printing world and became a museum preparator. Doris and Patrick moved to Los Angeles and after a time became printers at Gemini G.E.L., which continued to emphasize lithography but employed them to work in etching. Later, Doris and her husband (whom she met at Gemini) started Simmelink-Sukimoto Editions. It is now located in Olympia, Washington, and is still in business.

Patrick later worked for some years at Graphicstudio, a print shop affiliated with the University of South Florida at Tampa. He now teaches at the Oxbow School, a private one-semester art-focused high school in Napa, California, credited with changing the lives of many teenagers. Stephen Thomas, the school's director, was a printer at Crown Point from 1975 through 1980, then taught high school in San Francisco until 1998 when the school's founders approached him about directing it. "Sometimes teachers in other schools ask me how we control the kids," Stephen told me. "But that's the wrong question. The question is how we get them going. We start out with the kids the way we would start out with artists at Crown Point Press: 'Here is some space, here are some tools and materials, here are some examples of what others have done with those tools and materials, and here is some time for you to work with them. We'll answer your questions and help however we can.'"

At Crown Point Press in 1978, the year I lost three printers at once, I still had Stephen Thomas and another fine printer, Lilah Toland, who had begun working with us in 1977. Fortunately, also, I was able to hire two new printers whom I had already started to train. Hidekatsu Takada had been my student at the San Francisco Art Institute, and David Kelso had been a workshop member back when Crown Point was in my Berkeley basement. David stayed with us only a year, then went on to found Made in California, his press in Oakland, which he continues to run in 2012. Takada would be a crucial member of the Crown Point staff for the next fourteen years. You will hear more about him as we go on.

In 1978 Nancy Anello joined us. She stayed four years, then moved to Bali and started a children's clothing business, but came back to work for short periods at Crown Point in 1986 and again in 1988. Peter Pettengill came to Crown Point in 1979. He stayed six years, then started Wingate Studio in Hinsdale, New Hampshire (his family home). It is still active, and Peter has trained printers who have started their own shops.

Somehow, we maintained five skilled printers during this time. An artist usually works with us only a week or two to create a project, and we do the edition printing after he or she has gone. Because etchings are so time-consuming to print, I've learned that for each printer on the staff we can plan on handling only one-and-a-half artists in a year. In 1977, our first year of serious publishing, we published six artists and did two projects for Parasol, so there were eight projects. I did everything but print, with three support staff. Altogether, Crown Point, in addition to me, had eight employees, five of them printers.

Years earlier, I had visited Petersburg Press in London—publishers of the Beckett/Johns *Foirades/Fizzles* I mentioned in Chapter 9—and was taken past what seemed like dozens of people at desks to the back room where two printers were working in lithography. Lithography is much faster to print than etching. I knew that Petersburg also published etchings printed elsewhere, but even so I couldn't believe there were so many support people and so few printers. At that point, I thought the printers were everything. As time went on, I learned the importance of the people at the desks.

I can look back on years when Crown Point Press had as many as twenty-two employees. But with the country having been in or near recession since 2008, in 2012 we are down to eight people, plus me, the same as in 1977—except that now we have three printers instead of five, and five support staff members instead of three. In 2012 we plan to publish three artists, the correct number for a staff of our present size. In 1977 we produced eight artist-projects, two of them for Parasol. We had enough printers to do that, but (after subtracting the two Parasol projects) I had the work of six artists to sell with no gallery in which to show the art and hardly anyone beside myself to handle it. I have learned a lot since then.

In 1977, along with Richard Diebenkorn and Pat Steir, Crown Point published Chris Burden, Tom Marioni, Terry Fox, and Vito Acconci, all conceptual artists. Conceptual art was not something that most people at the time associated with printmaking.

Chris Burden, at Tom's suggestion, came from Los Angeles to work with us. His was the last project printed by John Slivon, and as John remarked later in a videotaped panel discussion, "Chris Burden came in and said he wanted to make money, and I said, 'That's illegal.'" When we found out he wanted to make Italian money, we decided to risk it.

Richard Diebenkorn, *#2* from *Nine Drypoints and Etchings*, 1977. A portfolio of nine drypoints and hard ground etchings, 18 × 11 inches.

Chris chose the ten thousand lire note to copy because it features a portrait of an artist, Michelangelo. We used photoetching to reproduce the bill as well as we could. A local paper maker, Don Farnsworth, made paper, including the intricate watermark, as close to the original as possible. We printed the front and back images of the bill, actual size, on two sides of a larger sheet of paper, in register, with the watermark in the right place. We did not cut the bills out of the sheet, which Chris signed and numbered. We sold the print, titled *Diecimila*, in a green folder that Kevin made for us. The edition is thirty-five.

Pat Steir had already done a print called *Marking Time* early in the year. Tom Marioni's new project was a set of seven mezzotints titled *Landing*. He used two burnishing tools, one in each hand like drum brushes, in a repeated polishing action to make six tiny hovering figures, light against a dark ground, and one larger image, along with a title page with a photo of the spaceship from the movie *The Day the Earth Stood Still*. San Francisco artist Terry Fox rigged a pendulum out of plastic tubing hung from the ceiling and dripped acid on a copper plate in automatic concentric circles to make his print *Pendulum Spit Bite*. (Spit bite is the name of the aquatint process he used.)

Finally, there are Vito Acconci's penises. Yes, that's what they are, a row of them (not actually his—we got them from porn magazines). The print is called *Come Up and See Mine Sometime: Sex for Sale*. When I asked Vito to make etchings, Mae West's "Come up and see me sometime" and the associated catchphrase "Come up and see my etchings" just popped into his head. (There is a James Thurber 1937 *New Yorker* cartoon showing a lobby where a man is saying to a woman, "You wait here and I'll bring the etchings down.")

Beyond sex, selling was Vito's main theme. His second print is called *Bite the Bullet: Slow Guns for Quick Sale (To Be Etched on Your American Mind)*, and the third is *The Selling of Five Americans and a Place for One World Citizen*. In the 1970s, many avant-garde artists were making intellectual art for a small audience, so they had not much expectation of selling. The economy was bad then, too. I suppose Vito (unlike most of our artists) thought that making prints would necessarily be about selling. But his prints didn't sell, at least not right away—I think we still have some of the penises in inventory.

The way I was able to handle selling this group of prints almost by myself was, for the most part, to bundle everything together as a subscription. We did that only for the first three years—our artists were, in the long run, too disparate to sell together—but somehow, back in 1977, our first subscription was a big success. Two local museums, the Oakland Museum and the San Francisco Museum of Modern Art each bought a set, and so did about a dozen collectors, one of whom promptly gave all the prints except the Diebenkorns to a charity auction. We laughed about this later when, at the

Basel Art Fair in Switzerland, a French collector looked around our booth and said, "I recognize most of these names, but who is Di-ben-korn?"

What were we doing at the Basel Art Fair, so difficult to get in, with Crown Point's first offerings to the print publishing market? It was the summer of 1977, and we showed the work from our first publishing program. The following year we returned to Basel and featured John Cage's prints from January 1978. The possibility of exhibiting in art fairs began with an invitation to the magazine section of a 1977 fair in Bologna. I was able to add a small booth for showing our prints. Then, I applied for a booth in Basel and got in. I still can hardly believe it.

We had started our magazine, *Vision*, in 1975. Tom Marioni was the editor, and Crown Point Press the publisher. We produced one issue in 1975 and got out two more in 1976, so three existed by the time we received the invitation to Bologna.

For the first issue, *California* (1975), a dozen artists from Northern California and a dozen from the South each designed two facing pages. The issue also had

articles by Vito Acconci and Claes Oldenburg, New Yorkers who had spent time in California, along with Tom's assessment of the art scene here and a picture essay by me about a great work of early "outsider" earth art, the Underground Gardens of Baldasare Forestiere in Fresno, California.

Vision, Eastern Europe, 1976.

The Crown Point Booth at the Basel Art Fair, 1978, with prints by John Cage.

Tom Marioni's text in the second *Vision, Eastern Europe* (1976), begins this way: "Art is a poetic record of the culture, and people understand the culture of the past by studying the art and products of past civilizations." The art of the Eastern European political bloc, closed to us, demonstrated how culture was developing behind the Iron Curtain. The cover of the Eastern Europe issue is by Czech artist Milan Knizak. He exhibited the drawing in 1971 and spent six months in jail for disrespecting the Soviet symbol.

Tom went first to Yugoslavia, where he got works for the magazine from a number of young artists, including Marina Abramovic, whose photo in *Vision* shows her standing, staring ahead while a man affixes a chain around her neck. In 2011 Abramovic became the first performance artist to be given a full-scale featured exhibition at the Museum of Modern Art in New York.

After Yugoslavia, Tom continued on to Hungary, Czechoslovakia, and Poland. In Budapest he visited an artist named Gábor Attalai, who took him to an underground art gallery called the Young Artists' Club. Attalai told him about an artwork that a Czechoslovakian artist named Jan Mlcoch had exhibited there. In his home country, Mlcoch had bandaged his chest and put a layer of earth filled with earthworms inside the bandages. He had shown the worms on his chest in his exhibition, and Attalai explained to Tom that Mlcoch had brought the worms to Hungary without papers, passports, or permission. That was the point of the piece to Attalai. But when Tom met Mlcoch in Prague and reported Attalai's praise, Mlcoch laughed. "Artists in Hungary are more political than we are," he said. "That piece was about my relationship with the worms."

Tom remembers the Hungarian artists as being more political than any of the others, and as we talk I think of the Hungarian revolution in 1956 when I was in Europe. Back then, I did not understand why the United States did not come to Hungary's aid. In 2012 the news is full of stories about Syria, in the midst of a rebellion being murderously crushed by a dictator. In front of me is a cartoon in the *Economist,* February 2012. The first panel shows two figures on a diving board, one figure labeled "The West," the other "Arab League." Cries of "Help!" are coming from below. "My conscience tells me to dive in headfirst," says The West. The next panel shows where he would be diving. Below the board are sharks with gaping mouths and enormous teeth; a tiny figure labeled "Syria" flails among them.

"However," says The West, bending down to grasp the diving board, "my central nervous system tells me . . ."

The third issue of *Vision, New York* (1976), featured pages (eight each) designed by a dozen artists from New York, including Carl Andre, Sol LeWitt, Hans Haacke, and Walter de Maria, who asked that his pages be blank sheets of a different paper from the one used in the rest of the magazine. *Vision* was printed by a local printer, a friend of Tom's, and he was able to accommodate us. (Special treatment like that would be hard to find today.) Tom considers the blank sheets an "original work" of de Maria's. We had such a work, also, in our first issue: Los Angeles artist Michael Asher asked that his two pages be glued together. Tom and I glued them by hand in all one thousand copies. *Vision* was typeset by Dave Blake, a Berkeley man with a typesetting machine that looked like a flattened wedding cake with great tiers rising up against the wall. He typed our texts into it. We took the pages home and laid out and pasted up the material on our dining room table.

After the first three issues of *Vision*, some time elapsed, but eventually we did two more issues. There were five altogether. In 1980 we produced a series of phonograph records to document an artists' conference called "Word of Mouth" held on the island of Ponape and sponsored by the Museum of Conceptual Art and Crown Point Press. I will tell you about it later.

Vision's fifth issue, in 1981, was called *Artists' Photographs*. Fifty-six artists from sixteen countries sent photographs at Tom's request. We held an exhibition of the photographs at Crown Point Press and presented single-sheet reproductions of all of them as the final issue of our magazine. Tom's introduction said the photographs were by "artists who design projects and create works of art in whatever material or medium is necessary to the idea of the work. . . . [The photographs] were not documentations of art works; they are photographs that are art works."

At the art fairs in Bologna and Basel in 1977, we promoted our first three issues of *Vision*, and we had a booth in each fair to display our prints. I knew that Tom would be busy with the magazine, and although he is always glad to help Crown Point, he doesn't like to appear in any role that could be construed as proprietary. So I asked a friend, Helene Fried, to come along to help with our booths. I still didn't have a gallery person on my staff. Helene was director of the gallery at the San Francisco Art Institute, where I had taught, and she had done a small Crown Point Press show there. Kevin was

Chris Burden, *Diecimila*, 1977. Front side of a color photoetching printed on both sides of the paper, 3 × 6½ inches.

seventeen by then and he knew the material well, so he, also, was fine for the job.

In Bologna, Helene, Kevin, and I were sitting in the booth when we saw four uniformed policemen marching down the aisle two abreast. They stopped and encircled our booth. A crowd gathered, and one of the policemen picked up our Chris Burden print, *Diecimila* (the facsimile ten thousand lire note), which we had displayed with its portfolio on a table. It was without a frame because of the printing on both sides.

The policeman was gesticulating and speaking rapid Italian. I answered in English, pointing to the uncut sheet and the artist's signature, but he continued talking to his compatriots as if I hadn't said anything. The men had removed the print from the case and were handing it back and forth, turning it over, holding it to the light to see the watermark. Helene was making gestures trying to get them to be more gentle with the paper, but that didn't worry me much. Paper is among the toughest of art materials. I was worried, though, when one of them showed me some handcuffs.

Kevin slipped away and quickly reappeared with someone to translate. More volleys of Italian, more gestures. I suggested that the translator tell them the price of the work. I pointed to it on our printed price list. The policemen exchanged disbelieving glances. I repeated what I had said earlier about the value of the art being more than the value of the money, and this time it was translated. The translator pointed to the artist's signature. One of the policemen laughed. Then the others joined his laughter and they all (literally) threw up their hands and left. We were selling the signed, fake *Diecimila* for $1,000. An actual *diecimila lire* bill was worth $10. (The "fair market value" for *Diecimila* now, if you could find one for sale, is $10,000.)

CROWN POINT PRESS
1555 SAN PABLO AVE.
OAKLAND, CAL. 94612 USA

This is a symbolic object

DIP IN WATER — WATCH THE ACTION

In Basel, we handed out compressed sponges printed with the Crown Point Press name and address and "This is a symbolic object." Our booth was small, sparsely hung, and out-of-the-way. Someone dubbed it "the curious corner." "Is there anything in here?" a man inquired as he poked his head in to look without entering. We did sell some things. And we met people.

I was delighted when one of our visitors looked carefully and lengthily at every print on the wall, then said that the work was beautifully printed. He gave me his card. He was Aldo Crommelynck, the French printer—admired by me—who as a young man had worked with Picasso and in 1976 with Jasper Johns on *Foirades/Fizzles*. In 1986, eight years after I met Crommelynck at the fair, Pace Editions brought him from his home in Paris to New York to print for them. He printed many fine etchings for American artists. He died in 2008 at the age of seventy-seven.

My most important connection in the summer of 1977 in Basel was with Margarete Roeder. She remains one of my closest friends and still has a gallery in the same place in New York as she did then. It is in an upstairs loft at 545 Broadway in SoHo, a few blocks from the loft on Greene Street that I had briefly pictured as my own living and working space. SoHo was beginning to assert itself as the dominant art area in New York. Tom and I would visit Margarete, sleep on a small platform above her gallery storage area, go out for coffee in the morning, and often run into Chuck Close, who lived around the corner. The major galleries were there, too, in great cast iron and windowed loft buildings on streets partly made of brick.

Margarete Roeder was a lifelong friend of John Cage's, and it was she who, in 1977, had given me his address and recommended me to him. Before I met her, Tom had already suggested that I invite John to work with us. He was a music composer, not yet a visual artist, but his scores were graphic. He had studied painting in his youth, and his ideas had influenced important

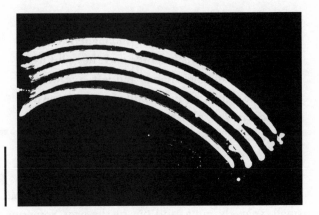

Joan Jonas, *Rainbow*, 1979.
From *Hurricane Series*, a portfolio
of five color aquatints,
23½ × 35½ inches.

artists including Jasper Johns and Robert Rauschenberg (and, of course, Tom Marioni).

Margarete is Austrian by birth and has many European connections. At Basel in 1978, with John Cage's work on the wall in our booth, she suggested we develop a show to travel in Europe. We didn't then have enough work of John's alone, but we formed an idea for an exhibition of Crown Point Press prints called *Music, Sound, Language, Theater*. It included John Cage (music), Tom Marioni (sound), Robert Barry (language), and Joan Jonas (theater).

In 1980 the *Music, Sound, Language, Theater* exhibition began its travels. In just over a year's time, Margarete had been able to arrange sponsorship by the United States Information Agency and to find museums in Europe to show the exhibition. It traveled for five years; the two best-known museums that showed it were the Tate Gallery in London and the Stedelijk Museum in Amsterdam. We produced the catalog at Crown Point (the printing was done at the same shop that printed *Vision*). It was under the direction of Robin White, our first publications director, whom I had hired in 1977.

Starting with John Cage in January 1978, Robin interviewed artists who worked at Crown Point, and we produced the interviews in our irregular periodical, *View*. The second issue was on Robert Barry, who worked with us in February of the same year. Barry is among the most radical of conceptual artists in that he has made some art that is literally invisible. For example, he exhibited an empty gallery that contained a sign saying that the top third of the room was filled with radio waves. Here is Robert Barry's description of how he came to do that kind of work: "A few years ago when I was painting it

Joan Jonas with proofs from *Hurricane Series,* 1979.

seemed that paintings would look one way in one place and different in another place. Although it was the same object, it was another work of art. . . . I finally gave up painting for wire installations. Then I started using thin transparent nylon monofilament. This led to my use of materials that are invisible or at least not perceivable in the traditional way. Although this poses problems, it also presents endless possibilities."

Words, used individually, as themselves, can be a material "not perceivable in the traditional way," and Barry is generally considered a language artist. For his prints he used a magnifying glass and hand-lettered words around the edges of copper plates, writing backwards because of the reversal inherent in printmaking. One print, *Untitled,* for example, has three words spaced evenly along the plate mark of each side of its rectangular shape: DISTANT IRRELEVANT HOW / AGAINST LOST WILLING / DENY CONSIDER ABSENT / UNCERTAIN BEFORE ENDURE. The ink is silver gray. Barry said the blank space in the center is "a space in which we can function; we can move, interpret. We can find out." The prints are impossible to reproduce, but if you spend a moment or two with one of them, it is strangely engaging; your associations with the words settle over you.

Joan Jonas, the fourth artist in our *Music, Sound, Language, Theater* exhibition, is a pioneer video and performance artist whose first prints, done at Crown Point early in 1979, are images (a rainbow, a sun, a heart) from a performance called *Mirage.* Robin White describes *Mirage,* in *View,* as "a composition composed of elements that are moving: video, drawing, actions . . . ," and Joan breaks in to say, "Theater comes into that also—using theatrical devices. I use the idea of video as I use everything else. All those fragments in there, from different sources, back and forth. Magic shows, also, they were a big influence on me as a child."

The European trip to the art fairs that Tom, Kevin, and I took in the summer of 1977 had been a business trip with ramifications that went on and on for us. In 1978 the three of us made another big trip in the opposite direction, across the Pacific Ocean. That trip, which also turned out to have ramifications, was intended simply as an escape for me.

My mother had retired in 1977 from teaching abroad and had moved to Berkeley. She was living in an apartment near our house and was eager to travel again. I was starting to feel bogged down in working on our first publishing program. So I took a five-week period in the summer when Kevin was not in school and we didn't have any artists at the press, and booked a freighter trip from San Francisco to Hong Kong. My mother took a longer trip, getting on the ship in San Francisco, but to save time Tom, Kevin, and I flew to Honolulu, where we joined the ship. We flew back from Hong Kong and she returned on the freighter.

There was a small group of passengers, and the ship stopped at many insignificant islands all across the Pacific to unload goods. I took photographs and made notes; the trip provided the material for my final *livre d'artiste*, called *Paradise* (plate 7). It also provided us with our first experience of Ponape, which would become a collective memory among thirty-six people who went there with us two years later.

Ponape is in the Caroline Islands, about halfway between Hawaii and Japan. When we first saw it, we thought it was an accidental shape outlined by clouds, but as the ship moved closer, great angular cones appeared. They were covered by vegetation with one large bare rock dominating. The island suddenly was wreathed with a rainbow, like a halo. The big rock became a sheer cliff above our heads, and the pleated texture of the slopes broke down into layers of palm and banana trees. People were standing along the shore and along the pier. It seemed that everyone on the island was there to meet the ship.

Ponape is 164 square miles and has 17 miles of roads, all unpaved and of firm red clay. The houses, with tin or thatched roofs, are on stilts and open all around at window height. The daytime temperature stays between eighty and eighty-five degrees the entire year, and rain (which bothers no one) comes and goes constantly, along with a breeze that makes the heat comfortable and keeps the bugs in check. In the middle of the jungle, on the side of a hill with the lagoon below and a strange volcanic cone above, is a hotel, a group of thatched huts on stilts, without window glass but with self-generated electricity, ceiling fans, and plumbing, clustered around a "longhouse," an expanse of wooden deck with a bar, tables, and wicker lounge chairs under soaring thatch. The Village Hotel was the only hotel on the island then—I see now on the Internet that there are four. On the Web, the Village Hotel looks the same as when we discovered it thirty-five years ago. The original proprietors are still there. The island is called Pohnpei now.

Bob and Patti Arthur, a couple from Los Angeles with four children, had designed the hotel in the native style and worked with local people to build it; they were running it and living there. The ocean is warm around Ponape and the waves gentle, but the beaches are strewn with volcanic rocks, so tourists, the Arthurs told us, were mostly scuba divers and would come in groups. Before we left San Francisco, Tom had been planning an artists' conference for the Museum of Conceptual Art. We sat at the bar on the Village Hotel's great platform and looked out over the ocean on all sides. "This is where you should have your conference," I said.

We went swimming under a waterfall in an idyllic pool, and then a small boat took us toward what appeared to be a large log fort. The "logs" are prisms of basalt each longer and larger than a person; they were split from the conical cliffs seven hundred years ago and transported twenty miles to that spot by outrigger canoe. Our boatman pointed out the permanence of the structure in a place where jungle, salt, and typhoons see that nothing lasts. "It's good," he added, "that the Japanese, when they occupied us during the war, didn't have any use for it. Otherwise, the Americans would have bombed it and we wouldn't have it anymore."

As our little boat bumped along the lagoon on the way back to the ship, a double rainbow fell down before us. You can look around anywhere, almost anytime, in Ponape and see a rainbow.

On the island of Ponape, 1980 (clockwise from bottom center): Dorothy Wiley, Marina Abramovic, Joan Jonas, Daniel Buren, Chris Burden and Mary Corse.

11.

Escape Now and Again

On January 15, 1980, thirty-five artists and other art people, with one baby in arms, boarded a small plane in Honolulu for the once-a-week flight to Ponape. Some of us had come from California, but others were from New York or Europe where winter was locked in. After a few hours, the plane stopped for refueling at an atoll. The loudspeaker said we could get off and stretch if we liked. The ocean was right next to the plane, a few steps from the runway. We all took off our shoes and ran into the water. A few went too far and got completely wet. There was a nice breeze, and the lightweight clothes we'd put on in Hawaii mostly dried before we reboarded.

For the rest of the flight, people cruised up and down the aisles, introducing one another, laughing, talking. Bryan Hunt was passing around his Walkman, a new gadget we all thought was tiny, only barely larger than the (big) cassette tapes it played. "If this plane were to crash," someone said, "the headlines would say, 'John Cage and some others died.'"

Tom Marioni had named the conference "Word of Mouth" *Vision #4*. Twelve artists each gave a twelve-minute talk. Since LP records lasted twenty-four minutes, he had specified twelve-minute talks so we could put two on a side. Later we presented three records in a box. The records are white—"because it felt like we were landing from a flying saucer when we got off the plane in Ponape," Tom remembers.

The plane circled over what looked like a green dot in a blue sea, and we landed abruptly on a short white runway made of crushed coral with a great green rocky cliff at one end and the sea at the other. Against the cliff was a new

Ponape, January 1980.

Joan Jonas, Bill Wiley, John Cage, Dorothy Wiley, and others (left).
Daniel Buren with a dancer (below).

Robert Kushner speaking (left), with Cage, Bryan Hunt, and Marina Abramovic to his right.

Wiley, Brice Marden, and Tom Marioni (left).
Brice and Mirabelle Marden (above).

low building. Shirtless workers in jeans hustled our bags from the plane into a big square hole in the building's side, visibly pushing them onto a moving carousel. A man in a grass skirt and an inspector's cap hustled us inside to claim them. The airport building was full of people, many in grass skirts, some (men and women) topless. They clapped and whistled as we filed past. We learned later that word had circulated that we were an American rock group.

In front of the airport was a flatbed truck with fourteen white wicker chairs from the hotel dining room strapped on the bed in two facing rows. There was also a "bus" with long benches facing one another, and a few private cars. Our caravan slowly made its bumpy way up the side of the rocky outcropping, and finally we were on the hotel's great longhouse platform with Bob and Patti Arthur and their staff serving drinks as the sun went down into the ocean below.

We would take the next plane out a week later. There was no television. People didn't carry phones back then, and there were none in the rooms, but the hotel's office had a phone we could use if necessary. The conference agenda was simply to have an artist talk before dinner each night and another after dinner. We recorded the talks, but not the following discussions, and although almost everyone had a camera and a couple of artists had brought eight millimeter film equipment, we did not, ourselves, document. I assigned my son, Kevin, who was eighteen, to take photos—I thought that would keep the "official" photography unobtrusive.

Everyone, sooner or later, went swimming under the waterfall and in the ocean, made a trip to the ruins in a little outboard motorboat, and spent time on the great longhouse platform eating, drinking, thinking, and talking to whoever was around. Laurie Anderson and a few others attended a local funeral; most of us watched (and some joined in) a dance the villagers held, and some of us tasted a narcotic drink pounded and twisted out of a root before our eyes.

Most of the twelve artists who gave talks were not well known at the time, but their names are familiar today: Marina Abramovic, Laurie Anderson, Chris Burden, Daniel Buren, John Cage, Bryan Hunt, Joan Jonas, Robert Kushner, Brice Marden, Tom Marioni, Pat Steir, and William T. Wiley. We saw them as representing the art-world avant-garde, a mix of Tom's selections and mine, East Coast and West, and two from overseas. The trip was a joint project of Crown Point Press and the Museum of Conceptual Art. It was the first year Crown Point made a profit, and we used the money to go to the South Seas.

Thirty-six people made the trip because that was how many the hotel could accommodate. Brice and Helen Marden brought their baby daughter, Mirabelle. From San Francisco, we had with us a favorite curator from the San Francisco Museum of Modern Art, Suzanne Foley, now deceased, and a gallery owner, Paule Anglim, who still supports advanced art. There were a couple of art writers, a couple of art collectors, a couple of college art gallery directors, and several younger artists, some of them companions of the participants. Tom likes to say we were "a microcosm of the art world."

Everyone had been invited either by one of the artists who gave talks or by Tom and me. People other than the participating artists paid their own way, and Crown Point paid the bulk of the balance. Tom's nonprofit MOCA rounded up enough donations to bring Marina Abramovic from Yugoslavia and Daniel Buren from France, and the National Endowment for the Arts paid for the phonograph records to be pressed. Of course, we didn't use any government money for the trip itself.

"It was a wonderfully crackpot idea," Robert Kushner told Grace Glueck, who wrote an article about it for the *New York Times* shortly after we returned. Brice Marden told her the idea was "slightly rarefied," but added, "the trip was important because now I have a whole new idea about the Coast, and how its being out there in the Pacific has really had an influence on its culture." Bob Kushner went on to tell Glueck something that I've heard often over the years from people who were there: "One of the major positive things was making friends and being able to talk with people I'd never get to know otherwise." I thought the quote in Glueck's article that summed up Ponape best was from Melinda Wortz, a professor at the University of California, Irvine: "The idea was romantic and unreal and totally irresistible."

Grace Glueck quoted me as saying, "The conference brought together artists with an individual, expressive approach that is beginning to modify the recent emphasis on reductivism in art." It sounds stilted to me, but I think I was exploring an idea close to that in my print publishing at the time. I doubt that I used the word *expressive*, but I know that I thought something romantic was stirring in our world after the sobriety of the seventies. Perhaps *romantic* is not exactly the right word, either. The art I'm thinking of has a direct relationship to the way we live our lives. Tackling this art in etching was

Daniel Buren, *Framed/ Exploded/Defaced*, 1979, installed in Crown Point's upstairs Oakland gallery with prints by John Cage.

somewhat daunting because most of the artists involved were not painters; they didn't normally work flat. Some of them wanted to use our medium in ways that had never been asked of it before.

Daniel Buren, who was at Ponape, had come to Crown Point from France the year before our trip and had made a work that was not only his first print but also his first framed work of any kind. He called it *Framed/ Exploded/ Defaced*. Since 1965 all Daniel's work has been stripes, usually pasted on walls, as he says, *in situ*. The art magazine *Modern Painters* in 2011 called Daniel Buren "France's most celebrated contemporary artist . . . once controversial, now revered." His stripes occur in both expected and unexpected places—on museum walls framing other art, or out in the world, at the historic Palais Royal court in Paris, for example, framing life itself. "The point of the stripes is just a little signal for something else," Daniel has said.

Setting out to help Daniel re-create his stripes as an etching, Lilah Toland, the printer in charge, decided not to try to paint them on a plate. Hand-painted lines always waver a bit, and Toland asked Buren if the stripe widths must match exactly. He replied, "Not exactly. They can vary within a millimeter." After checking a metric ruler and finding a millimeter to be just a little wider than the edge of a fingernail, Lilah decided to cover a large square plate all over with an evenly bitten aquatint, then mask out the stripes in printing. Daniel was delighted that the edges of the stripes are absolutely straight, and also that the uncolored stripes are absolutely white. The mask eliminated any trace of the plate tone normally present in etchings. We printed the work in an edition of forty-eight. The first print in the series is yellow, and for each subsequent print the printers added a measured amount of red to the yellow ink. Most of the prints are orange of various shades, but the first is yellow and the last is red.

Daniel had the printers cut each print into twenty-five equal fragments, and he asked us to frame them all. (We made twelve hundred frames.) Once he had decided on the width of the molding for the frame, he instructed that we cut down each square so that when the fragments were framed and put tightly next to one another, the "defaced" print was the same size as when first printed.

If you bought the print, you received a boxful of framed fragments with detailed instructions on how to "explode" them to fill any wall. If there were space enough on the wall, you could hang other artworks between the stripes. "I think people who have the etching will have something which is very close to a contradiction, but still as perfect as possible as an etching," Daniel said in *View*.

In 1979 Crown Point brought two artists from Europe to work with us. Daniel Buren was the first, and the second was Jannis Kounellis, a Greek artist who has lived in Italy most of his life and is the primary figure in the influential art movement called *arte povera* or, in translation, "poor art." Jannis's early work—a brazier filled with coal or bundles of wool attached to a steel bed frame, for example—placed humble yet symbolic materials in the context of high art. As his work became more complex, he sometimes created "living pictures." In his most famous piece he filled a gallery with tethered horses. In another work he sat motionless on a horse holding the mask of a Greek statue to his face.

Arte povera was named and described by Italian art critic Germano Celant, and Jannis Kounellis is featured in his 1969 book of that title, which also includes Italian, German, English, and American artists, some of whom are associated with movements called process art, anti-form, and earth art. Celant wrote that *arte povera* developed "in opposition to the consumerist ambiguity of pop art and the rigidity of minimalism." Because those movements were mainly American, *arte povera* is usually seen as European or European influenced.

Jannis said, in *View*, that his art is based on the "accumulation of history," and he speculated that American artists mainly reject history. "The square," he said, "eliminates completely the possibility of accumulation."

Jannis Kounellis in the Oakland studio, 1979
(above). Kounellis's *Untitled*, 1979. Photoetching
with aquatint, 29 × 21 inches (right).

Perhaps because he was working in the United States, he started his first print
at Crown Point with a large dense black square. Then he created "accumulation" by arranging flowers, printed in blue, in a rectangle around the outside
of the square. That image is called *Untitled*.

Jannis's second 1979 etching, *Manifesto per un Teatro Utopistico,* is rectangular, like *Untitled*, but this time the "accumulation" forms a rectangle around an
empty center rather than a square. In beginning this work, Kounellis shopped
in used-book stores for old family photographs. He arranged twenty-one of
these around the edges of the rectangular plate. At the last minute, he added
a photograph of a picture of a burning house to the frame. Many of the photographic images are of houses with people in front of them: old people and
children, black people, white people. One group is Chinese. Our country is a
utopian theater. There is possibility in the empty space in the center, but it is
also possible that the fire in the burning building will spread.

Vito Acconci, having tested our seriousness in 1977 with his prints of
penises and guns, returned to Crown Point in 1979 to make a huge ambitious
installation work that took us three years, working off and on, to complete. "I
feel like I've left 'wall' out of my work," he said, "and prints force me to really
think of 'wall.' " Before he began work on this project, he had only done one
wall piece, called *Wall Drawing*, the term that Sol LeWitt was using for the

With Vito Acconci (seated) and printers (from left) Paul Singdahlsen, Peter Pettengill, and Nancy Anello, 1979.

work he was doing at the time. Vito's *Wall Drawing* was not a drawing at all, but many actual ladders fastened to a wall to make a grid.

I remember looking out the window of the Oakland studio and seeing Vito and his chief printer, Nancy Anello, walking down the street with a huge aluminum ladder they had bought and managed to propel from the hardware store through a half-dozen blocks of downtown. The first of his set of three wall prints was the photographed image of the ladder, extended to twenty feet high by accumulated individually framed prints. The work is titled *Twenty-foot Ladder for Any Size Wall*. You can leave off a section or two if your ceiling is low.

"The way I thought of these pieces," Vito said in *View*, "was that I was starting with the basic notion of plate. Plate can have image, plate as image can be added to another plate as image. As these plates are added, they start to overlap, then paper is added to paper, and starts to correspond to the form of the room. So you could have a twenty-foot ladder and a twenty-foot airplane wing. Plate becomes image, becomes paper, becomes wall, becomes room."

Vito and printer Stephen Thomas assembled a model airplane from a kit, and we photographed a wing, then enlarged it to ten feet and made two sets of plates, sectioning the image. The second set is reversed, so the piece,

Two Wings for Wall and Person, is two wings, flesh colored, hung at shoulder level with a gap between them just big enough for a person to stand in. Both the ladder and the wings evoke a longing to escape.

Vito's third print, *3 Flags for 1 Space and 6 Regions* (plate 11), shows the United States as a central space, with China and the Soviet Union encroaching on it. Vito, in a magazine interview, spoke of his immigrant father doing piecework, sewing bathrobes in their apartment in the Bronx. "It wasn't until I was twelve or thirteen that I realized you didn't have to be Italian to make music or art. . . . All my life, I've never had particular skills, particular talents. I've just had will. I see myself as a drudger."

Vito brought the three flags with him from New York and later did several works of sculpture using them. At Crown Point he pinned them up on the wall and the printers photographed each one. Then they made transparencies that Vito moved around to form different relationships. He finally decided to show the Chinese and American flags obscuring the Soviet one. This turned out to be a presentiment of world events. A dozen years later, the Soviet Union was dissolved and China and the United States began to lock horns just as the United States and the Soviet Union had been doing at the time Vito made this work of art.

Daniel Buren, Jannis Kounellis, and Vito Acconci are very different artists, but all three use theatrical and/or decorative approaches and at the same time remain connected to conceptual art; they retain a sculptor's sensibility and they focus on ideas. Robert Kushner, who, like Daniel Buren, came to Ponape with us, broke radically from that sensibility and stepped away from conceptual art to focus directly on the theatrical and the decorative. Bob's work placed him in direct opposition to a culture of avant-garde painters who for the preceding thirty years had used the word *decorative* pejoratively. He and a few other artists, supported mainly by the Holly Solomon Gallery in New York, changed that culture by developing what they called pattern and decoration art, the forerunner of much painting today, including Damien Hirst's spots.

Bob Kushner has said that he started making decorative art "because you weren't supposed to." That changed after he made a trip to Iran (anyone could travel there then), "saw incredible works of genius and became aware of how intelligent and uplifting decoration can be." Bob had come to decoration from performance art and an interest in costume; at that time he insisted that

Robert Kushner, *Nubiana*, 1982. Aquatint with sugar lift and spit bite aquatints and soft ground etching with stenciling in gold paint printed on two sheets of paper, 36½ × 51 inches.

the costumes he made were art only if they were being worn. His trip to the Middle East in 1974 changed his approach: "The garments interested me a lot, especially the veil that the women wear. As soon as I got home, one of the first things I did was to try to cut one out just to see what it would feel like—and when I did, I realized very quickly that there was this big, sort of flattened half circle shape that I could paint on." In this way he shifted from conceptual art to painting.

Bob Kushner's mature style uses an abundance of multicolored, multi-surfaced fabrics as support for his paintings. The etchings he made at Crown Point in 1980 (and continued to develop with us for more than a dozen years) are figurative works that involve decorative materials, colors, and textures. *Nubiana,* one of his first prints with us, for example, is on Japanese paper in which leaf fragments are embedded. Printed leaves are included in an image of two dancing figures, along with black and white textures and flat areas of gold. The two bodies in *Nubiana* face each other while the faces look away. They are on individual sheets of paper designed to be shown together.

Joel Fisher, who worked with us in 1980 for the first time, also used two sheets of paper side by side for a single print. In his *First Etching*, the paper itself is the artwork—the plate was not actually etched but was inked and printed blank (there is plate tone). It bridges two sheets of paper that Joel made at the papermaking studio of Don Farnsworth. To make his paper, Joel pulped stacks of prints our printers had rejected as they worked on editions at Crown Point. We had been printing some fine-line prints by Sol LeWitt and rejecting a lot of them because of tiny skips of the ink in lines that don't cross other lines—this is extremely difficult work to print. The colored fragments of ink from the rejected prints remain linear in the paper pulp and are identifiable in the new sheet. The other identifiable elements in Joel's paper are flat bits of color from Robert Kushner's work.

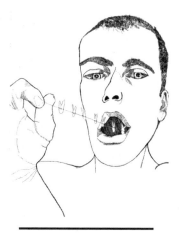

Robert Kushner and Joel Fisher, with their different approaches, set the tone for an exhibition I assembled for Crown Point Press in 1982 called "Representing Reality: Fragments from the Image Field." This show traveled, under arrangements made by Margarete Roeder, to the Contemporary Art Center in Cincinnati. In the "Representing Reality" catalog essay, I described the artists in

Francesco Clemente, *Self Portrait No. 2 (Teeth)*, 1981. Hard ground etching, 8 × 6 inches.

the show as creating "milestones along the road" to a new type of painting variously called at the time wild painting, new wave, energist, neo-expressionist, and trans-avant-garde. (The names that stuck were neo-expressionist and trans-avant-garde.)

Francesco Clemente, who was just beginning to exhibit his work in the United States, is the only artist in the show who was actually seen by the art world as a neo-expressionist/trans-avant-garde painter. The others, the forerunners, were Joel Fisher, Robert Kushner, Pat Steir, Günter Brus, and William T. Wiley. My idea may have been something of a stretch—it's a diverse group—but critic Robert Atkins, reviewing the show for *California Magazine*, explained it well:

> *They have dispensed with the traditional notion of figure and ground—an object or person depicted in front of a background—and instead regard their images as a nonstatic stream of consciousness or metaphorical field. Their prints are ravishing.*

My longest stretch was the inclusion of Günter Brus. He lives in Vienna and was part of an infamous performance art movement there in the 1960s in

Günter Brus, *Grosse Erdangst I*, 1982. One of three hard ground etchings with spit bite aquatint and drypoint, 23½ × 35½ inches.

which his naked body was stressed in public, sometimes even receiving self-inflicted wounds. Günter Brus pioneered forty-five years ago an "endurance" art of the sort that Marina Abramovic, in 2011, made famous with her exhibition at the Museum of Modern Art in New York. In 1970 he gave up performance art, called *aktion* art in the German-speaking world, and began to draw representationally. "Abstraction in recent art ended with the *aktion*. From now on, the laws of the wonder world hold sway," Brus wrote in the early seventies when performance art in the United States was just beginning to take hold.

Because of Günter Brus's position in the history of performance art, it was exciting to have him travel to Oakland, California, to work with us, and his prints—which have to do with his fear of earthquakes—show what I called "an easy slippage in and out of another time, another place, often dense and dark and smelling of the earth."

In my essay for the exhibition catalog, I talked about scientific attitudes toward reality and concluded by quoting from an interview I had read with Michel Poniatowski, a French scientist who discussed the coming age when computers would dominate our lives. "Einstein defined the relativity of time and space; nonlogical physics defines the relativity of objects," he said. "Everything becomes relative, not only time and space but the object contemplated in relation to time and space."

This seemed to me to relate to a statement by Francesco Clemente, in

William T. Wiley in Oakland, 1978 (above). Wiley's *Working at CPP*, 1978. Soft ground etching, 11 × 10 inches (right).

View, that his paintings are "crossing points for images." I ended my essay with the thought that new science combined with "a new vein of art built on the same assumptions" argues powerfully "for the existence of a changed world."

William T. Wiley, the San Francisco Bay Area artist in our "Representing Reality" show, filled his prints with dense networks of drawing and writing. In one of them, *Working at CPP,* 1978, we are looking through what might be the opening of an earthy cave to see a hand with a crown serving as a cuff above it. The hand points a finger toward a press that bears an image of a rectangle divided into four squares. Below the press is written, "thanks, kids," and in another spot there is a handwritten lament (I have provided punctuation):

> *I guess people might think, myself included, there was another time we were closer to, that this wasn't always our harmony, to rattle around like this, here and there, around the planet as savage as ever, some continual distant echo observed from some spot thought to be just a little more advantageous, outrageous, certain things become uncertain. They might feel they have no choice. Think for certain this uncertainty. We now understand.*

John Cage reading in the street-level Oakland gallery, Crown Point's twentieth birthday celebration, 1982.

12.

─────────────────────────────

Don't Try It Alone

We were in a new decade. I had hired Crown Point's first gallery director, Thomas Way, in 1979, and before he started work with us, in order to have a gallery for him to direct, I rented a room on the floor below our studio. Smaller than the studio, it also was a nice room, with big windows looking out over San Pablo Avenue. You had to climb a flight of narrow stairs to reach it from the street, and the street was in Oakland, a city not often visited by art collectors, but we were able to fill it with people at least when we had openings for shows. Most of the time, however, the gallery served as an office for Thomas, who always seemed to be on the telephone. He often traveled to New York, where Margarete Roeder let him use a desk in her space.

In 1981 the hat store on the street level of the building in Oakland went out of business. We had peered down through the skylight at the big room where the hats were made, but had never been beyond the narrow aisle of the street-front store. The aisle was lined on one side by a pair of long green cabinets where the hats were displayed; those cabinets are now in our Crown Point Press bookstore in San Francisco.

When the hat store took down its sign, an older sign was revealed: Feather's Bird Nest. Tom and I walked through the door at the end of the narrow store, and suddenly we were in a four-thousand-square-foot open space, oddly angled, beautifully proportioned. I imagined how it must have looked as an aviary, with birds singing, some in cages, some flying around. But when I described this vision to someone who had lived in Oakland a long time, he said he thought the space had been a dance hall during the war. Whatever

Staff and family ready to work on the street-level gallery space, Oakland, 1981 (top).
The first exhibition in the finished gallery space, 1982 (bottom).

it had been, it would become the most beautiful art gallery ever to be seen. The ceiling shot up twenty-two feet to the skylight we had looked through, a skylight two hundred square feet in size. Lining the glorious central space was a mezzanine with delicate decorative railings, lit by a smaller skylight.

Never mind that this beautiful space was on a street that people in the art community normally didn't come near. The rent was reasonable if we took it "as is." We got going right away, cleaning, painting, and repairing.

The photo at left shows eighteen people, thirteen of them staff members, not including me. I am in the second row at the far left, Tom is next to me, and in front on the right is my mother, Clare Brown. Kevin is behind her between two of our printers. Thomas Way is the man with the beard, leaning into the picture from the back row. You can see only his face. Shortly after we opened the new gallery in September 1981, Thomas Way resigned.

Just a week ago, as I write this, I was at a party seated at a large round table, and in the middle of a conversation with the person on my left, I looked up and caught the eye of a man with graying hair sitting across from me. His wide smile brought recognition. "Richard?" I said tentatively.

"Richard Pinegar," he affirmed. "You gave me my first job in the art world. I was just out of school. I did everything you or anybody else needed done." And then, to the laughter of everyone at the table, he told the story of the goose.

"Diebenkorn was coming back to work at Crown Point, and he wanted to use zinc plates. The printers had been using only copper, which doesn't bubble in the acid. Zinc bubbles, and you need to wipe away the bubbles with a feather from a waterbird. Really, a waterbird. The acid destroys brushes, but waterbirds have a wax coating on their feathers. The printers needed a feather from a waterbird."

Having set up the story, Richard continued, "I walked over to the lake in Oakland with Lilah, the printer, and we couldn't find any feathers on the ground. But there were geese waddling around. Lilah said, 'Sneak up on one,' and I did! I made a grab for the tail, and it pecked at me and flapped, and squawked and ran, and there I was lying on the ground with a big feather in my hand! The goose was not very happy."

Later, Richard turned to me, speaking quietly. "Did you ever locate Thomas Way?" he asked. "I left Crown Point soon after he came. He was still working for you then. But I heard he stole some prints."

"Yes," I answered. "And he vanished without a trace. The police recovered most of the numbered edition prints he sold to galleries in Los Angeles. But there were also Diebenkorn proofs that belonged to me that he got out of my storage area, and those are completely gone." Then, to my surprise, one of my mother's sayings (borrowed from *Hamlet*) popped out: "Forget the slings and arrows of outrageous fortune." And I added, "I've forgotten about Thomas Way now." And, it's true. I have almost forgotten. I can't remember the details of the recovery. One thing you should know, however: if the buyers of the stolen prints had asked for a documentation, which every publisher supplies with every print, they wouldn't have lost the money they "invested" in that work.

And here's something that would be funny if it weren't serious: We recovered a print that Thomas painted on. It must have been Thomas who did it—it certainly was not Diebenkorn. A once beautiful, signed, and numbered, black and white Diebenkorn print had been ruined. I said to the gallery owner who was showing it, "How could you possibly have thought Diebenkorn painted this? It's terrible."

The gallery owner replied, "Well, I didn't think it was a very *good* Diebenkorn." Before she bought it she had asked for an authentication. She showed me a sheet of plain typewriter paper on which was typed: "I, Thomas Way, authenticate that this print was hand painted by Richard Diebenkorn in the Crown Point Studio," (signed) Thomas Way.

After Thomas had resigned from Crown Point, he moved to Los Angeles, where he got a job with a gallery there. In December 1982, for the enormous sum of $12,000, I bought my second computer, a Vector. Unlike my earlier Zenith, it was equipped with a database program, and Wendy Diamond, our manager, began to enter our inventory (which was handwritten in notebooks). She noticed something funny about a notation concerning a (supposed) sale of a set of the newest Richard Diebenkorn prints.

I thought it was simply a paperwork mistake and called Thomas in Los Angeles to ask about it. He wasn't at the gallery that day, so I left a message asking him to call me back to help us figure out a discrepancy in the records about a Diebenkorn sale. After he received the message, he disappeared.

There are lessons to learn from every misfortune. I learned from this one that it is important that publishers give every print, including every proof, a unique designation. Although Crown Point recovered most of the stolen numbered prints, the proofs, which belonged personally to me, were impossible to recover. Back then I had artists sign all the artist's proofs simply "AP," so they weren't differentiated from one another. A proof, marked AP, of Diebenkorn's *Large Bright Blue* (plate 18) came up at auction a few years later. It went for more than $100,000 (the selling price when we published it in 1980 was $5,000). I thought perhaps the auctioned print (a proof) had been stolen from me, but I could not have proved it because we had marked other APs in the same way.

The Thomas Way disaster at Crown Point had a silver lining. It allowed the entrance of Karen McCready into the life of Crown Point Press. She carried us to a new era of professionalism and good fortune. Pace Editions, affiliated with a powerful painting gallery, was (and still is) the most visible place showing contemporary prints in New York. Richard Solomon, a graduate of Harvard Business School and owner/president/founder (in 1968) of the editions arm of the Pace Gallery, is a giant in the print world. Pace publishes mostly the prints of New York painters, in all print media. It started as a publisher without a press, but Solomon now oversees three print shops as well as two

Karen McCready, 1983.

print galleries in New York. In 1982, however, there was only the one print gallery, downstairs from the Pace Gallery on Fifty-seventh Street.

Karen McCready, then Pace Editions director, was sitting at a small desk in the middle of the gallery when I quietly asked if she might be interested in working with me at Crown Point. "Start at the top," I thought. She smiled in a neutral way and wrote something on a piece of paper. It was her home phone number.

Right after Thomas left, I had hired a young woman, Fredrica Drotos, to take care of the gallery we had so beautifully installed in Oakland. I knew we were at a turning point. I thought I would hire a local gallery director and also, if possible, someone from New York whom I could bring to California to be a right-hand person for me and guide the sales program overall, giving

Fredrica Drotos and Margarete Roeder at the Chicago Art Fair with Tom Marioni's diptych, *Train Windows*, 1982.

us more reach into the New York market than we had so far been able to accomplish.

Karen had another idea. She would open a stand-alone print gallery for us in New York. By stand-alone, she meant not attached to a painting gallery but having the professional standards of the gallery she was then directing. There were several print galleries in New York besides Pace. Castelli Graphics mostly showed prints produced at Gemini G.E.L. by artists in the Castelli Gallery, and the Marlboro Gallery, similarly, had a print component. Multiples was originally an excellent print gallery (since 1965), but in 1977 it became the Marian Goodman Gallery, and by 1985, when we started our New York gallery, Marian Goodman was a high-level contemporary art gallery with some prints in the back room. Brooke Alexander, a print publisher of seriousness and style since 1968, showed prints along with drawings and other unique works in his gallery. His gallery is stand-alone but is not entirely for prints. All of those galleries are still in business now, in 2012. The Crown Point Press gallery that Karen McCready created is not, but it did continue for ten years, 1985 to 1995.

Karen located our gallery in New York at 568 Broadway in a big gallery building at the corner of Prince Street in the developing art district called SoHo. She hired a young architect, Denise Hall, who designed a lovely, simple, welcoming space. There were framed prints in exhibitions and in an "open storage" area, and also prints in drawers. People found it a pleasure to visit, and many came, and purchased. "Kathan likes to live on the edge," Karen said in a 1997 interview published in an exhibition catalog. That's probably true. But Karen was there with me on that edge—or, in the case of the New York gallery, I was with her.

Crown Point Press turned twenty in 1982, the year Karen joined our staff. Fredrica Drotos installed a John Cage show in our Oakland gallery, and we produced a catalog with descriptive texts by printers about the prints Cage had done up to that time. An edited version of my introductory essay for the catalog, "Changing Art: A Chronicle Centered on John Cage," was published in *Tri-Quarterly* (spring 1982) and also anthologized in *A John Cage Reader*, a hardcover book published by C. F. Peters that year. Versions of our Cage exhibition (thanks to Margarete Roeder) traveled to the Whitney Museum of American Art in New York, the Philadelphia Museum of Art, and the Albright-Knox Museum in Buffalo, New York.

To celebrate our twentieth birthday and his seventieth, John Cage read a new work of his poetry, "Composition in Retrospect," to an overflow crowd in our Oakland gallery. Afterward there was dancing. Our beautiful Feather's Bird Nest space was infused with activity and goodwill. In the etching studio, Ed Ruscha came up from Los Angeles to do his first prints with us; Wayne Thiebaud made a new color print, *Sardines*; and Richard Diebenkorn produced *Blue Surround*. We also did new projects with Francesco Clemente, Joan Jonas, Robert Kushner, Tom Marioni, and Pat Steir.

Crown Point had done only etching for twenty years, and after the twentieth birthday celebration I wanted to add something else. One reason for this was simple restlessness, but also I had in mind to try something that was not so strictly limited in the number of prints we made of each image. Etchings can be printed in big editions, but it is not generally practical to do so because each individual print is so time-consuming. My notion of making large editions was not so much about commerce (we haven't ever had a

The Crown Point Gallery at 568 Broadway, New York City, 1987.

Conference in Baja California (clockwise from bottom): Fredrica Drotos (back to camera), Karen McCready, Wendy Diamond, and Deborra Stewart-Pettengill.

really large audience) as it was about an exploration of printmaking as a readily available, relatively inexpensive way for people to own art.

At that time, 1982, before the wide use of ink-jet printing, there were only four ways to print anything: relief (woodcut, linocut), intaglio (etching, engraving), planographic (lithography), and stencil (silk screen, pochoir). I rejected lithography because it was being done well by so many others, but I thought we would make a stab at the remaining two: stencil and relief. The relief (woodcut) project turned out to be more consequential than I could have imagined; it went on for ten years in Japan, and we extended it for a time to China. I will tell you first about the stencil project, short-lived and somewhat frivolous, but full of delight for those of us who were involved.

I had the notion that stencil printing was at its best in printing fabric, and I began thinking about printing art on something wearable. One of the great things about prints is that they are art in an unpretentious form, and I was thinking of trying something more lighthearted than our etchings. In my mind I could hear John Cage saying, "I always go to extremes," and I remembered conversations with various artists who appreciated seeing art out in the world as well as on the walls of homes, galleries, and museums. Those artists included theorists about decoration like Robert Kushner and also advocates of good design like Sol LeWitt. (LeWitt designed several scarves in his lifetime for various manufacturers; his work for our project is a kimono.) Another reason for our "Pure Silk" adventure was that Deborra Stewart-Pettengill, the wife of printer Peter Pettengill, was skilled in sewing and stencil printing. She

Crown Point's silk project at I. Magnin, 1984. Tom Marioni with a model wearing the garment he designed; William T. Wiley's robe hangs on a stand between them (right). A store window displaying Sol LeWitt's prints and his kimono (below).

was the one who figured out how to get each artist's design onto the fabric, and did most of the printing and sewing, too.

Before starting production, I collected the six people, all of us women, who were concerned with this project, and we took off to Baja California, a short flight from Oakland, for a three-day planning conference. I included Deborra, who made the garments; Mady Jones, a consultant I hoped would teach us how to sell them; Wendy Diamond, our Crown Point general manager; Fredrica, who ran our California gallery, and Karen—it was a good way to welcome her to Crown Point. We sat on the beach and talked and laughed. We held formal meetings around a table under a big tree. There was a mariachi band at the hotel every night, and one morning in the pool Karen organized us into a water ballet.

At first I titled the project Louise Brown Pure Silk in honor of my grandmother's lingerie business, but eventually Mady persuaded me to switch to Crown Point Pure Silk so that Crown Point could "own" the project; she felt the silks would benefit from the Crown Point name. Using our name on clothing demonstrated, I thought, our voluntary separation from the "snob factor" in the art market. We produced short kimono jackets, pajamas, a robe, and a few scarves, all made to order. The pieces were not editioned, not signed, and not presented as art. The Society for the Encouragement of Contemporary Art at the San Francisco Museum of Modern Art held a fashion show of our work, and around Christmastime, 1984, we displayed our garments in two big windows of the I. Magnin department store on Union Square in San Francisco. The store sold the items for a week in a "special event" covered by a full-page article in the *San Francisco Chronicle*.

After that, we shut the project down. We were spending too much money on making the pieces, and it was difficult to find occasions to actually wear them—I suppose, as clothing, they were a failure. But as art they are dazzling—you should see them! The artists are Vito Acconci, Robert Barry, John Cage, Joel Fisher, Joan Jonas, Joyce Kozloff, Robert Kushner, Sol LeWitt, Tom Marioni, Ed Ruscha, Italo Scanga, Pat Steir, and William T. Wiley. You *can* see the pieces if you call the Achenbach Foundation in San Francisco. Our silk project is part of the Crown Point Press archive there.

The story of the Crown Point Press woodcut project starts on a cold morning in Tokyo in 1980. My husband and I, wrapped in quilts, are lying on a straw-mat floor listening to resonating temple gongs that have awakened us. It is barely light but we can see delicate clouds forming as we breathe. A paper door slides open, and a brown-robed woman with a shaved head is offering us cups of steaming tea. "Good morning," she says in English. "Chanting meditation is in fifteen minutes if you care to attend." We pull our clothes over our nightclothes and then wrap ourselves in the brown robes we find folded by our beds. In the temple, half awake, we absorb the murmuring of voices punctuated by bells and gongs, then join the monks in a rustic dining room for a breakfast of fish, seaweed, rice, and pickles on pottery dishes.

Tom Marioni and I were in Japan with a book publisher, Richard Newlin, and his wife, Yoko Saito, who was born in Japan. It was she who arranged for us to spend a night in a Buddhist temple not as tourists but as guests. We never repeated the experience—our subsequent trips to Japan were very different—but neither of us has forgotten it.

Newlin, of Houston Fine Arts Press, published in 1980 a catalog raisonné of Richard Diebenkorn's etchings from 1949 to his first in color, done that year. Tom designed the catalog, and I edited it; we were in Tokyo to work with Newlin and the printers of the catalog on its production. The book accompanied an exhibition that Margarete Roeder circulated between 1981 and 1983 to twelve museums, including the Minneapolis Institute of Arts, the Brooklyn Museum, and the San Francisco Museum of Modern Art.

After I returned from that trip to Japan, Hidekatsu Takada, our printer at Crown Point (he is originally from Kyoto), and I made contact with Tadashi Toda, a printer in Kyoto working in the *ukiyo-e*, or "floating world," tradition. Our project with him went on for ten years.

The *ukiyo-e* style of printing from woodblocks in watercolor ink was at its height in the seventeenth century, the Edo period. In the brochure announcing our project, I quoted a Japanese art history book: "The people of the Edo period made light of everything in the world and demanded what was open-hearted and brilliantly clear in spirit." I thought the words conveyed not only the feeling of seventeenth-century Japan, but also a brightness and confidence that was in the air in the United States in 1982.

Ukiyo-e prints historically were not produced in limited editions. Most of the cost is in creating blocks and proofing with the artist. There might be as many as fifty blocks for a single image, and as in all forms of printing each matrix must be inked for each print. Even so, it is much faster to print woodblocks than it is to print etchings. My idea was to produce these prints in large editions so they could be more reasonably priced than our etchings— but the secondary market, where popular prints are resold after editions sell out, had its way with that idea.

We sold Wayne Thiebaud's *Dark Cake* (plate 12), for example, when it was released in 1983 in an edition of two hundred, for $1,000, and if you bought it in combination with other prints, you could have paid as little as half that. In 2007 an impression was sold at auction for $60,000—but another, exactly the same, went for $30,000 in 2011. This seems to show that edition size doesn't make a difference to the market—"it's the economy, stupid" as the political slogan goes.

The generally small edition sizes in which we print our etchings are mostly a function of using our printers' time wisely, but I learned from the woodcut project that if we occasionally make a larger-than-normal edition, it probably won't affect the market response. All in all, I have to say, markets are capricious, and the art market is especially so.

Like most art professionals, I don't recommend thinking of prints as investment. Most of the people who buy our prints live with them. Generally they cost about as much as a piece of furniture, and their values remain in that range, increasing (usually) with inflation. A very few take on investment status and shoot up in value; it's difficult to know in advance which ones they will be. The investment game must be played not only

with willingness to risk, but also with
experience and a lot of luck. But, as
one of our clients said to me, "Stock
certificates are no fun to look at." And,
if you do want to play that game, the
print market has a lower price point
than the one for unique works. Also,
because there is more than one impression of a print out there in the world to
be assessed, "fair market value" prices
are continually available from publishers and auction houses.

Hidekatsu Takada and Tadashi Toda, 1982.

The printing skills of Tadashi
Toda, our printer in Japan, had been handed down through his family since
the Edo period, and Toda was working with his father mainly printing decorative fans when I first met him. His father died during the years of our project,
and Toda died some years after our project ended. The printing tradition is
handed down in families, and since Toda had no sons (and, he assured us, his
daughter was not interested), his skills died with him. He did, however, teach
for a time at a woodblock institute that our printer Hidekatsu Takada was
instrumental in starting. "I told the people in Japan," Takada said, "that for
some reason Japan gave up on the idea of preserving the watercolor woodcut
tradition, but Crown Point took it on. Now, it's time for Japan to take the
responsibility back." Takada says that in Japan people see him as American,
and in America people see him as Japanese. But he thinks of himself as
American. He became a United States citizen in 1992.

In traditional *ukiyo-e* printing, the artist creates a drawing that a carver
traces onto many blocks, separating the colors by eye; then he carves the
blocks. After that, the printer prints a trial image, and finally he works with
the artist to make alterations, mainly in color balance. After I asked Chuck
Close to work with us in Japan, we sent a drawing to Toda that Chuck had
made with an airbrush—this was the way he typically worked at the time.
Toda told us the image was too smoothly refined to be carved into wood. So
Chuck invented another way of image making in which he used a grid, as he
had before, but instead of filling the squares with tones, he translated the
image square by square into colored squiggles, splotches, or spots. The new

Toda in his home studio with Chuck Close.

approach was perfect for woodblock, and it turned out to be useful to Chuck later in another way.

About two years after we did the woodcut, Chuck Close suffered a spinal aneurysm that has confined him to a wheelchair since that time. He paints with a brush strapped into a special glove. With tremendous will he was able to refine for use in his paintings the method of working he had created for the woodcut.

A Japanese woodcut printer builds up the image slowly by printing transparent layers; there are fifty-one blocks in *Leslie* (plate 13), the image by Chuck Close that Toda is working on in the picture above. For our project, we would travel to Kyoto and go every day to Toda's home where his studio was on the floor above the living space. Following the directions of the artist, translated by Takada, Toda would make proof after proof until the balance of colors was exactly right.

Most of the works Toda prepared for our artists in advance were amazingly good before the artists even began making adjustments, but this was not the case with Helen Frankenthaler's image, which ended up being called *Cedar Hill* (plate 14). Some thick areas of paint in the drawing couldn't be suitably translated into this transparent medium. We all could see that something needed to be done.

Helen decided to start over, and she asked that we find some plywood of a sort she had used in the United States to make woodcuts. Takada came up with a striated sheet, with a texture built into it. She carved a few marks

Helen Frankenthaler in the studio at Cedar Hill in Japan, 1983.

herself, and at her direction Toda carved others—the marks in the plywood appear white in the print. The color shapes are from the original image, printed from blocks cut by the master block carver Reizo Monjyu.

In Toda's studio, Helen was impatient with the time it took to make each proof. "Toda should have an assistant," she said. So the next day there was a man in the studio introduced as "Toda's assistant." The day's work progressed as before, with the assistant sitting quietly cross-legged, his hands folded. "The assistant doesn't do anything," Helen said. "He is not yet trained," Takada explained. That was the end of the assistant's employment.

Helen was not comfortable sitting all day in the cramped space above Toda's home, so, through Shoichi Ida, a Kyoto artist and friend (Crown Point later brought him many times to California to work with us), we temporarily rented a large studio by the side of a hill covered with cedar trees. Helen liked that studio, but in her printmaking in the United States she was used to a different approach to proofing than the one we were using. We worked with Toda in the same way we proof with artists in California. The printer makes a proof, the artist studies it and decides what should be changed, then the printer makes another proof incorporating the change, and so on until the finished print appears. Helen, however, wanted to make choices from samples the printer would prepare. This led to very long days for Toda, who worked to make all the tests she asked for.

Day after day, Helen would appear at the studio, ask for samples of different colors and different ways of printing or positioning a mark, and then leave. The next day she would choose what could be used—or reject everything—and set out more tasks. After almost three weeks (we had planned on ten days), we had an image, but it needed refinement. I asked Helen to dictate to me exact instructions for finishing the print: "on left edge, a purple quality, like painted color only lighter" and "the edges must be softened, bleeding into the wood grain." I have six pages of notes like this. I normally don't keep a diary, but in rereading my notes I discovered I had also written a description of a single day in which we made a print that incorporated all the instructions.

Yesterday, the most amazing thing: we worked, Toda, Takada, and I, as a team. We moved at Toda's pace, measured, steady, attentive, intense. He crouched over his printing board for twelve hours almost without rising, printing continuously but never rushing anything. At the end, as it neared midnight, he wanted to take a short cut; Takada insisted on the long and sure way and irritation flared for a moment. Otherwise, no break in the attention.

Toda ate almost nothing, moved almost not at all, graceful movements, small movements, regular breathing. Takada and I came into his orbit, quiet, attentive, ready with a careful judgment when he wanted it. Too red? More transparent? Overlapping? I studied each test proof, all of us did, with body more than mind. Our progress was a step at a time. We built the print. And at each stage we could see we were right—there was an almost disbelieving recognition. We were being given this. It was not coming from us. My judgments were not my own.

The work is a work that I could never have made, and none of us individually could have made, yet all of us did make for Helen. The radiance of yesterday happens rarely and grows drop by drop. The miracle is the short time, one day following a rhythm. I have felt this before in working with artists, but not so purely. And so, out of tribulation, revelation. We were given it, partly by Helen but mostly by some force outside us all. Things fell into place within us and around us. Ida's appearance about nine with food and confirmation, excitement at the beautiful thing we were making; the girl next door bringing strawberries—everyone hanging there fascinated, discussing quietly how to achieve this or that instruction, laughing once in a while with Toda saying something in Japanese, I the observer but part of it, easy, not forcing politeness.

And then, when we were leaving, sudden tiredness at one a.m., and in trying to pull an iron gate shut, everyone pulling, somehow it fell quietly on Toda. No one screamed. He thinks his arm is not broken, but it will be swollen. He will come anyway tomorrow, even if he cannot print, to show Helen what we did.

Until a few days ago, when I searched for and found my notes on this project, I had mistakenly remembered, believed, and even written that Helen had been with us when we executed the finishing work on the print. But the notes are clear. This is a strange story about a print that was made entirely under circumstances unconsidered by the artist. Nevertheless, it is an indisputably successful work of art.

A critic suggested that Frankenthaler's woodcut is "more interesting" than the other woodcuts we did in Japan because she did not use the traditional approach but made wholesale changes on the spot. I think Frankenthaler's print is beautiful, but I don't find it more interesting than the prints by Chuck Close and the other artists who adapted their work to the circumstances of the venerable tradition that Tadashi Toda offered to them.

Helen Frankenthaler died in December 2011 at the age of eighty-three. Although she was younger than the abstract expressionists, she shared their approach to art making, embracing the immediate and harboring suspicions about using the intellect in painting. Yet she was absolutely skilled at her work, as you can see by looking at the woodblock print that she created by remote control. Evidently, she had been so clear in her instructions about what was needed that we were able to pull it off by following them.

Remote control was not something you would expect of an artist of Frankenthaler's generation. But after sculptor Tony Smith in 1962 ordered a sculpture over the telephone from a steel fabricator, the issue of whether "the artist's hand" was necessary in a "true" work of art was settled. Of course, sculpture has been fabricated for centuries, and photography through its entire history has employed technicians. Even in painting, where the work of the hand shows, artists traditionally have had assistants, and by the 1960s Andy Warhol was making paintings in a place called the Factory and using silk-screen printing as one of his tools to do it.

In the printmaking field, however, the "artist's hand" issue has taken longer to settle than it has in other areas of art. In 1986 the *Print Collector's Newsletter* held a discussion about our woodcut program in Japan, and someone on that panel lauded Frankenthaler's *Cedar Hill* because she had been so "hands-on" in making it. The discussion was in New York, and I, far away in California, was not invited. But Alex Katz, who had by then made his woodcut *The Green Cap* with us in Japan, participated. In plate 15 you can see his finished print, and at right is a working proof on which he made notes to help Toda understand the changes to be made. Katz, in the panel discussion, made the hands-on, hands-off point clearly.

"I've worked with silk screen, and there's less contact, almost less contact, than on the things done in Japan in woodcut," he said. "In silk screen I did several prints that were cut film. I didn't cut the film, someone else cut it. I didn't feel there was much difference. It was

Working proof of *The Green Cap* by Alex Katz.

the same story—lighter or darker, brighter, thicker or thinner ink—the same words I would use to a printer in New York I would use to a printer in Japan."

One of the members of the panel said our woodcuts were "reproductions," and Katz answered in this way: "If these were like dull reproductions, there wouldn't be any controversy because we've seen a lot of those and nobody talks about them. But these things really buzz. It has to do with the personality of the printer. What you have is alive out there."

Alex and Ada Katz in Japan, 1985.

Richard Diebenkorn in the Crown Point studio, Oakland, 1982.

13.

RICHARD DIEBENKORN

SEARCH FOR SOMETHING ELSE

One day in March 2012, Richard Grant telephoned me. He and his wife, Gretchen, Richard Diebenkorn's daughter, had *Blue* (plate 17), one of our woodblock prints, on their dining room wall "forever," he said, and, noticing it was a bit rumpled at the edges, he sent it to a conservator to be flattened. I interjected that we could have done that for him (paper breathes and often changes with the weather, but it can be rejuvenated). "Thank you," he said, "but I'm calling about something more bizarre. The conservator said that this print has been painted!"

"Any chance that Dick added something before he gave it to you?" I asked.

"Not a chance. It came directly from Crown Point."

"Then I wonder who the conservator thinks painted two hundred of them," I laughed. Such is the power of Tadashi Toda's skill.

Richard Diebenkorn made two trips to Japan for our project there, and for the first one, in 1983, he sent two drawings: one that he had made especially for the project and one that he hadn't. He told me he wanted to see if Toda would deal with the two differently, or if he, himself, would. *Ochre* (plate 16) was based on the drawing Dick made with Japan in mind, and over the years it has become a talisman for me of memories of my many trips there.

Ochre is in a horizontal format, earthbound, and some Japanese-like motifs are in the upper-right corner of the image. When Dick saw Toda's first proof, he broke into a delighted smile. Looking from the print to the drawing, I could see that the shapes in the print were simpler, and the whole more

Toda sorting proofs of *Blue* (above). Takada
with the drawing for *Ochre* and a partial
proof of the print on the wall (right).

transparent and flatter. Dick made only a few changes, removed one block for
further simplification, and lightened the color a shade or two. He said he was
afraid that if he messed around with it, the strange quality Toda had captured
would disappear.

For *Blue*, on the other hand, he added blocks, and asked Toda to proof
over and over with color changes. When it was time to leave, the print wasn't
quite finished, and proofs went back and forth across the Pacific a couple of
times before we were able to release it in 1984. Dick's third woodblock print,
Blue with Red, done on another trip in 1987, was more problematic. When
we first saw it, it wasn't holding together, Dick said; it had the wrong blue,
and lots of other things were wrong with it. He seemed a little dismayed and
asked me how to proceed. "Where to begin?" he wondered. "It wouldn't be
productive to simply tear it apart."

I suggested that he think first about where new blocks would be needed,
and he decided to add blocks in the blue area especially. That got him started
about how to hold the pentimenti, or "accidental," material in the field—it
needed to be covered more in some areas and less in others. By the time
we left Toda's that day, Dick told me we had made a lot of gains and he now

thought it would work. After ten days of concentrated effort, it was finished.

In Chapter 10, I used one of Dick's studio notes as my subtitle: "Attempt What Is Not Certain." Here is another of those notes: "*Do* search. But only to find other than what is searched for." I've adapted that one to be the subtitle for this chapter: "Search for Something Else."

Richard Diebenkorn was born in 1922 in Portland, Oregon, and moved with his family to San Francisco when he was two. He drew locomotives as a child, he has said, and medieval heraldry as a teenager. In this he was inspired by a reproduction of the Bayeux Tapestry given to him by his grandmother, who was an artist, writer, and civil rights lawyer. He and his wife, Phyllis, married while both were studying at Stanford University, and Dick served in the Marines in World War Two, assigned to a photographic map-making division in Quantico, Virginia. He spent a lot of his spare time in museums, especially the Phillips Collection, in Washington, D.C.

Dick almost went to Japan, he told me as we set off for Kyoto in 1983. Just before the end of the war, he was in Hawaii awaiting orders to be part of an invasion, a backup plan, he realized later, if the atomic bomb had failed in its purpose.

Near Toda's home in Kyoto is the temple complex Daitoku-ji, an active monastery usually not full of tourists. Often, in all our projects, while Toda was printing a correction, we would walk there as a break from our work. Within the Daitoku-ji grounds is Daisen-in, a simple wooden structure, built in 1509, surrounded by a dry landscape garden, a Zen Buddhist garden

Part of the dry landscape garden at Daisen-in, Kyoto.

containing raked gravel, rocks, and only a few low plants. The garden at Daisen-in has been maintained by monks for the past five hundred years in essentially the same form; its theme is life's journey.

As we entered, we crossed a bridge over a narrow space, the gravel raked in wavering strokes: childhood. Behind the building, the garden becomes turbulent, the raked lines, embedded with rocks, moving toward a dry rock waterfall: the dangerous obstacles of youth. Then, at the building's far side, a complicated but confident pattern develops, the rocks in balanced groups, the raking falling into curves. Finally, as we rested on the stepped apron of the smooth wooden floor at the front of the building, we faced a long rectangle of mainly straight lines with two peaked mounds of gravel settled among them. At that time, my life was in the period represented by curving lines and substantial rocks. Now, I understand the straight lines, the gravel piled into simple forms. As I write this, I am thinking of my own life and the place held in it by each of the artists who sat with me at Daisen-in, and remembering especially Richard Diebenkorn, who died in 1993.

As I sat at Daisen-in with Dick and other friends, someone said that Kyoto had been originally designated as the site for dropping the first atomic bomb. Throughout the war, Kyoto was time and again protected from ordinary allied bombing raids because of its historical significance and its art. Then, as American military strategists planned their greatest destructive demonstration, they argued that the new bomb's power would be most visible if used on a city with a low level of previous damage. Fortunately, the one highly placed man who had held out for Kyoto's dispensation throughout the war prevailed again. I can't vouch for the truth of the story, but it leads to thinking that sometimes one person with courage and conscience exists in the right place at the right time.

Kyoto is full of gardens. Let me tell you about two more: Ryoan-ji and Katsura. I have chosen those two, and Daisen-in, because they are so different from one another. Daisen-in, which I have described, tells a story. There is an idea behind it, and if you don't look for that, you will see something beautiful, but you may miss the garden's complexity. This relates to conceptual art. You expect a conceptual artwork to have meaning, so, with that expectation, you search for a clue in its title, perhaps, or look for kinship to a life experience.

Ryoan-ji, the most famous dry landscape garden in the world, is a single long rectangle of raked gravel holding fifteen stones of various sizes.

You cannot see all fifteen from any viewing angle, and it is probably impossible to make sense of the arrangement of the stones, though mathematicians frequently try. The Ryoan-ji garden was built between 1488 and 1680; the date is uncertain because it was destroyed and rebuilt several times in that period.

The garden at Ryoan-ji, Kyoto (above). A view of the pond at Katsura (below).

When John Cage was visiting Ryoan-ji, he told me, he asked a monk if he thought the stones could just as well have been placed anywhere in that space, and the monk answered that they could have been, to the same effect. Cage, in prints and drawings titled *Ryoanji,* traced outlines of fifteen actual stones, or multiples of that number, and placed them, using a chance-invoked system, in rectangles defined

by the proportions of the garden. Cage's work, like Ryoan-ji itself, is "the music of the spheres." A search for meaning is rewarded, but the point is that there is no precise point.

Katsura, the garden I think of as linked to the art of Richard Diebenkorn, is not a dry landscape garden in a confined space. It is a strolling garden of living trees and plants built around an imperial villa, Katsura Rikyu, so beautiful that it influenced architect Walter Gropius after his visit there in 1953. Katsura was conceived by a prince named Toshihito, who began its construction in 1619 when he was forty years old. He died ten years later. Construction stopped but was eventually revived by a tea master who accepted the commission, a brochure told us, with the assurance of no limitation in time or money, and no interference. He, also, died before the garden was complete.

The garden at Katsura—I can hear Dick saying this—is marvelously unwieldy. It has two hills, a lake with tributary streams, and bridges of stone and wood. It has a tower, a shrine, a platform for watching the moonrise, and four teahouses, each with a controlled view. Thousands of stepping-stones form a path up and down the hills, and as you walk you must look down during some periods in order to keep your footing. When you look up again, landing on a larger stone, there is a view that causes you to catch your breath. You see the graceful Katsura Rikyu far below, perhaps, or the lake with a slender sod-covered bridge, framed by a window of trees. Sometimes you see a gardener working with pruning saw and tape measure. Trees and shrubs have been kept to their assigned sizes for centuries, so the perfect scenes are always there.

But, of course, the scene that startled you is not perfect, and it is not always there. As the Katsura website says, there is "a sense of vulnerability." There has been rain and snow and hail and mud. Plants have died and been replaced, become thicker if not taller. At Katsura, there are plenty of pentimenti, to draw a parallel to Diebenkorn's art with its partly painted-out marks, fingerprints, smudges, and blots.

Dick would put things in, and he would take things out. "I like to have some impulse to go against what I'm up to, in a sense," he once said in an interview. But changing and correcting isn't easy when you've carved your drawing into a sheet of metal. If you want to remove a line, you have to do it physically using a scraping tool. Dick did this extensively, and traces of his removals and changes are visible in all his prints.

In printmaking it is common to keep a mirror nearby because plates print backwards from the way they are drawn. I learned, however, from a 1987 New Yorker profile titled "Almost Free of the Mirror" that Dick also used a mirror when he painted. He told Dan Hofstadter, the New Yorker writer, that he was trying to give up the mirror. But, he went on to explain, "by looking at a picture's mirror image, I could see it as something foreign, unfamiliar, and so address myself to its previously hidden flaws."

Dick's use of the mirror, I think, was connected to his doubting, which was fundamental to his way of working. When I asked him about the word flaws in the article, he said it wasn't the right word to describe what he was looking for. He accepted lots of flaws—in fact, I have seen him create them

With Dick and proofs of his first color etchings, 1980.

deliberately, pushing his fingers into a soft wax etching ground, for example, to create a shadow area out of fingerprints in the finished work.

Dan Hofstadter used a phrase, "the overlapping and interpenetration of the forms," that reasonably describes what Dick was looking for when he studied a painting or a print in progress. I will add something more general. I think the content of Diebenkorn's work, like the garden at Katsura, concerns the flow of things in the universe. When he fixed a moment of that flow in a painting, drawing, or print, he would say, "That's OK. Now it's working." And the art creates, in people engaged with it, a catch of the breath, a sense of pleasure and maybe also of vulnerability.

Sebastian Smee, writing in the *Boston Globe* in 2012 about an exhibition of Diebenkorn's "Ocean Park" works organized in California at the Orange County Museum of Art, put it this way: "Diebenkorn's built-up surfaces, with their erasures and ghost lines, their scuff marks and pooled stains, draw you into a process, a history of their making. They transform the act of viewing into an elastic, involving experience, not just a sudden all-at-once hit." But he also raised a question about beauty. He talked about "California hedonism" and pointed out that Diebenkorn is "deeply indebted to Matisse." He called Diebenkorn's paintings "some of the most beautiful works of art created in America, or anywhere else, since the Second World War," and then added that "some undertakers of modern art contend that Diebenkorn was the end of a line—the last important studio painter still concerned with building on the inheritance of Cezanne, of the School of Paris, of Mondrian, of de Kooning. They may or may not be right."

Picasso called Cezanne "the father of us all." In Chapter 5, I wrote about Matisse's refusal to accept Picasso's position of connecting violence with modernity. And now, we are (tentatively) being advised to forget not only Matisse, but Picasso—and Cezanne, even de Kooning, who came along much later. If Diebenkorn is at the end of that line, what other line is there? I have the April 2012 issue of *Art News* here on my desk and have been reading an article that describes art that meets Smee's "sudden all-at-once hit" description.

The article is by Richard B. Woodward and is titled "When Bad Is Good." Woodward writes that "bad taste often passes for avant-garde . . . and whereas kitsch in art was once to be assiduously disdained, art that traffics in sentimentality and bathos behind a dancing veil of ironic laughter has become highly prized." One of those "highly prized" works of art is a model of a human skull by Damien Hirst, who made the "spot paintings" I mentioned in Chapter 7. The skull, titled *For the Love of God*, is cast in platinum and studded with more than eight thousand diamonds. It is (according to *Time* magazine) "said to be worth" $79 million.

A retrospective exhibition of Hirst's work opened April 4, 2012, at Tate Modern in London, and *Time* mentions that a museum gift shop, "the final room" in the exhibition, features a limited-edition plastic skull "garishly" painted and priced at $58,000. Museum gift shops used to be called museum bookstores, but things have changed.

Japan, the country that continues to care for Daisen-in, Ryoan-ji, and Katsura, has produced a kitsch artist almost as famous as Hirst. Takashi Murakami, born in Tokyo in 1962, makes paintings and animations of sweetly colored animals, flowers, and children with big eyes and wide smiles. In 2007 Murakami was given a retrospective exhibition at the Los Angeles Museum of Contemporary Art, and the exhibition had an "embedded boutique" for Louis Vuitton, for whom Murakami designs products. Also on sale in the boutique were multiples. Paul Schimmel, curator of the exhibition, told a Web blogger, "Takashi found exactly the point that would irritate both me and Louis Vuitton. He took the materials he had printed for various [Vuitton] products and had them stretched like paintings and made into a very large but numbered edition."

Anyone visiting Japan can see roots of Murakami's art in comic books, signs, Pachinko machines, the "Hello Kitty" statues in stores, and even the Buddhas in some monasteries. In the same way, you can see forerunners of Damien Hirst's art by looking back to Frankenstein and other dark tales of the United Kingdom. Think about Salvador Dalí and the surrealists. And then, in your imagination, cross the ocean and in the United States look at the most popular videos on YouTube or the most successful movies measured by box office receipts. Then take a look at Andy Warhol.

Warhol said, "Just look at the surfaces of my paintings and films and me, and there I am. There's nothing behind it." Diebenkorn said, "A successful art-work stands for an artist's being; it contains the whole person." I have a nagging worry that in this moment in history a commonly held connection to beauty and complexity is drifting away. But I also know very well that when the art market elevates a trend, artists begin looking for something else.

The next "something else" will most likely not be work that looks like Diebenkorn's, but I don't think it will look like Hirst's or Murakami's either. Possibly it will entail pursuing art as a skill-based pursuit, a way of becoming a whole person. Or, if searching for a whole person is too old-fashioned, too inner-directed, we could consider instead cultivating "a basic sense of good order," as David Brooks puts it in a *New York Times* op-ed column on April 12, 2012. He uses Dashiell Hammett's "noir hero" Sam Spade as an example, call-ing Spade "allergic to self-righteousness." Brooks says that "he is motivated by a disillusioned sense of honor. . . . Each job comes with obligations, and even if everything is decaying you should still take pride in your work."

Richard Diebenkorn saw printmaking as "a way of drawing." In 1980 Dick worked with color aquatint for the first time, painting the acid directly onto rosin-prepared plates. His skill in handling a brush gave him immedi-ate results with this process. Two of his most admired prints, *Large Bright Blue* (plate 18) and *Large Light Blue* (plate 19), are part of the first etching project in which he used it. The two prints share the same plates. The light blue version is a partial "ghost"—only the top part of the image received

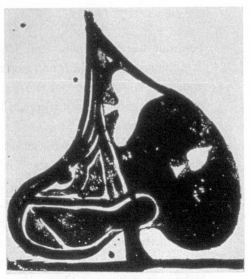

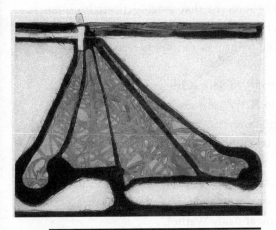

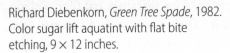

Richard Diebenkorn, *Green Tree Spade*, 1982.
Color sugar lift aquatint with flat bite
etching, 9 × 12 inches.

Richard Diebenkorn, *Sugarlift
Spade*, 1982. Sugar lift aquatint,
16 × 14¾ inches.

new ink; the light blue field resulted from ink residue in the plate after *Large
Bright Blue* was printed.

In 1981, and also in 1982, Dick worked in the print studio mainly with
images of clubs and spades, a motif that appears, in whole or in fragments,
in drawings and paintings as well as in prints made off and on over his entire
working life. The *Clubs and Spades* prints are mostly aquatints, some in color,
some not. They demonstrate Dick's use of printmaking as a way of firming
up an idea by making many permutations of it. *Sugarlift Spade* and *Green Tree
Spade*, shown here, are two of my favorites. Dick's original name for *Sugarlift
Spade* was *Spade Slouching*. In *Green Tree Spade* he added a separate little plate, a
jaunty top to the tree, outside the print's plate mark.

I don't think anyone in history has made color aquatints more beautiful than those of Richard Diebenkorn, and in one short period in 1986 he
made three of his most beautiful: *Indigo Horizontal*, *Red-Yellow-Blue*, and *Green*
(plate 20). He began work on *Green*, his largest and most sought-after print,
in early October 1985, after a two-year absence from the etching studio. The
largest plate he had worked on before *Green* was *Blue Surround*, twenty-two by
nineteen inches. Our plates are made from roofing copper that comes in long
sheets. We cut them down to the largest plate size our press can accommodate

and wait for direction from an artist as to how to cut them further. Printer Marcia Bartholme later recalled how *Green* began.

> *We had just finished cutting down some large sheets of copper when Dick walked into the studio. A full-size thirty-six-by-forty-five-inch plate was lying on the table. Dick immediately went over to it and walked around it, tilting his head to see it in both horizontal and vertical positions. An hour later, Takada and I were astonished to be pulling a line image in cadmium red off this plate. I use the word* astonished *because we assumed Dick would not work that large, that he preferred the intimacy of smaller prints. I was to learn very quickly that with Dick absolutely nothing should be assumed.*

Dick developed his print images mainly by using collage. After the printers pulled a proof, he pasted or pinned cutout paper shapes to it until he got something he thought might work. Then the printers helped him figure out how to put the changes he wanted into the plates. Often this required scraping away something already there. Marcia continued the story:

> *For the next five days we had a hard time keeping up with him. Takada and I had begun to realize the complexity we were facing given Dick's predilection for going back into plates again and again to build up layers of texture and color, and sometimes to completely change whole sections. Then on the sixth day, work on* Green *came to a standstill. Dick said he was frustrated with the size of the plates. He decided to abandon the print. We took the proof off the front wall and put it up at the back of the studio.*

Dick started work on a smaller print, still larger than any he had done before. It was later named *Indigo Horizontal*. The printers became completely involved with it. They were beginning to forget about the big green print on the back wall. "Then, one afternoon," Marcia recounts, "I turned around to see Dick pasting some printed paper from *Indigo Horizontal* on the *Green* proof."

Dick began a new plate for *Green*, using a technique he'd liked in the smaller print. There were only four days left of his planned two-week working time. Besides *Indigo Horizontal*, he had started a multiple-plate image that he abandoned after a lot of work on it. We had begun the project with Marcia as

The Oakland studio, 1986, showing proofs of *Green* (right),
Red-Yellow-Blue (center), and the abandoned print (left).

chief printer along with Takada as assistant and an apprentice. In addition, by this time, I had called in the two printers who had been editioning in our other studio. So five printers (all we had) were starting work at nine in the morning and sometimes not leaving until midnight. Dick would leave before dinner, but the printers would stay to etch plates he had finished drawing, then proof the result for him to see first thing the next morning. Marcia continued her story this way:

> *We made steady progress on* Green *in the last part of the second week. We were always working with Dick's collage elements. Sometimes we would painstakingly measure and trace the exact location of a new line or color area, then mark the location on the plate for him to work over with acid or a drawing tool. At the other times he would look at the proof and say something like, "I'll just wing it here," and begin drawing on the plate without any guidelines. Once we etched a triangle shape that came out three inches from where it was intended. Dick liked it, so it stayed.*

We finished the project with OK to Print proofs of *Indigo Horizontal* and two smaller prints but without completing *Green*. Three months later, at the end of January 1986, Dick came back and worked with all five printers for another two weeks. He spent most of the time on *Green*, but also he created the color print titled *Red-Yellow-Blue*.

On the very last day of the project Dick added a seventh plate to *Green*, not full-sized like the others but a narrow strip that ran along the bottom of the image and changed its proportion. It widened a band of brown ink already there and was the final touch. The "something else" that he pursued was, in his words, "something other than what is searched for."

The project that included *Green* was unusual in that Dick almost gave up on *Green*, and he did give up on another, smaller color print that he later referred to as "the one that got sick." In all the years I worked with him, I can't remember any other instance of his abandoning a print once he had begun serious work on developing it. He prodded and changed everything, and rarely let go of anything he had started. "Certainty may or may not come later," he wrote in his notes to himself. "It may then be a valuable delusion."

With Dick and printers Lilah Toland and Nancy Anello, 1980.

In my room at the
Tawaraya Inn, Kyoto, 1987.

14.

THE MIDDLE EIGHTIES

TELL THE TRUTH

Elaine de Kooning was born Elaine Fried in Brooklyn in 1918. She met Willem de Kooning in 1937 when she was an art student and he had not yet had a one-man show. Elaine's art-school teacher had told her de Kooning was one of the two best painters in New York—the other was Jackson Pollock, and that judgment is now generally accepted. Elaine has described her early years with Bill as a time when they were "expert at living hand-to-mouth." Elaine and Bill were married in 1943 and separated in 1957. The two never divorced and began living together again on Long Island in 1975. Elaine died of lung cancer in 1989, four years after her project at Crown Point Press. Her husband, already afflicted with Alzheimer's disease when I knew Elaine, survived her by nine years.

After Elaine died, I asked her longtime assistant Edvard Lieber whether he thought she had tried to escape Willem de Kooning's stylistic influence. "I remember someone writing that she painted in his shadow, and she answered that she painted in his light," Lieber replied, and added, "Lots of other artists were more derivative of him than she was."

Elaine's work was mainly figurative, and she spent many years painting portraits. She painted two official portraits of President John F. Kennedy, who worked on his papers while she made studies that she developed on canvas later. One of her portraits hangs in the Kennedy Presidential Library and the other in the Truman Library and Museum. "I really wanted something that would incorporate not only my image of the president but also a collective image—the public image," she said in *View*. Elaine was social, and her

attitude toward her work was different from the solitary, inward-looking
approach of her husband and the
abstract expressionist artists of her
time. "Bill always thought that portraits were pictures that girls made,"
Elaine told a friend. "So I had that
area free."

When Elaine was working at
Crown Point Press, the studio was
generally full of people she had invited
to visit, some of whom she knew and
some who were brought by the ones
she knew. She kept working, hardly

Elaine de Kooning at Crown Point, 1985.

stopping to talk with them, but the visitors, along with the printers, clearly
felt connected to her. "She was wonderful," said printer Hidekatsu Takada,
"so vigorous, so interested in other people."

After we had finished printing Elaine's editions, I took the prints to her
studio on Long Island for her to sign. It was full of assistants and friends. One
of the guests was Minna Daniel, who edited Elaine's writings (published regularly in art magazines) and also those of John Cage—I had heard John speak
of her almost reverently. I must have mentioned that I wanted someday to
write about the artists I had been working with, because later I got a letter
from her with advice: "Don't, for heaven's sake, ramble," she wrote. "And, if
possible, avoid evaluations, which you may want to make, but they are bound
to get you into a peck of trouble."

Minna Daniel and I were dinner guests, and when it was time to eat
Willem de Kooning appeared. He was surprisingly small and trim, I thought,
very tidy and self-possessed, smiling and laughing with our little group at the
round kitchen table, completely integrated but not volunteering conversation
himself. He seemed relaxed and happy, especially when he interacted with
Elaine; I thought he had a kind of glow about him. Elaine said that although
he had become "forgetful," he was painting every day in his studio.

After de Kooning died, I saw an exhibition of his late paintings at the
San Francisco Museum of Modern Art, and I loved them. I thought they
reflected the person I met at dinner in 1985: open, smiling, graceful, glowing,

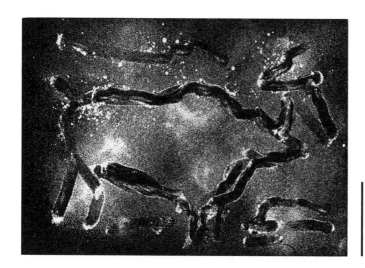

Elaine de Kooning,
*Torchlight Cave Drawing
No. 1*, 1985. From a
portfolio of eight aquatints,
each 12 × 15 inches.

without the bitter, desperate edges shown in his paintings from earlier times. The show was mostly panned, critics hinting at possible use of projections, of Elaine's or an assistant's interference in laying out colors, and so on. I remembered a story of Elaine's from back in the time when Bill worked as a window dresser in a department store. He borrowed an opaque projector, and he and Franz Kline projected little drawings of barns that Kline was doing then. That was when Kline became an abstract painter, she said. I had always wondered how Kline made such casual gestures on such a large scale, and reading the reviews of de Kooning's late work I wondered if he, too, early on, used a projector. Whether or not he used one, early on or later, how could there be anything wrong with doing that in order to have a starting point for a painting?

Those thoughts have come back to me fifteen years after the SFMOMA exhibition because I read in the *Brooklyn Rail* a review of paintings by a young artist named Charline von Heyl. "Artists like von Heyl," the reviewer commented, "have focused on the aspects of de Kooning's late work that made it suspect for that artist's traditional admirers: his use of projected images, the work's sense of formal dissolution, and its nagging intimations about the erosion of de Kooning's authorial control. I imagine that for von Heyl, the ways in which an abstract painting is disjunctive, incomplete, and contaminated are not faults, but are precisely the qualities that make it worth continuing to explore."

Elaine de Kooning said that her prints, made at Crown Point in 1985, were part of the culmination of her life's work. She began this work in 1983, after a trip to France to see the prehistoric cave paintings there, and continued developing the "cave paintings" theme until her death. "I felt a tremendous identification with those Paleolithic artists," she said in an *Art in America* interview. "I found myself deep in the caves imagining I was one of them, looking for surfaces smooth enough to paint on, noticing chunks of yellow clay on the ground that would be perfect to draw with. Prehistoric art was secret—hidden way deep as though they didn't want you to find it. The cave walls seemed to be teeming with animals before I saw my first actual prehistoric drawing. When I did see it, a crude and powerful bison, I was overwhelmed by its unexpected immediacy."

The cave paintings were important to Elaine because in prehistoric times, clearly "art was a very important part of the thought processes of the human race," she explained to Robin White in *View*. "And, disastrously, that is no longer true. I don't want to get into half-baked talk about right brain, left brain," she said, "but we did go off into the left brain, codified, rationalized. Our whole education system is based on that; art is almost squeezed out of existence. . . . You know, I feel as though my desire to go back [to the cave paintings] is like trying to touch home base. How did it all begin?"

Elaine de Kooning thought in the mid-eighties that art could be our salvation in a world "confronted with mass extinction." But, she added, "some of the people now who are attracted to art would have gone into commercial art forty years ago, where they always made money. In the past, artists were the ones who made other artists' reputations. Now, reputations are fabricated by people interested in protecting their investment. They are involved with a value system based on merchandising concepts rather than aesthetic principles."

Hans Haacke, coming from an entirely different place and making entirely different art, laid out some of those "merchandising concepts" in an exchange with interviewer Paul Taylor in 1986 in the magazine *Flash Art*:

> *Are you implying that politics has become spectacularized?*
>
> Politics, as mediated by the press, has indeed become a spectacle. Clever politicians exploit that. Hitler was a master at it, and so is the actor, Ronald Reagan.

Would art play a different role in such a context where even the political seems unreal?

Let's not be fooled. Behind the spectacle, politics continues, as hard-nosed and real as ever. And if a policy is built on fiction, its results are nevertheless felt in the world of reality.... What is really frightening, though, is the degree to which fiction is taken for reality at the Reagan White House. Reagan's "star wars" defense concept comes straight from the dream factory. If global policy is developed along the lines of a Hollywood script, we may very well blow up the world....

Is the idea of historical progress being discarded?

I would like to believe in a utopia, a more humane society, at peace with the environment. But I confess I'm not very confident. We are getting drained already by the struggle not to let things slip further into barbarism.

A quarter century later, in 2012, I picked up the *New York Review of Books* to find a quote from the venerable historian Tony Judt: "We are likely to find ourselves as intellectuals or political philosophers facing a situation in which our chief task is not to imagine better worlds but rather to think how to prevent worse ones."

Hans Haacke was born in Cologne, Germany, in 1936. World War Two ended when he was nine. His father, who had been a city official in Cologne, refused to join the Nazi party and became unemployable but kept himself and his family alive. Haacke came to the United States in 1961 on a Fulbright grant to continue art studies that he had begun in Germany and Paris. He returned to Cologne after two years, then moved permanently to New York in 1965. His wife, Linda, is American, but Haacke has remained a German citizen. In 1993 he represented Germany in the Venice Biennale and won the Golden Lion award for the best pavilion.

I visited the Venice Biennale that year. It takes place in a commercial fairground. Permanent highly styled buildings owned by the world's most powerful countries are interspersed with walkways, shade trees, and ice-cream vendors. The German pavilion is an imposing Fascist-era building; *Germania,* the Italian word for "Germany," is engraved on its facade. Inside, Haacke had lettered the word again, this time in giant letters on a curved white wall. The enormous exhibition hall was empty except for flat icelike shards of marble dense from wall to wall, clearly the remains of an elegant floor that Haacke had caused to be broken up. Not only did the willful destruction create a kind of beauty, but it was shocking in its understated symbolism.

Crown Point Press has published two works by Hans Haacke. We completed the second, which I will tell you about first, in 1982. Called *Upstairs at Mobil: Musings of a Shareholder,* it was an enormous project: ten large prints that hang tightly together to make a wall-size work. Haacke bought ten shares of stock in Mobil Corporation and received a stock certificate engraved with an image of the familiar winged Mobil horse and various decorative corporate seals. We enlarged this in our darkroom to nearly six feet by nine feet and transferred it in sections to ten plates. We printed it in the black, brown, and red of the original certificate. Layered under each panel in blue is a printed "musing" in Haacke's writing. Here is one.

> *Mobil's public relations people make a killing through support of the arts. Although our tax-deductible contributions are hardly equal to 0.1 percent of our profits, they have bought us extensive goodwill in the world of culture. More important, however, opinion leaders and politicians now listen to us when we speak out on taxes, government regulations, and crippling environmentalism. The secret for getting so much mileage out of a minimal investment is twofold: a developed sense for high-visibility projects at low cost and well-funded campaigns to promote them. Mobil, in fact, ranks lowest among the 50 companies which give most in proportion to their pretax profits. Museums now hesitate to exhibit works which conflict with our views, and we need not cancel grants as we did at Columbia's Journalism School. The art world has earned our support: "Art is energy in its most beautiful form!" Mobil makes my money grow!*

Hans made ten facsimiles of his stock certificate and cut each one into ten pieces. We glued the matching piece onto each sheet of the large print. We made an edition of ten of this print, the proofs included in that number. Six were for sale. In addition, Hans created one unique work that he sold through his dealer. To make this, he started by cutting up his original stock certificate and gluing the sections into the panels we had printed. Then he hand-wrote his texts over the panels in blue.

ARE THE RICH A MENACE?

Some people think they are, so let's look at the record.
  Suppose you inherit, win or otherwise acquire a million dollars net after taxes. That would make you rich, wouldn't it? Now, what's the first thing you'd do? Invest it, wouldn't you?— in stocks, bonds or in a savings bank.
  So, what does that mean? It means that you have furnished the capital required to put about 30 people to work.
  How is that? National statistics show that for every person graduating from school or college, at least thirty thousand dollars of capital must be found for bricks, fixtures, machinery, inventory, etc. to put each one to work.
  Now, on your million dollar investments you will receive an income of sixty thousand, eighty thousand, or more dollars a year. This you will spend for food, clothing, shelter, taxes, education, entertainment and other expenses. And this will help support people like policemen, firemen, store clerks, factory workers, doctors, teachers, and others. Even congressmen.
  So, in other words, Mr. Rich Man, you would be supporting (wholly or partially) perhaps more than 100 people.
  Now, how about that? Are you a menace? No, you are not.

TIFFANY & CO.
FIFTH AVENUE & 57TH STREET
NEW YORK

Advertisement in The New York Times, June 6, 1977

The 9,240,000 Unemployed in The United States of America Demand The Immediate Creation of More Millionaires

Hans Haacke, *Tiffany Cares*, 1978.
Photoetching, 29 × 41 inches.

Tiffany Cares, 1978, Hans's earlier print, is in an edition of thirty-five. We had heavyweight deckled paper specially made so the work would resemble a card from Tiffany & Co. There are two texts on the sheet. On the left side is a direct copy of an advertisement Tiffany put in the *New York Times* on June 6, 1977, titled "Are the Rich a Menace?" It lays out the classic "trickle-down" theory of wealth: if you own a million dollars and invest it, you are putting "policemen, firemen, store clerks, factory workers, doctors, teachers, and others, even congressmen" to work. In fancy Tiffany-like script opposite the ad is Haacke's message: "The 9,240,000 Unemployed in The United States of America Demand The Immediate Creation of More Millionaires."

The message, Hans said in Robin White's 1978 interview with him in *View*, is that "you have to have a small number of people making tremendous fortunes so that they can put other people to work." What Hans Haacke calls "a handout theory" involving tax loopholes and low taxes for the rich is used,

Hamish Fulton, *Porcupine*, 1982. Color etching on three sheets of paper, 93¼ × 22¾ inches.

he says, "to legitimize exploitation." That theory is a mainstay of the Republican Party. In 1978 when Hans created *Tiffany Cares*, Jimmy Carter, a Democrat, had taken over the presidency from Republicans Nixon and Ford, and the country's economy was slowly emerging from a recession. In four years, however, Carter was unable to fix high unemployment. He lost his bid for reelection, and when Hans created *Upstairs at Mobil* in 1982, we were in the beginning of the Reagan years.

That year, as Crown Point Press began its program in Japan, I wrote that there was a "brightness and confidence in the air in the United States." I think it was true in the first years of Reagan's presidency. However, he pressed quickly into lowering taxes and giving special breaks to large corporations, and his presidency ended with the country in recession. This happened again, more severely, in Republican George W. Bush's two terms in the 2000s. As I write this, in the election year of 2012, thirty-four years after Hans created *Tiffany Cares*, "trickle-down economics" is clamoring its way into television and radio ads again.

Hans considers himself a systems artist; that is, as he said in *View*, he believes that "forms and patterns of behavior in one set of phenomena have an equivalent in another set. So that one can view the world as a whole rather than as autonomous departments." Although he is considered the father of political art, he doesn't like the label. "Every time I hear it I cringe. The term reduces the work to a rude, one-dimensional reading. Worse, however, it implies that works not called *political* have no ideological and therefore no political implications. This is a myth cherished by everybody who promotes art but does not want to be seen as promoting one set of interests and ideas over another. Every product of the consciousness industry contributes to the general ideological climate."

In 1982, the same year we published *Upstairs at Mobil*, Crown Point Press published *Porcupine*, by the English artist Hamish Fulton. I think of Haacke's work and Fulton's as two sides of a coin—both concerned with how an individual functions in the world, both part of the "consciousness industry," both telling the truth. Fulton, along with Richard Long, is a pioneer of what in England is called land art; land artists create art by walking. Fulton and Long were students at St. Martin's School of Art in London in the late 1960s and have remained friends since that time. Long is better known, possibly because on his walks he often makes subtle sculpture works in the landscape and photographs the works or, on occasion, transfers them home to be exhibited in a museum.

Hamish Fulton describes his approach in this way: "I don't make sculptures in the landscape. My beginning was in 1969 when I visited the American West. I took landscape photographs and made works with small titles and texts. This put me in the category of conceptual art. I was in various exhibitions in which the uniting characteristic was photography."

Hamish doesn't think of himself as a photographer, however. "I'm not interested in mediums, the medium of photography, or sculpture," he told Robin White. "I'm really interested in the place, in the weather, in the rocks. . . . When I start out, I'm starting to learn about the way the place looks—and then eventually I feel relaxed in that environment and I feel good. So then I might take a photograph." He goes on to explain what he means by feeling good: "Let's say you go on a seven-day walk. After four days, your mind is not the same as when you started. It has slowed right down and is starting to work in a slightly different way. Your thoughts are somehow silhouetted, and you can identify them."

There is no photograph in Hamish's etching. Robin asked if he intended the work to function the same way as one of his photographic works, and he replied, "Yes, this is a continuation." He used "a notebook that functioned like a camera" and brought back some pine needles to the studio. "When I saw the pine needles on the snow, I got the idea for the etching." He pressed the needles into a wax ground so they would etch directly into the printing plates. Hamish's print is narrow and tall, the height of a standing person. A poetic text is etched in a column over the pine needles.

The fourth artist emphasized in this chapter, subtitled "Tell the Truth," is Rammellzee. At breakfast on Sunday morning, February 26, 2012, I opened my *New York Times* to the Arts and Leisure section and there, filling the bottom third of the front page, was an article, "Art Excavated From Battle Station Earth." Oh, I thought, someone's copying Rammellzee. I looked more closely. It *was* about Rammellzee! But, he had died two years earlier and hardly anyone had seemed to notice. Reading, I found that a show in a gallery was coming up, and a group of works were on display at the Museum of Modern Art in a show of "print-influenced" work, and that Rammellzee was the author of "one of the most talked-about pieces in 'Art in the Streets,' a sprawling graffiti survey [in 2011] at the Museum of Contemporary Art, Los Angeles." I knew his work had been in that show; I didn't realize it had been noticed.

I turned the page to continue reading, and was surprised. There was Rammellzee, the rest of the article filling a whole page and including a big picture of him in costume with a mask, his "letter racer" sculptures all around him, and a smaller photo of him painting, and another of him with the most famous graffiti artist of them all, Jean-Michel Basquiat, taken in Los Angeles in 1982, two years before Rammell came to Oakland to work with us. The *Times* quoted a studio assistant of Basquiat's as saying that Rammellzee was "our T. S. Eliot. In terms of his ideas Jean-Michel was white bread compared to Rammellzee and I think he knew it."

I invited Rammell to work at Crown Point Press on the suggestion of artist Francesco Clemente, who had worked with us several times since 1981. "He's the real thing," Clemente had said. "He has a developed philosophy, he makes art all the time, nonstop, and he is really smart."

I don't know the name Rammellzee was born with, but he was born in 1960 in Far Rockaway, Queens, New York. He told me his father was a New York City policeman, but there is apparently no other information available about him before he became Rammellzee. "I am a gentleman who was trained in the trains," he told us. "I studied art four stories underground with the rats and the bats and the cats and the dogs."

Some "writers" who created subway graffiti in New York in the late 1970s were pulled into the international art world. In the 1980s Rammell sold enough paintings in Holland alone that in 1987 the museum of the town of Gröningen gave him a ten-year retrospective, filling five rooms with his art entirely borrowed from Dutch collections. I learned from the *New York Times* article that he was "courted" by New York dealers "for years" but was not taken on; it is unclear whether this was his decision or theirs. Rammell made it clear to us that in his graffiti work he was not like the writers who "were amateur enough to run into the trains and let out an emotional attack." He said he was "a mere mechanic in quantum strategy," not an artist. Admitting to being an artist, he said, "would be like losing all my old laws and coming to the crazy-ass society."

The theory behind Rammell's work begins in the Middle Ages with monks who ornamented letters in manuscripts and chanted Gregorian chants. Rammell saw graffiti writing and rap music as related to these monks. (I learned from the *New York Times* article that Rammellzee "was a renowned 1980s M.C., and his 1983 collaboration with K-Rob, the twelve-inch single 'Beatbop,' became a hip-hop landmark.") In his subway writing he revived the Gothic tradition of the ornamentation of letters; this was the beginning, he explained, of a historic period called Gothic Futurism.

Most of the graffiti writers' work, Rammell told me, was based on "fame emotions." But he moved "from ornamentation to armamentation, from styles of competition to styles of weaponry." The central image in Rammellzee's *Palladium Protractor, Chase to Assassination (Gothic Futurism)* is a laser tower that rotates on its base while a tanklike spaceship, called Ikonoklast Panzerism, chases Diseased Culture. His second print is subtitled *Future Futurism*. In it a single red orange shape, a "Luxturnomere," bristles with daggerlike appendages and is silhouetted before a deep space.

By 1984, when I invited Rammellzee to work with us at Crown Point Press, Tom and I had turned a little garden structure in the backyard of our Berkeley house into a guesthouse. We added a bathroom and a comfortable bed, and artists who stayed with us could have privacy in their comings and goings. When we picked up Rammellzee from the airport, he sat in the backseat of the car and played rap music at full volume on a large boom box. When we got home, we were frazzled and sent him out to the guesthouse immediately. Tom was leaving for Europe the next day, and he suggested I should send Rammellzee back to New York and forget the project.

At three in the morning the telephone woke us. It was an art critic in

Rammellzee, *Sirpier-E-Ule's Luxturnomere, Staff Landing (Future Futurism)*, 1984. Color sugar lift aquatint with soft ground etching, 24 × 36 inches.

Rammell in the Oakland studio with his *Palladium Protractor, Chase to Assassination (Gothic Futurism)* on the wall.

New York whom I slightly knew. "Rammell's at the corner of Solano and Key Route," she said, naming two streets about a mile away from us. "He went out and forgot to take your address or phone number so he called me. Could you get him?" It wasn't a good start, but Rammell did apologize.

My son, Kevin, who was twenty-three at the time (a year younger than Rammell), was living at home, and he and I and Rammell spent two weeks of evenings together. I cooked a large amount of food—Rammell and Kevin were both enthusiastic about eating. We laughed a lot, went to the movies, did some sightseeing. Rammell spent a lot of time reading our encyclopedia. Kevin remembers his "crazy intelligence, his physics language—like the things I studied in school were in him too, but they came out in a different way." Rammell called Kevin "Homeboy." Back then, I hadn't heard the term before, and it suited Kevin, so I thought Rammell had made it up for him. But after a couple of days in the studio, Peter Pettengill, Rammell's printer, became Homeboy too. I understood it was a compliment.

The following January in 1985, John Cage stayed in our guesthouse. We took him to the movies to see Jim Jarmusch's *Stranger Than Paradise*, a comedy of non sequiturs about young people in which Rammellzee had what the *New York Times* called "a scene-stealing cameo" as a fast-talking "money man." John loved the movie, and over the next two weeks as we worked on his prints, if anything seemed mysterious or out of sequence, he would exclaim, "Stranger than paradise!"

Over the next sixteen years, Rammell telephoned me from time to time to tell me what he was doing. He told me he was making "Letter Racers" out of skateboards by attaching toys to them; he told me he got married. "Her name is Carmela," he said happily, "Carmela Zee." If I wasn't there when he phoned, he would leave a message: "Just tell Kathan hello. Don't call back. I'll call another time." He left such a message just a few days before he died on June 28, 2010, of heart failure. It's hard to believe. He was not quite fifty.

The mid-eighties were busy years for Crown Point Press. We had a staff of eleven in Oakland, and in addition Karen McCready had two assistants in the New York gallery. In Japan, Tadashi Toda was by this time printing for us full-time. Francesco Clemente created his unforgettable self-portrait titled *Untitled* (plate 21) in Japan in the mid-eighties, and in the same period we also published memorable woodcuts by William T. Wiley (plate 22), Wayne Thiebaud, Robert Kushner, Robert Mangold, Pat Steir, Sylvia Plimack Mangold, and other old friends, as well as by several artists new to us, among them Eric Fischl, April Gornik, Alex Katz, Al Held, and Judy Pfaff.

Karen McCready joined me on a Japan trip in which Toda worked with Al Held and Judy Pfaff back-to-back. "The artists' initial reactions when the proofs were unveiled were of awe," she wrote in our newsletter, *Overview*. "How can this process of printing with transparent watercolor pigments be so rich and detailed? How can so much be accomplished by only a single wood-carver and a single printer in a tiny studio?" Our woodcut project had come along just in time to supply Karen with more inventory than we could have produced in etching—she needed the prints in New York.

Karen had suggested that I invite Al Held to work with us at Crown Point. He didn't think he was interested in etching, but he did want to go to Japan. My invitation to Judy Pfaff was at his suggestion. She, too, said she did not want to do etching. Both artists ended up doing monumental bodies of work in etching, but they started with us in Japan.

Bill and Shirley Brice with Shino, Okay, and Yuki at the Tawaraya Inn, 1987.

I was traveling to Japan twice a year, staying two weeks to a month at a time, and I had fallen in love with the place, especially the place we stayed, the Tawaraya Inn. As our taxi from the airport would approach the inn through Kyoto's narrow streets, I would feel a happiness that was physical, a letting go of my muscles in anticipation. Just a few more minutes and we would be there. Twenty-five years have passed, but the memory comes quickly to my mind.

We get out of the taxi and I poke my head through the door. Suddenly, gracefully, we are surrounded by friends—the shoe man is first, then Yuki and Okay, the two housekeepers who always care for me, then Mr. Yamaguchi, the manager, all welcoming, smiling, bowing. Mr. Yamaguchi pays the taxi. We give our shoes to the shoe man, slip into red slippers, and glide down the narrow hallways, glimpsing little gardens, lanterns, and a single flower in a hanging section of bamboo.

In the room where our artists usually stay, paper doors frame a tiny garden with a moss-covered pond and lighted stone lantern—Diebenkorn called the lantern "the house across the street." I leave my guests to get settled and make my way upstairs to the oldest part of the inn, built about 1810. A door slides open, and I see the straw-matted floor, the lacquer table with legless chairs, the alcove containing a hanging scroll and a vase with flowers, just as I left them, except the scroll and flowers have been changed to suit the season.

Yuki brings a cotton robe and a mild clear soup in a lacquer bowl. After I've had a bath in the deep wooden tub, the others in my party join me in my room—all of us, having bathed, are wearing patterned cotton robes—for a meal in which each dish is presented simply on a lovely piece of china, on a tray, or in a small basket. The chinaware dishes don't match one another, and my favorites appear: a little yellow teapot, a rectangular plate with a brush painting of bamboo. I feel as though my guests have come to my home, which is kept this way always for me.

As Yuki and Okay bring the food, they laugh and chat with Takada, who tells everyone the story

William Brice, *Kyoto*, 1987. Color woodcut, 36 × 23¾ inches.

of how Okay, who is nearly eighty years old, once knocked on the door to his room and he called out, "Don't come in, I'm naked." She replied, "I don't mind," as she walked in. Traditionally, people in Japan don't have private space, but they are given privacy by other people not noticing private acts. There are no keys at the Tawaraya and hardly anybody waits for an answer after knocking.

Illustrated here is a woodcut by William Brice: a faint mountain partly obscured by a white rectangle containing water-shapes. There are big stylized images of rocks in the foreground. The title is *Kyoto*, and it is Kyoto at its most meditative. It's surprising that Bill created the drawing for the woodcut before he had actually seen this beautiful place.

Bill and his wife, Shirley, were longtime friends of Dick and Phyllis Diebenkorn's. The four of them, with Takada, Tom, and me, took a driving trip in Japan visiting small museums and staying in country inns similar to the Tarawaya but more rustic. Bill, who died at the age of eighty-seven in 2008, lived most of his life in Los Angeles. He was an influential artist, a longtime teacher at UCLA, and a great traveling companion.

Bill was the son of comedienne Fanny Brice and he told us many stories, mostly funny, but the one that sticks in my mind is sobering. Bill described visiting his aged father, the flamboyant gambler Nicky Arnstein. (I remember the movie *Funny Girl*, where Barbra Streisand, who plays Bill's mother, belts out, "Nicky Arnstein, Nicky Arnstein, Nicky Arnsteinnnn.") Arnstein,

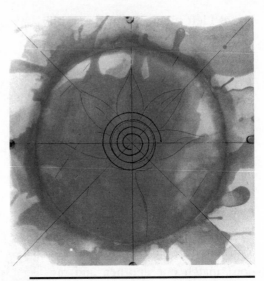

Shoichi Ida, *Well From Karma-Trap in Echo #12,* 1989. One of eight color aquatints with soft ground etching and drypoint printed on gampi paper chine collé, 18 × 18 inches.

when his son visited him, was living in a rented room shared with an old show-business friend. "It was the shoes that got me," Bill exclaimed. "Many pairs of them, lined up and running down the center of the room, his facing his bed, the other guy's facing his bed, the whole line making a demarcation."

Back in Berkeley, Tom and I entered what we fondly remember as "our Japan period." Perhaps I thought that if I could replicate something of the Tawaraya, the happy relaxation that I found there could be carried home. We laid down tatami mats in our bedroom, slept on a futon, and built a niche in the wall for a scroll and flowers. We made a hole in the floor so we could sit at a low lacquer table and look out a big window at the maple tree in our garden, a gift from the Crown Point staff on the occasion of our marriage in 1983. Our biggest building project at home was a bathhouse with a deep tub and a shingled roof. John Cage, who was staying in our guesthouse while the bathhouse was being built, called his assistant in New York and had a large round rock sent by Federal Express so we could install it in the floor.

Remembering our Japan period, it seems appropriate to end this chapter by talking about Shoichi Ida, an artist who—by virtue of his heritage—is different from the four at its beginning. "When you look at a wall," Ida said in *View*, "you can't see what is happening on the other side of it, but you can try to perceive what is happening. But I don't want to break through that wall to discover what's behind it. Rather, I have a romantic approach. I don't confront a situation immediately and directly."

I met Sho at a party given for him by a Berkeley artist who had spent time in Kyoto, where he lived. When we were trying to find a *ukiyo-e* woodcut printer there, Sho recommended Toda. From the mid-eighties to the mid-nineties Shoichi Ida made forty-three etching editions at Crown Point Press, working in all three of the locations we had since 1984. He died of cancer in 2006.

In 1986 Sho worked in Kyoto with Toda to make a woodblock print titled *Garden Project—Wood, Paper, Fire and Rain*. He asked Toda to print on both sides of a thin translucent paper into which he burned tiny spots. "The Japanese garden is very controlled," he said. "The Japanese like to control the relationship between nature and human beings. They must have a relationship with nature in their lives. That's why they have to find a way to hold a piece of nature close to them."

Connie Lewallen, interviewing Shoichi Ida, asked if his art was about self-discovery "as opposed to telling a story or communicating an idea through your work." He answered, "Right," but pointed out that self-discovery is "proof of human creativity. . . . Look at this stain on this table. You might remember who made it right after it was made, but eventually, years later, it becomes an anonymous record and you recognize only that somebody made it." This, also, is a way of telling the truth.

Crown Point's new gallery at 871 Folsom Street, San Francisco, 1986.

15.

THE EARTHQUAKE

Know That You Are Lucky

Lucky, lucky, lucky me
I'm a lucky son-of-a gun
I work eight hours and sleep eight hours
That leaves eight hours for fun.

Looking back on the years from 1986 through 1989, I can't get the old "Lucky Me" song, with its locomotive rhythm, out of my head. This chapter begins in January 1986. In that month, Richard Diebenkorn completed his monumental print titled *Green*, our Oakland landlord gave me notice of a substantial rise in the rent, and I decided that before the end of the year we would move Crown Point Press to San Francisco. The rest of 1986, and the following three years when Crown Point was at 871 Folsom Street, San Francisco, went by at locomotive-like rhythm and speed.

It must have been a warm winter in 1986 because I remember blossoms in February on Benvenue Avenue in Berkeley, where Dick and Phyllis Diebenkorn lived when they came up from Los Angeles. The sun was out. I was carrying final proofs of *Green* wrapped around a tube, the tube in a double-walled long thin box, our Crown Point packaging for safe transport of our prints. I paused for a moment, looking at the flowers, before approaching the house. My parcel was precious, Dick and Phyllis would be welcoming, and Crown Point was moving to San Francisco. Everything was going to be fine. I can close my eyes now, feel that box in my arms, and see the flowers. I was happy.

Wayne Thiebaud in the Oakland studio, 1985 (above),
and in the new San Francisco studio, 1989 (opposite).

Tom was taking the bus from Berkeley every day to his studio in San
Francisco on Third Street in the South of Market area, called SoMa. SoMa
was rundown then, with a lot of residential hotels, but the city had a plan for
its redevelopment and had already constructed, at Howard and Third streets,
the Moscone Convention Center, where the Democratic Convention was
held in 1984. (Reagan was president; the Democrats went crazy and nomi-
nated Walter Mondale for president and Geraldine Ferraro for vice president, a ticket I supported but that had no chance of winning.) Yerba Buena
Gardens, two square blocks above the mostly underground convention center, and a city-sponsored art gallery and theater were planned (all of them
opened in 1993). Tom scouted the neighborhood for a place I could rent.

Folsom Street runs along the back of the convention center parallel to
Howard, and in the block between Fourth and Fifth there was a "For Lease"
sign. It was on a brick building that had survived the 1906 San Francisco
earthquake but would not survive the one that was to come. The building
had no seismic bracing, but it did have a freight elevator—we had carried
many large sheets of copper one at a time up three flights of narrow stairs in
Oakland, so the freight elevator seemed marvelous to us.

The top floor at 871 Folsom Street had skylights and big factory windows with a north-facing view of low industrial buildings. Paradoxically, in moving to the city we lost our city views; our studio on San Pablo Avenue in Oakland was in a building of stores and offices on a street near City Hall. Our new block in San Francisco contained two vacant lots (parking lots, in fact). Across the street, next to a gas station, was a simple neighborhood restaurant named Windows West. It seemed moored on a street without a neighborhood; we were very glad it was there.

I asked Denise Hall, the architect who had designed our New York gallery, to design our new space, and she essentially had her office in Windows West on her frequent visits to our construction site. Wendy Diamond, our manager at Crown Point, coordinated the project and kept Denise connected to what the contractor was doing. I went back and forth from Oakland to San Francisco a couple of times a week, more often when Denise was in town. I also went twice to Japan. That year I oversaw four projects there, by Bryan Hunt, Sol LeWitt, Pat Steir, and Chuck Close. Chuck's project was filmed by CBS television and became a segment of the program *CBS News Sunday Morning*, with Charles Kuralt. It aired in early 1987.

When Denise was finished with the Folsom Street studio six months or so after I signed the lease, it was the most beautiful loft space I have ever seen, full of natural light and with lovely proportions. The lease was for ten years, and we put in large-capacity electricity, a heating and ventilation system, and complicated plumbing. It has always been difficult for Crown Point to borrow (our business is not really comprehensible to banks). The landlord provided some "tenant improvements," but nevertheless I spent pretty much all the money I could round up. The result was thrilling.

At first, there was nothing art-related nearby, but a few months after we moved in, Adrienne Fish rented our building's ground floor and opened a gallery and art bookstore (the best place in the city to find out-of-print exhibition catalogs). She named it 871 Fine Arts. About a year later, Cheryl Haines started the Haines Gallery in the building next door.

Green was the last print we editioned in Oakland, and, in the final months of 1986, Diebenkorn's three aquatints called *Folsom Street Variations* were the first art created in the new studio. Robert Hudson, who lives in Cotati, a small town north of San Francisco, made two prints in Oakland in 1986 and two in San Francisco the following year. Hudson has made an original contribution to art with his polychrome sculpture, intricately constructed

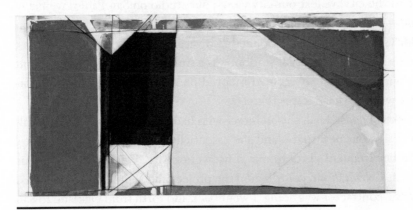

Richard Diebenkorn, *Folsom Street Variations III (Primaries)*, 1986.
Color aquatint with drypoint, soap ground aquatint, and flat bite etching, 12 × 26 inches.

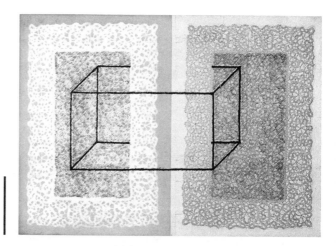

Robert Hudson, *Green and Red Rhyme*, 1987. Color soft ground etching with aquatint, 17 × 24 inches.

of disparate actual objects and then painted, often with details that give the illusion of flattening or increasing its volumes. His art is always concerned with space. In the etching *Green and Red Rhyme* he pressed two lace doilies into wax grounds and etched them in different ways. Then he joined the rectangular panels of lace by precisely drawing a three-dimensional box.

The most complicated projects Crown Point did in the crossover time between Oakland and San Francisco were by Al Held, who came from New York several times in that period and continued to work regularly with us for the next seven years. We have on our list a print of Al's titled *Oakland* and another titled *SF*, both dated 1986. There are two other prints of his dated the same year.

The previous year Al had made a trip to Japan for our project there but had refused my invitation to make etchings. "Like a lot of painters in New York at the time," he said a decade later in a panel discussion, "I thought of printmaking as a second-class activity." He liked Crown Point, however, and showed up in Oakland with an idea that made sense to him. Engraving, he explained, is printmaking at its core. After all, this is how the plates for printing money are made. He figured that if he could make a really big engraving, that would be something. But, he was aware that mastering the skill to the level he would need would take a lifetime. Engraving is done without acid. The craftsman pushes a sharp faceted tool through the metal to create a clean line, narrowing or swelling depending on the angle of the tool and the pressure exerted. Al asked me to look for someone who could engrave his plate for him.

Al Held, *Straits of Magellan*, 1986. Hard ground etching, 35¾ × 44¾ inches (above). *Putu*, 1989. Color aquatint, 35½ × 44½ inches (below).

I found an old man who had engraved currency for the United States government. Al and I and a printer drove out to visit him in the country near San Francisco. He had invited two other engraver friends of his, and we sat by a river in the sunshine listening to stories about counterfeiting and espionage. The engraver lived in a little house trailer, and he had a little desk with his tools on it in a corner of the trailer. He engraved a test plate as we watched. It was a couple of inches square, and he detailed it beautifully.

Then Al broached the subject of a three-by-four-foot plate. He would have preferred larger, he said, but that was the biggest size our press could handle. The engraver exchanged a panicky glance with one of his friends and promised to think about it. After that day, he never returned my calls.

Back in Oakland, Al started work on an image on our largest plate. He drew its outlines in a wax ground and the printers began ruling thousands of closely spaced lines into the forms that Held had defined. We etched those lines into the plate to make a very large black and white traditional hard ground etching that Al titled *Straits of Magellen* because, I think, it was to him an exploration and a discovery.

Al Held was born in 1928. He died in 2005. He came to maturity at the time abstract expressionist artists like Willem de Kooning were at the height of their power and some younger artists, looking for something else, did not want the touch of the hand to show in their work. Many were making flat paintings, and Al started there, but shifted to working with geometric forms and grand illusions of depth, creating, as he said, "three-dimensional grids, twisting and moving in space." At the time he first worked with us, his painted surfaces were very smooth. He hired assistants to do most of the fill-in painting in his studio.

At Crown Point, Al didn't mimic his paintings. Although he asked the printers to rule his fill-in lines, he did work on his plates, and he tried all our processes. The small prints called *Oakland* and *SF* are in drypoint, and have lines with a rough character. In *Straits of Magellan*, the hard ground etched lines are crisp and smooth, but lines cannot be perfectly spaced by hand and the feeling overall is somewhat irregular. Al liked this print very much. After working with hard ground and extensively using the labor of the printers in *Straits of Magellan*, he shifted gears entirely to make a soft ground etching, *Pablo 7*, that he drew on seven plates entirely by himself. He began work on *Pablo 7* in 1986 in Oakland and finished it in San Francisco later that year.

A year later, in 1987, Al came back and tried color aquatint, painting acid on his plates using spit bite. This led to a body of work in watercolor that he continued for the rest of his life. For artists, it's one thing, then the next thing, then the next thing. I'm glad that Crown Point has been able to be a part of the chain.

Al made one large color aquatint in each of the next seven years, all prints of our maximum size, almost three by four feet, a very large size for work with so much detail. The prints are tightly constructed according to a plan, and are complex, ambitious, and subtle. *Putu*, made in our Folsom Street space in 1989 just before the earthquake, was named for the baby of printer Nancy Anello and her Indonesian husband, whom she had married during her sojourn in Bali. And in 1992 Held named his greatest print *Liv* (plate 23), in honor of the daughter born that year to printer Renée Bott. These prints had so many plates and the color inking was so complex that they required at least six printers working at the same time to print each impression. If we had not had such a large staff at Crown Point then, Al Held's major work in printmaking would not exist.

We had three years at Folsom Street, from summer 1986 to fall 1989. Our first full year there, 1987, was the twenty-fifth anniversary of Crown Point Press. Riva Castleman, the print curator at the Museum of Modern Art

"For 25 Years: Crown Point Press" at the Museum of Modern Art, New York, 1988.

Judy Pfaff at the opening.

Judy Pfaff, *Six of One-Tatoes*,
1987. Color woodcut,
39½ × 57 inches.

in New York, visited me. Although Bob Feldman had given to the museum a print from every edition Parasol Press had published, the work we had published ourselves was very sparsely represented, she said. The museum had purchased a few works from us, but money for print purchases was hard to come by; most of its collection had been donated. She would have liked to be able to represent us more thoroughly in print exhibitions, but generally the museum did not exhibit work it did not own. I agreed to a one-time donation: she could choose one work from our available inventory from each of the artists we had published, provided the artist was willing to forgo his or her commission. Before the year was out, Castleman had mounted an exhibition, "For 25 Years: Crown Point Press" in the museum's print galleries. It was on exhibit from November 20, 1987, to February 9, 1988. (The possibility of a special exhibition was not mentioned at the time we made the gift.)

The exhibition at MOMA was a boon to our gallery in New York, where Karen McCready, now with three assistants, was creating shows and selling our prints well. In California, we didn't do anything to celebrate our twenty-fifth anniversary—it seemed to me we were just getting started. In fact, I was too busy to figure out how to celebrate; the "Lucky Me" locomotive was careening along at breakneck speed. I hired four printers in 1987. Brian Shure, Mark Callen, Pamela Paulson, and Daria Sywulak joined Renée Bott and Larry Hamlin, who had come with us from Oakland.

We did ten etching projects at Folsom Street that year, nine of them with artists who had worked with us before. The new artist to us was Bertrand

Lavier, who traveled to San Francisco from France. He is an installation artist who puts real-world things into strange juxtapositions. "When I put a fridge on a safe, the result seems to float between two separate things," he has said. Bertrand abstracted the images in his etchings from a comic strip in which, he told us, "Mickey Mouse had some adventures in the Museum of Modern Art." He copied the images in his three prints, titled *Untitled Modern Painting I* (plate 24), *II*, and *III*, from the small "paintings" shown on the museum walls in that strip.

In 1987 we also did two unusual projects, the first a gigantic one in San Francisco with Judy Pfaff in which she made woodcuts from plywood parts that she carved, assembled, and glued. The second was with Alex Katz. After Alex had made woodcuts with us in Japan, I asked him to make etchings, and in 1986, the year we moved from Oakland, he did that in the New York workshop of Jeryl Parker. We published that work, and we arranged for Doris Simmelink, a very fine printer whom we had trained at Crown Point in the early days, to go there to run the project. The following year Alex came to San Francisco to work at Folsom Street. He created *Reclining Figure* (plate 25) and two smaller prints, working (at his request) with Doris again as the lead printer. Doris editioned the prints in her studio in Los Angeles. In both cases, Crown Point published the work, but after one more project with us in 1990, Alex and Doris (not unreasonably) cut out the middleman and Crown Point was no longer involved.

There is still more to tell about the year 1987. In April I went to Japan with Wayne Thiebaud and stayed on to work back-to-back with Richard Diebenkorn and then Bill Brice. (I talked about that trip in Chapter 14.) Later there was another trip, in December.

I had made an important addition to our staff: Connie Lewallen had agreed to leave her job as curator at the University of California's Berkeley Art Museum to become associate director of Crown Point Press. I needed to share some decision making, and I thought I should share some of the traveling too. Connie joined me on my December trip to Japan, and after that trip, which was with New York painter David Salle, I turned the Japan project over to her. Takada would continue to make trips with us until the end of the project in 1991, but he did not continue to work as an etching printer after we left Oakland. He started a gallery in San Francisco. "Printing is a young person's job," he said. It is true.

I didn't want to stop going to Japan, but I had another project in the works. After our trip with the Diebenkorns and the Brices, Tom and I continued on to China. Two years earlier, when we were still in Oakland, Sören Edgren, a scholar of Chinese printing and books, had telephoned me. He had seen an exhibition of our Japanese woodcuts, and he wondered if we might be interested in investigating the possibility of doing something similar in mainland China. Nixon had traveled there in 1972, and theoretically China was open to us, but in fact there was a lot of suspicion and not much interchange between our two countries, certainly not on a scale as small as ours. Sören, however, had a contact for us. He had been doing research at the historic woodblock printing company Rong Bao Zhai in Beijing. He is a fluent speaker and reader of Mandarin Chinese.

The Rong Bao Zhai woodcut printing shop on Liulichang in Beijing (top). A carver in the workshop (above).

Rong Bao Zhai is more than three hundred years old and for the past hundred years has been located on Liulichang, a narrow shopping street in the center of Beijing. Tom and I followed Sören into a hallway at the side of an art supply store and up a dark flight of stairs. A door at the top was flung open. I blinked my eyes.

We faced a long room with a wall of narrow windows from which light streamed in rays. Silhouetted against the windows were about a dozen people at tables piled with small irregular pieces of wood and rectangular stacks of paper. The people sat still, only their arms moving, lifting sheets of paper sideways, making fluttering motions. As my eyes adjusted I saw potted plants,

A garden in Beijing.

Tom Marioni, *Peking*, 1987.
Woodcut printed on silk mounted
on rag paper, 21 × 9½ inches.

thermos pitchers, and little ceramic dishes, some full of colors. Almost everyone was wearing blue clothes. I realized that the rays of light were visible because the whole room was filled with mist coming from a pipe running along the ceiling.

The water mist, which is released periodically into the room, keeps the humidity level constant. Because the ink is water-based and is absorbed into the paper, it won't look the same from one printing session to the next unless the paper is reliably the same dampness. And since paper expands and contracts as it becomes damper or drier, controlling the moisture in the room makes accurate registration possible.

My purpose on that trip to China was to see if there was a way our artists could work with craftsmen there; I hadn't brought any art with me. But as we met with the Rong Bao Zhai managers, I thought we should move ahead while they were interested. Their primary motivation was curiosity about us; our payment would go to the government and their subsidies wouldn't change. I asked Tom, who had accompanied me as my husband rather than as an artist expecting to work, if he could make a drawing right there. He said he would try. He had already purchased a large Chinese brush, a beautiful object. In the art supply store that was run by Rong Bao Zhai we bought some thin silk of the type used in painting and printing. We were staying in an old hotel that long ago had been a nobleman's house, and our room looked out on a once-formal garden with a tall weathered rock as its centerpiece. Tom's wood-cut, titled *Peking*, is a single brushstroke inspired by that garden rock.

Rocks like the one in the hotel garden were considered enchanted in ancient China, I read later. Currents of favorable forces were thought to run through the earth and escape through places of beauty, which focused luck on those who were in contact with them. The Sung dynasty, AD 960 to 1279, the age when the Chinese invented printing by creating the first woodblock prints, was also a time of high intellectual and aesthetic refinement that included the building of many rock gardens. The concept of rock gardens and the techniques of woodblock printing both spread to Japan in ancient days, and the Japanese modified them to suit themselves.

With Xia Wei and Bob Bechtle in the reception room at Rong Bao Zhai, 1989 (above). A Beijing street from inside a taxi (below).

Rocks in Chinese gardens are generally rougher in both their surfaces and their surroundings than those in Japan, and the same is true of the two styles of woodblock printing. In Japan, parts of an image are carved into blocks separated by color and all the same size. The Chinese assemble an image from a multitude of carved cherry wood blocks, as many as fifty for a complex image, all small and irregular. It's a unique tactile experience to

Early morning by the lake in Hangzhou, 1988.

handle them—each part of the image is carved right to the edges of its own block; nothing is wasted.

Traveling, as we did, in 1987 from Japan to China plunged us back in time. We had found Kyoto to be an old town with narrow streets and low wooden houses, yet full of cars, open-fronted Pachinko parlors, and bright lights. Downtown Beijing, by contrast, was full of bicycles, wide avenues, and big low dimly lit buildings—Soviet style. The first Kentucky Fried Chicken restaurant had just opened, and on the street around it people were crowding, pushing, and peering toward the door.

To cross a street we had to dart through a torrent of bicycles and hope to dodge the few cars weaving among them with horns sounding. Once, when riding in a taxi, Tom asked the driver why he kept his hand always on the horn. "Traffic safety," he replied. It is different now, but back then it seemed that only government officials and taxi drivers had cars. Bicycles carried everything: construction materials beds, even restaurants (complete with stools) were carried on wheeled bicycle carts. A restaurant owner would fry or steam food as long as customers were there, then collapse the kitchen and pedal on.

On that first trip Sören looked for someone who could translate for us in the future and renewed an acquaintance with a young woman living in

Beijing named Xia Wei. She was a great help to us, and I'm happy to say that as I write this in 2012 she and Sören have been married for almost twenty-five years; their son, Julian, is about to go to college.

Our project in China took place mostly in the years covered by this chapter, 1986 through 1989. After our first trip, I started taking Chinese language lessons, and Tom took some instruction in Chinese calligraphy. His second print made in China is the Greek letter pi rendered calligraphically. Pi symbolizes the imperfect, Tom says, because mathematically it is an infinite irregular progression. As time went on I began to think it symbolized our China program as well. Pi never repeats itself and is not logical.

It took the Rong Bao Zhai printers in Beijing two years to produce an edition of Tom's first print, *Peking*, and they were at the same time producing the blocks for a complex image of Robert Bechtle's, a street with two leafy trees and two cars. My Chinese teacher was from the town of Hangzhou, a former capital near Shanghai, and she knew an independent printer there. She and I traveled to Hangzhou to make the contact. I left Tom's pi image and also a drawing of Pat Steir's with the printer as a test.

Tom Marioni, *Pi*, 1988. Woodcut printed in red on silk mounted on rag paper, 12½ × 14½ inches.

Hangzhou is a beautiful city, built around a lake edged by a thin strip of public park filled with ancient trees and plants. Our hotel faced the park, and getting up early to walk there among people doing tai chi as the sun came up was unforgettable. I wanted to find a printer in Hangzhou so I could go there often.

Steir's "proof," mailed to us, looked beautiful, but when I arrived there with both artists, it turned out there was only one block and the subtleties were created by hand-painting on the print. I was horrified, but—thinking about it now—I can see that, from the Chinese point of view, if only a small number of "copies" (twenty or thirty, I had said) were wanted, it would be easier to paint them by hand than to cut all those blocks and print them.

There was no way that this printer could have understood my principle that "original" prints are similar impressions from the same matrix, and the very presence of a handmade matrix changes the image so significantly that the printed work is not a copy.

Tom's print was only one color, and the printer assured us he had carved a block and would bring a proof the next day. After our rejection of his interpretation of Steir's print, however, we thought he wouldn't show up. He didn't, but his wife did. She told us she had done the printing, which seemed to be quite good. After she realized Tom liked the proof, with great relief she took a package out of her handbag that contained the entire edition. The prints looked fine, but all were on translucent silk, unmounted, without a paper backing. When we asked about mounting, she said it was impossible. We paid the bill and brought the prints home, hoping we could mount them ourselves.

All our Chinese woodblock prints, printed on silk or thin paper, required mounting to a stronger sheet. This concept had become clear to us on our earlier visit when we were taken to the studio of a famous Chinese artist. The studio was small, with scrolls on the wall, brushes and an ink stone on a central table, and wadded-up rags piled in a corner. Saying he would show us his work, the artist went over to the corner and picked up an armful of the rags. He smoothed these out, one by one, on the table. They were pieces of silk, covered with brush drawings of mountains and trees. After we admired each one, he wadded it back up and tossed it onto the floor again, laughing at my surprise. "When they're mounted, they'll be like that," he said, pointing to the scrolls on the wall. Rong Bao Zhai, the professional shop in Beijing, mounted their prints as part of their production process.

At Rong Bao Zhai, the manager, Mr. Sun, had been doubtful about accepting the Robert Bechtle image that became *Potrero Houses—Pennsylvania Avenue* (plate 26). "Very difficult," he said, pointing to the leaves of the trees and the grille of one of the cars. I asked if they could do it, and he said they could, but added, "Why do it?" I couldn't explain why, except to say it would be a challenge to them.

On my first trip, Mr. Sun had said our artists should work with Chinese materials, so I had bought some Chinese watercolor paint, silk, and brushes, and had given them to Bob to see what he could do. He stretched the silk like watercolor paper and taped the edges to keep it flat, then painted meticulously on it. He gave up trying to use the Chinese brushes but did stick to the paints I had given him. The colors were muted, but Bob found them acceptable, since his colors normally aren't bright.

Bob and I traveled to Beijing in early 1989 with Tom and Karen McCready, our New York gallery director. Karen was a major force at Crown Point, and I wanted to be sure she understood this new adventure in China. We all were amazed when we saw Bob's proof. To the Chinese printers, not only was this an unfamiliar scene, but also Bechtle had used unfamiliar ways of placing forms tight together and unfamiliar flat brushes to paint the forms. The craftsmen at Rong Bao Zhai had carved forty-two blocks, and they were piled up on the printer's table when we walked into the shop. We handled the blocks as if they were toys, finding a bit of a tree here, a car taillight there. We couldn't keep our eyes off the proof, it was so lively. To see the cars sitting so securely at an angle on the street, to find the light on the tree so naturally rendered—the whole thing was a real achievement. The printers and carvers stood waiting. There was nothing to do but extend our congratulations.

"I really couldn't think of anything that could make it better," Bob told me later. "I found the whole thing rather emotional. There was such a powerful sense of place, and the character of the people was so strongly present. I still think about the scenery we saw on that trip, but what sticks with me even more is the feeling of the cities, the bicycles, the crowds, the way people looked at us—the juxtaposition of the culture being old and grounded and at the same time eager to catch up with the world."

The proof of *Potrero Houses—Pennsylvania Avenue* that we saw at Rong Bao Zhai had been mounted, and it was pristine, but it was just a single print. When we received the edition prints, although the printing was excellent, many of the prints were not pristine. In the mounting, brush hairs and bits of dirt were caught between the print and the backing sheet. These showed clearly through the silk, especially in the light-colored expanse of the

Professor Yang Yong Hua (at right) on a bus.

The Yellow Mountains near Hangzhou, China.

street. I hated to complain to Mr. Sun after the extraordinary work they had done, but it was necessary. He seemed surprised at my concern. "Nobody sees that!" he said. I thought there was nothing we could do about it at that point, and we threw away the worst of the flawed prints (in fact, we could have remounted them, but I didn't realize it at the time).

I asked Mr. Sun if he would be willing to allow his craftsmen to teach their mounting techniques to one of my printers, and I was amazed and grateful that he agreed. Back at our Folsom Street studio, Crown Point printer Brian Shure was struggling to mount the prints of Tom's image, now titled *Pi*. Japanese artist Shoichi Ida had been to San Francisco to work with us, and he used a technique called chine collé, in which the image is printed on a thin (usually) Asian paper that is mounted to a heavier sheet in the printing process. We had used chine collé before that, but Ida gave us practice and new ideas and helped Brian became a chine collé expert. Chine collé and traditional Asian-style mounting are inextricably linked.

Eventually Brian figured out a way to mount the *Pi* prints. After traveling to China to learn mounting at Rong Bao Zhai, and spending a couple of days with an expert mounter in Japan, Brian Shure wrote Crown Point's first techniques book, *Chine Collé: An Artist's Handbook*. It is now out of print but has been updated as *Magical Secrets about Chine Collé* (2009).

Between my first trip to China in early 1986 and the end of 1989, we had nineteen prints either produced or in process in China: two with Tom, two

Janis Provisor, *Long Fall*, 1989. Color woodcut printed on silk mounted on rag paper, 19½ × 14 inches.

Sören Edgren, Xia Wei, Brad Davis, and Janis Provisor with a guide after a rain in the mountains.

with Bob Bechtle, three with Pat Steir, four with Robert Kushner (see plate 29), five with Li Lin Lee, and three with Janis Provisor (I will introduce Li Lin and Janis to you shortly). We were working in shops in four different cities: Rong Bao Zhai in Beijing, a similar professional shop in Shanghai, a smaller shop in Suzhou, and an independent printer in Hangzhou (not the one who did *Pi*).

Rong Bao Zhai had declined to do a second Bechtle print, but the shop in Suzhou agreed to try it; Suzhou is a town of canals and gardens located between Shanghai and Hangzhou. Bob Kushner and Janis Provisor also worked there. Bob Bechtle's print *Albany Monte Carlo* (plate 27) has an interesting story. The proof he OK'd was very good, not as crisp as the earlier print from Beijing, but good. The edition, however, came back with the colors hopped up. "It looked like flames coming from underneath the car," Bob said. I called to see what had happened, and the reply was that they had received a source for brighter colors and had improved the print, which had

A democracy demonstration, Hangzhou, China, late May 1989.

been a bit dull, they thought. (They did reprint it for us.)

All that activity would have been impossible without the help and supervision of Yang Yong Hua, a former professor from Hangzhou who traveled with us, translated, and kept in touch with the printers when we were not there. We called him Professor Yang or the Professor, in keeping with the Chinese custom of prefacing with titles the names of people especially worthy of respect. Professor Yang had finished his university training in the early days of the People's Republic of China. He had studied Russian and taught it at Hangzhou University. When Russia fell out of favor, he was told to teach English, and learned it as he taught. During the Cultural Revolution, which began in 1966, he was made to wear a dunce cap and was persecuted, as were all university professors and other members of the cultural elite. He was sent to work on a farm during some part of that period. Chinese universities were mostly closed for ten years. In 1976 Professor Yang resumed teaching at Hangzhou University. He had retired before we met him.

My last trip to China (until much later as a tourist) was in late May 1989 with Janis Provisor, a painter of the "pattern and decoration" persuasion who is also a designer and believes in mixing art with life. In fact, she and her husband, Brad Davis, also an artist, actually moved to China a few years later. With Professor Yang's help they set up a small factory (still in business in 2012) with workers weaving traditional silk carpets to their designs. The trip in 1989 was their first China encounter. Janis worked in woodcut in both Suzhou and Hangzhou, and after that, Sören and Xia Wei joined us for a driving and walking trip in the Yellow Mountains, an ethereal landscape familiar to everyone who has looked at traditional Chinese painting.

Li Lin Lee, *In the Rainy Season*, 1989. Color woodcut printed on silk mounted on rag paper, 13 × 12½ inches.

Tom was not with me on that trip, but Brian Shure was along; he and the Professor went to Beijing after Janis finished her print. Brian received lessons in mounting there and also checked on proofs being made in preparation for a visit by Li Lin Lee later in the year. There, in Bejing in the last week of May 1989, Brian and the Professor landed right in the middle of the great democracy demonstrations in Tiananmen Square: thousands of young people were camped there, and a great hand-made statute resembling our own Statue of Liberty rose above them. It

Li Lin Lee (right) with a printer at Rong Bao Zhai, 1989.

was thrilling to Brian. The professor was afraid. "It will not end well," he said.

Everywhere we went on that trip, from the first moment we stepped off the plane, we saw democracy demonstrations. Students silently marched through streets, carrying placards, handing out leaflets. People would run out of offices and stores and walk with them for a block or two, then run back to work. In one store we were left all alone for a short time; a returning worker said to us in slow but clear English, "We want to be free, like you." Even in the Yellow Mountains as we stood on a high peak, we looked down to see far below a white line winding along. It was made up of demonstrators marching down a village street with their signs.

Late in the day on June 3 we said good-bye to our friends, and Brian and I made our way to Kyoto, where we would stay just two days so Brian could have a lesson from a Japanese mounting expert. We arrived the morning of June 4, and I stepped into my room at the Tawaraya, feeling the sweetness of being there again. Suddenly Brian, who had gone to his room just before me, pulled my door open. Tears were running down his cheeks. "Turn on the television, turn on the television!" he said. Yuki, who had followed me, and other staff people were behind us. We all stood and watched tanks rolling over bicycles, flattening them and the bodies of their riders, a sea of helmeted soldiers bayoneting young people, fires, people running, soldiers running after them, the square a great sea of anguish. The panic of the Japanese commentator's voice was clear to us even though his words were not. The broadcast was live from Beijing.

When I got home I asked my Chinese language teacher to translate the flyers handed us by the marchers in Hangzhou. One of them ended like this: "We know that students' duty is to study, but with the country in this way, how can we study? And with the country in this way, how can we use our knowledge?" We had projects with Robert Kushner and Li Lin Lee scheduled for November, but, I thought dismally, we cannot go—we can never go to China again. But "How can we use our knowledge?" kept ringing in my ears, and I asked myself if our not going back, on principle, would be of any use to anybody. I thought of Li Lin Lee, whom we planned to take on our next trip. His father had been a physician who had attended Mao Zedong but had fallen out of favor and was exiled. Li Lin lives in Chicago and had never been to China.

"Over and over my parents had talked about it," he said on his return. "So, arriving there, it felt like I had been before. I recognized it. But of course what I was recognizing were my fantasies for years." A photograph of Li Lin with a block carver at Rong Bao Zhai shows the excitement both felt at Li Lin's presence there. He speaks Chinese and was the only one of our artists who could talk directly to the workers. One of his prints is shown in this chapter; another, *Lucky Life*, is in plate 28. His work is influenced by Chinese New Year's greeting cards; these cards are still popular in China and are a major product of the woodcut studios still operating there.

"Li Lin was shaken at first by the fact that he felt so American in China," Brian remembers. "He said he had always imagined China as his homeland, but in fact, China turned out to be the only place where he had ever felt completely American." Brian went to China with Li Lin and Robert Kushner, who worked at the woodcut shop in Suzhou (see plate 29). I could not make the trip because the earthquake in San Francisco had occurred just two weeks before it. This was the last trip that Crown Point Press artists made to work in China.

Before this locomotive-like chapter ends on October 17, 1989, we must come back to San Francisco, where, despite my excitement about China, I did spend most of my time. Tom and I would drive every day across the Bay Bridge from Berkeley; his studio was just a few blocks away from our Folsom Street building. With six printers on our staff there, in 1988 we did etching projects with nine artists, including Tony Cragg and Anish Kapoor from England, Markus Lüpertz from Germany, and José Maria Sicilia from Spain. Wayne Thiebaud made three complicated color prints: *Country City*, *Steep Street*, and *Lipsticks*. Ed Ruscha made prints titled *Heaven*, *Hell*, and *Hourglass*. Richard and Phyllis Diebenkorn had moved in 1988 from Los Angeles to a farmhouse

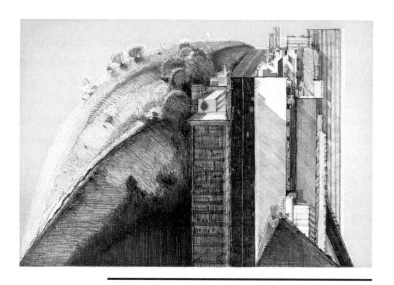

Wayne Thiebaud, *Country City*, 1988. Color soft ground etching with drypoint and aquatint, 22 × 32 inches.

The Crown Point staff at its largest, 1988. I am in the front row between Connie and Karen. Stephanie is third from right and Valerie is in the back row by the window.

in Healdsburg, a couple hours' drive north of San Francisco. Dick was unable to keep a scheduled work time with us in 1989 because of a heart-valve-replacement operation that had to be repeated that same year.

During our short stay at Folsom Street we had the largest staff in Crown Point's history: twenty-two people, four of them in New York. In San Francisco, Connie Lewallen, as associate director, was making arrangements with artists and overseeing some of our projects there, as well as traveling to Japan. She also revived our publications department (she produced nine issues of *View* in 1988 alone) and was assisted by a publications manager. We had a shipping manager and he had an assistant. We had a registrar and she had an assistant. We had a business manager; I think she had two assistants. And, of course, there were printers and gallery staff.

From the vantage point of 2012, I can see that the most important staff event in our Folsom Street period was the arrival of Valerie Wade in 1988. Since Fredrica Drotos left in 1982, we had had in California, sequentially, two gallery directors. Then Karen sent us Stephanie Bleecher, who had been with her since she started the New York gallery in 1985. Kim Schmidt and Meg Malloy (both of whom now work for power- ful New York galleries) remained with Karen in New York. Not long after the earthquake, Stephanie left us to go to business school; she became an executive with a bank. Valerie quickly became a key person. As I write this in 2012, nearly twenty-five years after she arrived, she runs pretty much everything day-to-day at Crown Point and is a much- valued partner to me.

Valerie in 1991.

Just before the earthquake I made two additional important staff decisions. In 1989 our business manager and our bookkeeper both left, and I hired Kyle Wood as business manager. He had gone to business school at Stanford, and I intended, finally, to actually let him run things for me; I confided in him that eventually I would like to take some time off to write a book. He hired Stacie Scammell as his bookkeeper/assis- tant. She is still with us, now as business manager.

In seventeen seconds between 5:04 and 5:05 p.m. on October 17, 1989, everything changed. An early game in the World Series was being broadcast by ABC television, so the first part of the shock was seen by people around the world before their screens went black. It was a lengthy shock and measured 6.9 on the Richter scale. I was sitting at my desk, talking with Stephanie, who was on a chair next to me. At first I felt just a little jitter underfoot—it happens sometimes in San Francisco. I turned to Stephanie to reassure her, then realized we were in a long deep rolling motion accompanied by crack- ing sounds and plasterboard falling. "Get under the desk!" I cried, pulling on Stephanie as I slid to the floor. She had become rigid, her eyes and mouth open wide, her fingers tight around the chair. I could not move her.

The air was white; I can still taste the grit between my teeth. This was not dust from falling fragments but mortar from between the bricks of my office wall. The shaking motion had ground it so finely that afterward I

October 18, 1989, after the earthquake.

removed a brick out of a seemingly undamaged section just by pulling with my fingers. Some bricks fell out into the street, creating a small new triangular window. The ceiling didn't fall in, but there were cracks, like on a hard-boiled egg, around each of the supporting columns.

Tom, in his street-level studio a few blocks away, stood in the doorway watching cars skid to the curb and street lamps sway. "I rode it like a bucking bronco," he said. The moment it stopped he picked up the phone and called my mother in Berkeley. Miraculously, the call went through and he ascertained that she was all right and told her not to worry about us—we would not be home that night. Then the phone went dead.

At Crown Point we all quickly left the building; there might be aftershocks, and it could collapse. There were hundreds of people walking in the street and on the sidewalk—I had no idea so many people were in our neighborhood. I had locked up after everyone was out and found myself walking aimlessly. The crowd was oddly quiet. I joined a group of people gathered around a car with its radio on. We were straining to hear. Those in front turned to tell the rest of us: "The Bay Bridge is down," they said, and the words were murmered through the group as everyone repeated them: "The bridge is down." I walked in the direction of Tom's studio, wondering if I would find him, and suddenly there he was, walking toward me on the street.

It was starting to get dark and the crowds were still thick. Some people had lighted a campfire and were standing around it. A few parked cars had their interior lights on; in one of them, someone was settling down for the night. We joined a line at a grocery store; flashlights flickered inside as the staff took orders and gathered customers' purchases for them. We bought some cold cuts, milk, and cereal and made our way to the Crown Point apartment. We had rented it for Denise when she was overseeing the building at Folsom Street and then, with so many artists coming from out of town, had kept it for their use.

The apartment complex was dark, but there were emergency lights in the stairwells, and we climbed the six flights to our unit and stood on the balcony looking out over a city that was dark except for a frightening wash of light in the direction of the Marina on the other side of town. Fires were burning there and we heard a drifting sound of sirens, but essentially everything was quiet and we could see only shadows. Luckily there was a flashlight in the apartment, and Tom had a pocket transistor radio that we listened to until the batteries went out.

The building at 657 Howard Street, built in 1922 for the *San Francisco News*.

16.

THE BUILDING

BEWARE DELUSIONS OF GRANDEUR

It is October 18, 1989, the morning after the earthquake. The electricity is not yet working, but the buses are running, and every single Crown Point employee is at work. We have a meeting to try to decide what to do. We know we will have to move, but where? And how? As we are sitting there, we have an aftershock, a brief tremble. I say that maybe everyone should go home, just in case, but nobody does. Instead, everyone starts getting organized, sweeping up and packing things in boxes.

Suddenly, the telephone, which has been dead, rings. It is John Cage calling from New York. I pour out our situation, practically in one breath. Remembering that moment, I can hear him speaking: "Kathan, dear Kathan, as you continue, which you will do, the way to proceed will become apparent."

Standing in front of me when I get off the phone is Robert Feher, our landlord. He is a real estate developer and he owns another building in the neighborhood. The building is concrete, seismically reinforced, alarmed, and climate-controlled. The main tenant is the Ansel Adams Center for Photography, but the basement tenant has recently moved out. I should go right now, he says, and look at it, and also I should take a look at a building at 657 Howard to see if it interests me long-term. He has a potential deal for it in place. There are some problems, but if I like it, maybe we can solve them together.

The Center for Photography basement is windowless and low ceilinged. We can put the prints there and also a few staff members who work mainly at desks. Kyle is on the phone with the equipment movers who brought our presses into the Folsom Street space almost three years ago.

They will take them to storage. He also arranges for the furniture to be moved and most of it stored. After a rather big aftershock (we had about a hundred between Wednesday and the following Monday, the paper said), I send everybody home and tell them to stay home Thursday and come back Friday morning. We'll have a rented truck then, and we can move the prints and whatever we will need in order to work in the basement space.

Tom and I walk around the outside of the Howard Street building with mounting excitement. It is beautiful, a low brick building among high-rises. We look carefully for cracks but can't see any. We have heard that the San Francisco Museum of Modern Art is considering building just around the corner. I call Feher to ask to see the inside, and he makes an appointment for Monday. I call my architect, Denise Hall, in New York, and leave a message on her machine asking her to come.

Friday morning, with electricity restored, I am standing in our print storage room, an interior room that I had last seen by flashlight. The floor looks pleated. Every one of our flat file print cabinets has tipped forward and the drawers are cascaded in layers. The prints are mostly fine, but we must set the cabinets upright in order to get to them. It takes two strong men to wrestle each cabinet into place so others of us can pull out drawers and load them into the truck, the prints still in them. Even though the sky is misting, close to rain, we can't take time to wrap the prints. On Thursday, while we were planning our move, the city installed a padlock and a big red tag on our front door: "Unsafe. Do Not Enter."

The back door is unencumbered, but we fear that at any moment an official will stop us and we will lose everything. I imagine our inventory locked in but unprotected against hoodlums or aftershocks, and me helpless against bureaucratic red tape. All our staff and a few friends are running fast, taking our things out the back, racing with framed prints and open drawers, hoping no one will notice the activity. We finish up on Saturday and Monday. Monday afternoon a crane is dangling the presses over the street on the way to storage. We have broken the studio windows and cut the ironwork with a torch so the crane can reach directly inside.

On Monday Denise arrives in time to tour the Howard Street building with Tom and me. Feher tells our escort that we're his "staff." Then Denise comes with us to Folsom Street and is running around trying to measure furniture and equipment as it's being taken out. I call our accountant and our lawyer to ask if they can see any way I could buy the Howard Street building. Feher, because of the demise of his Folsom Street space, is no longer in a position to buy it himself. He would, for a fee, assign his interest to me. The catch, he tells me, is that we must close on the property by the end of the year. The price he has negotiated is low, and there is a back-up bidder, so if I cannot obtain the title in nine weeks, the deal definitely will be lost. It will be difficult to meet that deadline, he adds.

The building is L-shaped with entrances on two different streets. When I first saw it, I thought of it as an animal asleep, its head on its paws at Howard Street, its haunches slung around to Hawthorne, with a separate little unrelated building nestled against its belly. It was breathing deeply, asleep. Now that I am inside, I feel it more strongly (probably the heating system, which is functioning perfectly). More than

Moving fast, taking everything out the back door (top). The press going out the front window (bottom).

a hundred people had worked here, and each had had his or her own cubicle; we keep losing our way and calling out to each other: "Where are you?" Even so, there is an accommodating volume, a good proportion, three floors with two light wells piercing what otherwise would have been a dark center, and factory-style windows on the street sides. It was built in 1922 for the *San Francisco News*, the main rival to the Hearst paper then. Good printing vibes, we say to one another.

Karen flies out from New York a week later, and she, Connie, and Kyle see the building. They are enthusiastic and think we should go ahead. Feher gives us copies of some materials he had gotten from the seller, and Kyle is glad to find a fairly recent complete appraisal from the Bank of America. "If they'll accept this, we have a chance," he says. "Otherwise the appraisal could take two months." With the help of my lawyer, I make an agreement with Feher and give him a cashier's check to take to the title company for a deposit, which is refundable if we can't get a loan or if the building fails its inspections.

My lawyer says the bugaboo right now is the environmental issue, and we should test immediately for toxic chemicals. Feher's service for his fee includes arranging and paying for inspections, and he has ordered the toxic one, but the report will take three weeks. It is already November 1. Kyle and I have an initial meeting with two lending officers at the Bank of America. Quite a few of our prints are hanging in the lobby and in a gallery behind it that displays works from the bank's collection. We drag the bankers through the gallery; they are polite but clearly uninterested in the art.

Five weeks have already gone by since the earthquake. Tom and I have been taking the ferry from Berkeley every day to work, since the bridge is out. A printer who lives in the East Bay has taken one of our small presses to her studio so the printers from over there don't need to come to the city every day; the San Francisco printers are working in Brian Shure's studio, which is equipped with a press. Everyone else is jammed into the basement space, but Valerie and the sales staff are getting ready to move into a temporary gallery space on Market Street, at the edge of the SoMa neighborhood in a building that has a few other galleries in it.

In the basement of the Center for Photography,
left to right: Valerie, Connie, and Kyle.

We have a key to the Howard Street building now, and we take all the employees to see the inside. We drink champagne. We know it is premature, but it is good for our morale. I am so upbeat that I suggest the address be included in an ad we are preparing for the January issue of *Art in America*. I plan to pull it at the last minute if necessary.

Kyle is working on the loan. It is useful that he once worked for the Bank of America, the only choice for us because of the presence of the appraisal. Karen and her staff are rounding up a lot of cash, appealing to our clients to pay in advance for the Thiebaud prints we are printing now. She is also selling my proofs of our out-of-print editions. Connie is telephoning our artists to ask if we can hold their commission checks—all agree warmly. I am helping the printers set up a temporary studio in a storefront not far from our base-ment home base. I am also working with Kyle to get together all the material the bank wants. We find a structural engineer who will give us a rough esti-mate of the cost of retrofitting the building. He says he can't do anything else until at least February.

A bank officer calls me before he has received all the requested mate-rial and tells me that Bank of America is not interested in doing this loan. He says this is because the building is URM (unreinforced masonry—that is, brick), because we are not customers of theirs, and because our business is unusual. Kyle calls him back and tells him we have already incorporated the cost of a seismic upgrade in our estimates and talks him into at least looking at our financial material. The money has been pouring in from our marvelous clients, and it seems to me that our ability to raise enough cash for the down payment on such short notice without borrowing must be impressive. I call a San Francisco client who is influential in the community and tell him the story. "I'll have a word with someone at the bank," he says.

A few days later, Kyle and I meet again with the bankers, this time joined by a senior person who asks many perceptive questions about our busi-ness. It is clear we will need detailed plans for the seismic bracing, and we are having no luck finding someone to make them. I talk about this in our weekly staff meeting, and a young intern named Mira Desai speaks up: "My father is a structural engineer."

Raj Desai is a well-known engineer, completely acceptable to the bank, but—like all engineers after the earthquake—absolutely booked up, and also planning a family trip to India for the holidays. He can't believe we want to

The Howard Street side of the building (left). The Hawthorne Street side (opposite).

go ahead without owning the building. But we do. We ask him at least to schedule preliminary tests, and Denise is rushing to finish her plans because he wants to see them before he decides if he can take the job.

On November 20, Denise and I are having coffee at her "office," the Windows West restaurant; it is still functioning on Folsom Street. Closing time has arrived, and a waiter has pulled an iron gate across the doorway. I look up and see Kyle at the gate waving and gesturing. The proprietor lets him in, and he walks over and sticks out his hand to me; "Congratulations," he says. "The bank said yes." We drink champagne again. But it is still premature. This "yes" concerns only our creditworthiness. Whether or not the bank will accept the building is still a question.

Feher has been getting the inspections, and they have been coming up good: good heating and ventilating, good roof, good plumbing, good electricity. But now we have the environmental report. It is the size of a thick magazine and is full of information about neighborhood gas stations, and it talks about fluorescent lights (PCBs) and vinyl asbestos floor tiles (VATs) that we would remove anyhow. But there is something else: old blueprints show that the newspaper, back in the 1920s, had two tanks buried under the sidewalk, one for fuel oil and one for gasoline for their trucks.

Feher says, "Don't worry, the tanks are under the sidewalk, not on the building's property." But our lawyer says, "If even an infinitesimal quantity of solvent leaked into the soil, this deal is off." He says the sellers should

Architect Denise Hall.

indemnify us. I look up the word *indemnify* in the dictionary; it means "hold harmless." Kyle talks to the sellers. They say the price for the building is "as is" and there is no possibility of an indemnity from them. They locate, however, an old receipt from a contractor employed forty years ago to fill the tanks with sand. We talk to the bank. They say they'll get back to us.

It is December 1. Kyle has been talking on the phone to the bank every day for a week—a precious week we have lost—and now we are promised a commitment letter that will spell out all conditions. Kyle says his stomach is churning; he hasn't been away from his desk all day. We both jump every time we hear the little whistle of the fax machine. It is after six o'clock and everyone else has gone home. Finally the pages start coming through—lots of them; we are both reading as they come. The message is clear: Unless we can prove beyond a shadow of a doubt that the tanks have no toxic residue, the bank will not give the loan. Also, we must have finished plans and a detailed bid for the seismic work; the money for that will be held in escrow. We will need, all at once, not only the money for the down payment and Feher's fee, but also all the money for the earthquake retrofitting.

The company that is testing the tanks will drill into them sideways from the building to avoid waiting for a city permit. Their people are extremely busy after the earthquake but are going to "work in" our small job. We will have results in two weeks.

Denise is in my office, talking to Raj Desai on the phone. "Oh that's

Building a new foundation
in the basement.

great, Raj. Thank you very much; we appreciate it." Then, aside, to me, "He's going to do it." I am elated, then immediately dashed; Denise's tone has changed. "Oh, no," she says, still on the telephone. "Oh, that's too bad. There's no question about it? What will it entail? And the cost?" She hangs up the phone, crestfallen. The foundation of the building has failed its concrete test, so it will be impossible to tie the steel reinforcing braces to it. A new, anchoring foundation will need to be created in the basement.

A building across Hawthorne Street from the building-animal (which is still sleeping) has an "Available" sign on it, and Connie makes an appointment to see it. "It couldn't hurt to look, could it?" she says, and she, Kyle, and I meet the broker. There are seismic braces, and we examine them carefully. "Do you have any idea how much it cost to put these in?" I ask him. He doesn't. On the top floor, we cluster at the window looking down on "our" building, admiring it, until the broker asks if we've seen enough.

It is Wednesday, December 13. I speak on the phone with Muriel at the tank-testing company. She assures me they will be there with a rig early Friday and will give us a verbal report later in the day. Floor plans with little inverted Vs drawn over them are coming through the fax machine from Raj. I think there are an awful lot of Vs—seven, it looks like. Raj says this is just the locations of the braces; he needs the results of a soil test before he can do actual plans. The test was difficult to schedule, as it requires a rig small enough to fit into the freight elevator, and those rigs are in great demand these days. He got the date of Friday the 15th, but the tanks were being tested that day, so he scheduled it for Monday the 18th.

At nine a.m. on Friday the 15th I am at the building. Kyle is already there with some workmen. "They're finished," he says. "The gas tank is clean. But they weren't able to test the fuel tank." They drilled a number of holes and retrieved sand, but they could not find evidence of the actual tank. "Maybe it has rusted away," a workman suggests. "Or maybe we just didn't find it." Later Muriel assures me on the phone that the news is good. "If there are both gas and fuel tanks," she says, "it is the gas tank that we worry about. Fuel oil is also a controlled substance, but, unlike gasoline, it degrades in the soil with time." She explains that there is a gas main over the tank area, and other pipes

New seismic braces in a light well.

and wires from city utilities. If we want her company to continue, they will have to research the exact location of the utilities and get a permit from the city to drill through the sidewalk—impossible to do before the end of the year. Muriel agrees to call the bank officials to explain this. She will emphasize that any traces of fuel oil will almost certainly have degraded in the forty years since the tank was filled with sand.

Raj is leaving for India on December 22. Denise has lined up a contractor who is willing to receive the final seismic drawings on December 21st and give us a price on the 26th. It looks like we will have enough money if the price is within the range given in our earlier estimate. Denise optimistically has sent her construction plans for a preliminary check by the San Francisco building department, and learns that we will be required to install an electric wheelchair lift between the main floor and the shipping/loading dock three stair steps up. "It is possible," the plans checker said with a straight face, "that the shipping technician is handicapped." When Denise reports this, we are all so tired that we cannot stop laughing.

December 21 is the lowest point. The bank says it will require indemnity for the fuel tank from the sellers, and the sellers say they have a back-up deal and are not willing to indemnify us. In the hallway of our basement office, with several staff members standing there, Valerie asks me to OK the final proof of the *Art in America* ad. "Take out the Howard Street address," I say. "Put 'by appointment' instead." Kyle is walking toward us in the hallway. "My God, what did you just say?" he asks.

Raj has delivered his drawings on the 21st as promised, and Kyle and I meet with the seismic contractor and his subcontractors on the 22nd as planned. The contractor promises to have the cost figures at noon the day after Christmas. Kyle and I are at work that day, and promptly at noon the phone rings. The steel erector needs a couple of hours more; we are shooting for two o'clock now. At two he calls again. It is almost ready; he will fax it at the end of the day. By five o'clock we have it, a spreadsheet from a computer. The price is within the range of the original estimate, within the range that we can afford.

In the morning, December 27, Kyle takes the bid and the plans to the bank and asks again if there is anything to be done to modify their position on the tank. But there is not. I decide to call the president of the engineering firm that owns the building—so far, it has been Kyle and their lawyer who have been talking. I say that we truly love the building and we hope they might want us to have it; I tell him a bit about who we are and what we do. I say it seems that there is no issue, really, about a toxic threat, and if there turns out to be one, we would correct it, would not hold them to doing that even if they indemnify us. It is just that the bank insists on indemnification. He says he knows the tank is not toxic—he is an environmental engineer. He will think about this and call me back. At seven in the evening—Kyle and I are both still at work—he calls: they agree to sign. We call the bank. They already know.

First thing the next morning, December 28, Kyle calls the title company. The woman there, her name is Debbie, says she needs all the documents by noon today if the deal is to be recorded tomorrow, the last working day of this year. This surprises us—we had thought the closing would be tomorrow. We call the bank immediately, and about noon the young officer calls back. I overhear the call: Kyle is furious. "You mean, after all this, we are going to lose this deal because you can't do the paperwork?" he snaps. He puts the phone down. We are both stunned. We call Debbie at the title office and she says forget about noon, anytime today, she'll stay late, even as late as seven o'clock. "Keep pressing the bank."

Kyle calls the lawyer for the sellers, and at the same time I call the senior person we have sometimes dealt with at the bank. His secretary says he is in a meeting, but I explain the situation and ask her to call him. After a bit, he comes on the line. I thank him for all he has done and beg him to extend himself and his staff this last bit, and I tell him the title person is willing to stay late. He says, "Does it make so much difference?" I remind him that there is a back-up bid and we will lose the deal if we do not sign by the end of the year. "It makes a lot of difference," I say, and add softly, "We didn't ask for this earthquake." He is silent for a moment and then says he will see what he can do and call me back. Kyle, also just getting off the phone, says that the sellers are trying to reach the man I just talked to.

When the bank officer calls me back, he says he has a particular obstacle. No one is working this holiday week who can read the seismic drawings we sent them. He says that if I can get him some more detail—"how many bags of concrete, how many pounds of steel, for instance?"—he has someone "standing here right now" who can make sense of the material so they can know if the bid is reasonable. Can we fax him something immediately? Kyle has a beeper-signal number for the contractor and reaches him in the field. "I've never had a lender ask for that," he says, but, yes, he can provide it. He calls his office and has someone there fax to the bank a printout of the detail on which he based his bid. The whole thing takes only a few minutes. Half an hour later we get a call saying the bank has set up a four o'clock meeting at the title company.

It is nearly four o'clock before the bank tells us the exact amount for which our cashier's check should be made, so by the time Kyle and I obtain the check and get to the title company, we are late. Sitting around a conference table are the engineering company president and his lawyer; Feher; Debbie from the title company; and three people from the bank: the young officer and two women from the real estate division whom we have talked with on the phone but not met. They all stand up when we enter and applaud, crowding around us, smiling, congratulating, shaking hands.

Afterward, we drink champagne. And call Denise. The next day we have more champagne with the staff. Denise's permits are applied for, but the seismic drawings must still be filed. I call Raj's associate. "Oh, yes," he

The raw space above became my office (bottom) and part of a studio (center) that later became our gallery.

says good-naturedly. "About this matter, Denise called me, the contractor called me, you called me, and Raj called me from India. The matter is taken care of, rest assured."

A few days into the new year, a real estate agent telephoned me. He said his clients were the back-up bidders on our "657 Howard Street deal" and that they were prepared to offer me "considerably more" than I had paid if I would sell the building to them. It was out of the question, of course, but I asked him what they wanted to do with it. "They plan to gut it," he said. "Since it's a landmark facade, they would keep that, and go up as high as possible behind it." I thought about the previous owner at the closing, shaking my hand. "Enjoy the building," he had said. "It's a wonderful building, and it deserves the use you will give it."

After that, the building-animal woke up. It was hungry, of course. It is a beautiful animal but it eats voraciously. As I had been developing the renovation plans with Denise, it hadn't occurred to me that we should occupy only part of the building. I was enamored with it as a whole, and generally I like to fill things up. I have to admit I had delusions of grandeur.

The street-level space with the Howard Street address became a gallery, so large and beautiful that people were dumbfounded: "All this space for prints!" someone exclaimed, and someone else said it was "like a museum." Upstairs, we built three etching studios so we could have two

The new street-level gallery.

artists working at once, each with his or her own completely equipped studio, and still have another studio being used for edition printing by printers not busy with artists. We also built a large darkroom area for the photogravure process, something we had not had at Folsom Street.

Along with the studios upstairs, Denise created three offices—including mine, the most beautiful office in the world—and a large lobby with a library area under a skylight. Connie and our publications manager worked on that floor with me and the printers; there were seven printers then. The gallery staff, including Valerie and Stephanie; our businesspeople, including Kyle and Stacie; and the registrar were on the main floor. The shipping area was down there, too.

In the basement, along with storage, we built a lunchroom with a complete kitchen. We also had a "resting room" with a Japanese theme—it had a tatami mat floor and a futon bed. I justified it because often our artists would come from different time zones and need a place for naps. The kitchen was John Cage's idea; he had used a hot plate to cook for us until then. At the back of the building, with a separate entrance, Tom had his studio.

We held our opening celebration October 20, 1990, one year and three days after the earthquake had dispossessed us from Folsom Street. It went on all afternoon and into the evening, with different events happening on each of our three floors. In the gallery on the main floor there was a party, with music,

A celebration, 1990. I am in the second row with Valerie and Kyle. In front are Katrina Traywick and Russ Richardson.

champagne, and food, and an exhibition of the prints we had published in the preceding difficult year. All our staff members, including the ones from New York, were there.

Downstairs, in the basement lunchroom, videotapes showed the building's reconstruction and artists and printers working in our temporary studio. Upstairs, live demonstrations of etching, of Japanese woodblock printing, and of Chinese woodblock printing were occurring simultaneously in the three different studios.

Tadashi Toda, our printer in Japan, came with his wife from Kyoto. We brought Professor Yang from China, and a printer, thanks to Brian's perseverance, Sören's influence, and Professor Yang's connections. Hu Qin Yun, Master Hu, was the chief printer from the workshop we had used in Shanghai. She had done projects with Robert Kushner and Janis Provisor and was working on a print with Richard Tuttle. Richard was at the opening, and while Master Hu printed his image, he stood by and gave her suggestions about the color.

In our largest studio, with windows on Howard Street, our printers inked, wiped, and printed Al Held's latest large seven-plate aquatint. All day long, for seven hours straight, visitors filled the beautiful building. Afterward, we tried to estimate how many there had been, and we thought, perhaps, the number was in the neighborhood of a thousand.

The opening of Crown Point's new building, October 20, 1990.

Master Hu demonstrates Chinese woodblock printing (below). Valerie shows congratulatory scrolls from the Chinese woodblock workshop where Hu Shufu was master printer (bottom).

Tadashi Toda demonstrates Japanese woodblock printing (top). Master Hu prints with Brian, Richard Tuttle, and me watching (center). A big crowd in the main studio for an etching printing demonstration (bottom).

Greeted by Harry Parker, director of the Fine Arts Museums of San Francisco, at the opening of "Thirty-Five Years at Crown Point Press," October 3, 1997.

17.

THE NINETIES

MAKE SENSE OF WHAT YOU ARE DOING

The day after the grand opening of our Howard Street/Hawthorne Street building, I walked around our big gallery on the ground floor, quietly, by myself, looking at every print in the exhibition, and I was surprised. The show was titled "Post-Earthquake Prints" and contained the work we had published in the months of 1989 and 1990 that were loosely bracketed by the earthquake and the opening of our new building. I was surprised by the number of artists. Twenty were represented.

We included William T. Wiley, Wayne Thiebaud, and John Cage, who had worked at Folsom Street just before the earthquake, and Alex Katz, who had worked on prints for us in Doris Simmelink's Los Angeles studio. Another artist, Sherrie Levine, had worked in Oakland on plates that we editioned in 1990. But even if we don't count those five, the number of artist projects we managed is surprising.

We did four projects in Japan that year and six in China; traveling had become an integral part of our program. At that moment, however, I thought our China project unlikely to last, and with the dollar falling against the yen, Japan was becoming prohibitively expensive. Toda had received offers to print for other publishers, so we would not be leaving him without work if we began winding down there.

When the earthquake hit, Karen, Connie, Kyle, and I had begun talking about letting the Asian programs go and setting up a workshop in the South of France. Delusions of grandeur at its height, perhaps, but—thinking about it—if we had not had an earthquake and had stayed in our leased space on

Tony Cragg in the temporary studio, 1989.

Folsom Street, and if the country had not gone into recession, a program in France might have been just what we needed to keep providing fresh experiences for our artists and ourselves.

In 1990 in our storefront temporary studio, two old friends, Sol LeWitt and Pat Steir, had started projects that they completed in 1991, and we had done full-scale projects there with Tony Cragg, Richard Diebenkorn, and Gary Stephan. Tony Cragg is an English sculptor. In 1988, the year he first worked with us at Crown Point, he represented Britain in the Venice Biennale and also won the Turner Prize given by the Tate Gallery. Tony has said that his work is a "network of associations, relationships, techniques, and images," and one of his prints from 1990 showing rubber stamps in abundance was in my mind as we braved construction regulations. *Container Out of Control*, though it was done before the earthquake, became symbolic to me in general of the post-earthquake year at Crown Point Press. Unexpected offshoots, often humorous, sprouted one after another. In our "Post-Earthquake Prints" exhibition, most of the artists had four or five prints apiece. Tony had forty-one. He worked quickly and in small sizes.

Richard Diebenkorn, whose health was fragile, also worked mostly small that year, in black and white. He started a color work but did not finish it. I remember in the temporary studio a printer and I were sitting in our lounge area with Dick and he looked up and said, "Are you getting along well with your little friend?" We followed his amused glance to see a large rat boldly staring at us. The earthquake had disrupted the neighborhood below ground as well as above.

Gary Stephan put up with the rats, too, and also a flood one morning caused by street work. Gary is a New Yorker who pushes abstraction toward representation. "Above the world of man," he says, "there is a completely other time and significance. If you look at these pictures, you're a visitor in the space, but you're not really part of it. Our world is here, on the bottom, in shadows, and up there in the atmosphere, the molecules are dancing together or whatever they are doing up there."

To keep that perspective, and to remind me that Gary's prints were the first to be editioned here, I hung one of them in our Hawthorne Street entrance lobby, and it has remained there since the building opened.

Daria Sywulak, Gary's printer, remembers his good humor, his clowning imitation of Jack Benny, "shoulders slumped, arms crossed in front of him, and puffing nonchalantly on a cigar." At one point, Gary asked her if the printers ever accidentally dropped a plate. "No sooner did the words come out of his mouth than a large plate went crashing to the floor at the back of the studio where the other printers had been drying it off. We all laughed, but Gary turned serious after that and said, 'You guys are still in shock from the earthquake, aren't you?'"

Tony Cragg, *Suburbs (Softground Series) III*, 1990. Color soft ground etching, 10 × 8 inches.

Tony Cragg, *Container Out of Control*, 1988. Spit bite and water bite aquatints, 8 × 13¼ inches.

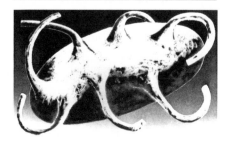

We did the renovation on the Hawthorne Street side of the building first, and soon after Gary completed his work the printers were able to leave the temporary studio and take his plates to Hawthorne Street to edition them. Tom also moved into his

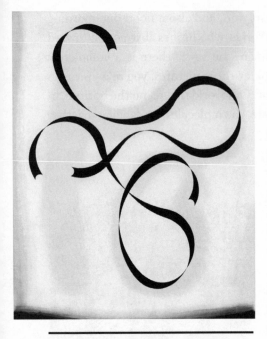

Gary Stephan, *1990 II*, 1990. Color aquatint with spit bite aquatint, 37 × 30 inches.

new studio, then on the Hawthorne side. The building has three floors: a lower level partly below ground (there are small high windows), a ground floor with one entrance on Howard Street and two on Hawthorne Street, and a single floor, which I'll call the upper floor, above the street level. We turned the upper floor over to studios and offices in our first iteration of the building's space; our gallery was originally on the ground floor and had the 657 Howard Street address.

In 2012, the two Hawthorne Street entrances, numbered 20 and 22, are the main entrances to the building. Howard Street provides a secondary entrance for a tenant, an Internet company, and the main entrance for Tom's studio. He moved to the Howard side of the building in 1995 when we rented 22 Hawthorne Street, his former space, to a restaurant.

When you enter the lobby at 20 Hawthorne Street, you see the Internet company's primary entrance off a smaller lobby and an elevator and stairs that take you up to Crown Point Press or down to Adrienne Fish's 871 Fine Arts. Adrienne founded her gallery and bookstore in our 871 Folsom Street building, moved to a big gallery building after the earthquake, and then in 2008 came into Crown Point's orbit again, this time on our lower level at 20 Hawthorne Street. Crown Point Press is on the upper floor. The second entrance on Hawthorne Street, number 22, leads to the ground-floor space that was originally Tom's studio and later became a restaurant.

In the lobby at 20 Hawthorne Street, to your right as you enter, is a print by Joel Fisher. It is seven feet high and four feet across. Four sheets of paper together create an image, titled *Tree*, made up of impressions of 119 small square plates, pixel-like and inked in earth colors. Joel made this work in the Crown Point studio while construction was going on in the lower part of the building. Because inking all those small plates took so long, we made an edition of only seven.

Two additional artists worked in the studios of the new building before we opened to the public: one traveled from Japan, and the other is a collective rather than a single artist. Katsura Funakoshi, who lives in Tokyo, is a sculptor who usually focuses on the heads and shoulders of his subjects. He has studied traditional Japanese wood temple sculpture, and his chief concern is bringing to life the person he is drawing or carving. In the etching studio, in *Dream of the Bird,* shown here, he drew his image by carving into an acid-resistant ground made mainly of soap and then etching the portrait of a man sitting still but ready to move at any moment.

Tim Rollins and K.O.S. (Kids of Survival) is a collective. The group had worked with us at Folsom Street before the earthquake and returned in July 1990 for a second project. Tim Rollins, who was born in 1955 and grew up in Maine, was teaching in a South Bronx high school when he founded, in 1982, an after-school program called the Art and Knowledge Workshop. Tim would read aloud to the kids who came to the workshop, partly to calm them down. Drawing materials were available, and while he read, the kids would draw.

Joel Fisher, *Tree*, 1990. Color aquatint on four sheets of paper, 68 × 40 inches.

Katsura Funakoshi, *Dream of the Bird*, 1990. Soap ground aquatint with drypoint, 36¼ × 31½ inches.

Kids of Survival, clockwise from left: Angel Abreau, George Garces, Nelson Savinon, Jose Parissi, and Annette Rosado. Tim Rollins is on the far right.

Eventually Tim started giving the kids book pages to draw on, and he organized the drawings into grids glued on canvas. He has educated the kids in art by exposing them to it, taking them to galleries and museums, and by letting them, as a group, decide which images to include in their finished works. "We're a meritocracy," he explains. Only kids who take a serious interest can remain in the group, and—because paintings have been sold—everyone gets a salary.

Tim brought with him to Crown Point in 1990 five members of K.O.S., ages sixteen to nineteen. The text he chose for both his projects with us is *The Temptation of St. Anthony*, by Gustav Flaubert. It is full of monsters and demons, and the kids created images of monsters, as Tim said, from Crown Point's "strange, sinister chemical processes."

"The kids were quick to develop variations on the spit bite process," printer Brian Shure recalled. "At least once a day Tim and the kids would hang all the proofs up on the wall and edit. It was very democratic. Even if only one person liked or disliked a certain image, he could sometimes convince everyone else." The resulting work is of high standard. Paintings by Tim Rollins and K.O.S. hang in many museums, among them the Museum of Modern Art in New York. I loved seeing our new studio populated by teenagers drawing and dancing to hip-hop music, full of life and purpose.

Like every construction project I've ever heard of, ours had cost more than was estimated—the container often seemed out of control. And, as we entered into our building project in 1990, the economy was slowing down.

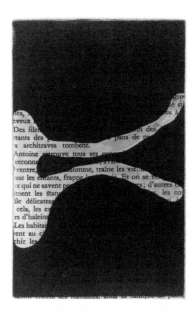

Tim Rollins + K.O.S., *The Temptation of St. Antony XVI–The Solitaries,* 1990. One in a series of soap ground aquatint and soft ground etchings on photogravure text chine collé, 4¼ × 2¾ inches.

There had been a stock market crash in 1987; at the end of the eighties a crisis had developed in the savings and loan industry, deregulated by Ronald Reagan in 1982. In 1990 George H. W. Bush was president, the first Gulf War was in process, and gas prices were going up. I wrote in my daybook in the little space under January 16, 1990, "Karen thinks the country's going to fall apart soon."

I noted on May 14 that our sales at the Chicago Art Fair were very low— none of the exhibitors did well. "The market is careful but not completely bad," Karen reassured me. But on June 12 she said, "Business is very bad. Dead. Our usually supportive dealers are now selling only their inventory." We moved our presses into the new building on June 13.

We finished out the year 1990 by publishing projects by three artists who had worked with us before. Francesco Clemente and William Brice were with us in early December in different studios at the same time, and José Maria Sicilia came in October from Spain. Sicilia did a series in which he embedded his prints in beeswax.

Since 1978, with exceptions only in 1988 and 1990, John Cage had spent at least two weeks of every year with us—in some years he came twice. He stayed with Tom, Kevin, and me in our house, cooking for everyone at home and in the studio, and working on his etchings. In 1988, the first year that we did not see him, he made his first working visit to the Mountain Lake Workshop in Virginia to make watercolors. Ray Kass, the director, set him up with a situation in which he could expand on the *Ryoanji* prints that he had made at Crown Point in 1983 by drawing around stones. Kass provided big rounded rocks for

John Cage, *HV2 25b*, 1992. One in a series of 15 related color etchings in three impressions each, 11½ × 14½ inches.

John Cage and printer Pamela Paulson with plates for *HV2* on the press, 1992.

John to use instead of stones, and brushes for him to use instead of etching needles. Some of the brushes were very large and specially made, and John used them to make oversized watercolor paintings on paper. The paintings are beautiful extensions of one aspect of the work he had done with us, and when he returned to Crown Point in 1989 he brought back to us what he had learned in Virginia about brushes and created etchings like *The Missing Stone* (plate 30), in which his marks are larger and looser than what he had drawn before.

Although John usually came to Crown Point in January, in 1989 he was with us in September, a month before the earthquake. At the breakfast table September 17, 1989 — "the sun coming up, a little thunder, quick burst of rain," I wrote in my daybook—John told me that he was "in a state of not knowing." He said he used to think he disliked harmony but had heard a work by new-music composer Pauline Oliveros that was "marvelous and harmonic." He had thought he didn't like drama, but had made an opera. Then he said (I wrote this down with quote marks): "All the work I have done with chance operations was to get away from gesture, and now I'm working with gesture." He sat quietly for a moment and then added, "My work has always been about changing the mind." He went back to Mountain

Lake in 1990 and missed a year with us. This was the year right after the earthquake, when we were mostly in the temporary studio.

We began 1991 with John working in our beautiful new building, and for a short time everything seemed right with the world. He had a way of making people around him believe that. In that year, as he had done frequently over the years, he designed his project so it would be complete when he left us. In *Smoke Weather Stone Weather* (plate 31) he made layers of images and smoked the paper as well, and from each set of plates he made for a print, we printed only one impression. Each print in the series of thirty-seven is unique.

Smoke Weather Stone Weather is less dramatic than John's watercolors and the related etchings of 1989. He named it for the weather, which, as he said, "remains the weather no matter what is going on." He said he "didn't want to have an image that would separate itself from the paper." I think *Smoke Weather Stone Weather* is the culmination, the full development, of John's work in which he used rocks or stones. I see the images as integrated with the "weather" as the body is integrated with the spirit.

In January 1992, John was back at work with us. As in 1991, he asked that everything be finished before he left—there would be no editioning. He made a series of small black and white prints called *Without Horizon* and a set called *HV2* in luminous pale colors. In the *Without Horizon* prints, we made as many as possible in the time we had and printed only one of each image. We ended up with fifty-seven prints, each one unique.

HV stands for "horizontal vertical"; John had made a set with that title in 1983 by inking rectangles of soft materials, foam and felt, and laying them out, some horizontal, some vertical, side by side on the press. In *HV2* he composed using the same method, but this time we inked rectangles of copper plates from the scrap pile. John asked that we keep one set of the fifteen images together; the Erzbischöfliches Diözesanmuseum in Cologne, Germany, now owns it. We made three impressions of each print in the series.

Without Horizon and *HV2* were the last prints John made. He died of a stroke later that year, on August 12, less than a month before his eightieth birthday. The day after we had word of his death, Tom and I came to work in the morning (it had rained the night before), and mushrooms had sprouted in a crack in the asphalt parking area outside the press. Nothing has ever grown there before or since. We looked at the mushrooms, and at each

Richard Diebenkorn, *Flotsam*, 1991.
Aquatint reversal with scraping,
burnishing, and drypoint,
24 × 18 inches.

Dick and printers working on
Flotsam, The Barbarian, and
Touched Red, 1991.

other, and both said, "John." I remembered John standing in our doorway in Oakland on January 1, 1978, his first day working with us. He was holding a handful of mushrooms. "I found these on the way here," he said. "We can have them with our lunch today."

Richard Diebenkorn worked with us in September 1992, just weeks after John died. "We talked about John Cage a lot," he said to Phyllis when she came to pick him up. Dick was fragile at that time—his strength had been in decline since 1989, when he had had two heart valve operations. Nevertheless, he worked at Crown Point in 1992 with extraordinary productivity. That is the year he made *High Green*, second only to *Green* as his most celebrated work in printmaking.

In 1991, a year before making *High Green*, Dick had completed *Touched Red* (plate 32), the color print he had started in the temporary studio in 1990. When he had set *Touched Red* aside, I thought it had reflected his delicate condition. In 1991 he added strength to the print without losing its sense of vulnerability. That year he also made *Flotsam*, an odd black and white print full of motifs that he had used over the years. There are spades, circles, Xs, crosses, and in the center a soft floating form that—in my fantasy—is an embodied psyche hanging there.

In creating *Flotsam*, Dick had used an ink transfer method to work on three plates with different versions of the same image, and when he returned in 1992, he released the other two in small editions with the titles *The Barbarian* and *The Barbarian's Garden—Threatened*. I saw those prints as humorous and ignored the pessimism that was also there. I looked instead to the vitality of *High Green*, new that year. I thought he would recover. But he did not. He died on March 30, 1993. In three weeks, he would have turned seventy.

When we moved into our Oakland studio in 1972, we found an abandoned chair that had been repaired many times with diagonal wires bracing the legs and a length of cord wrapped around a split in the rounded backrest. The chair seemed symbolic to me of how art and life proceed. I didn't know that the studio had once been Dick's, but in 1977 when he walked in to make prints, he said right away, "That's my chair." Yes, I thought. Of course. It's his chair.

On February 11, 1991, I inserted a blank page in my daybook and wrote the following:

Option One, Part One: *Sell the Archive.*
Maybe it would bring enough to pay off the construction loan. But it doesn't solve the long-term problem if the recession lasts. We can't go on spending more than we're making.

Option One, Part Two: *Scale Down the Operation.*
How to do it? Cut the staff.
Rent the street floor of the building and move everything upstairs. Close the New York gallery.

Option Two: *Go Out of Business.*
This option sees the whole thing as an artwork with the building as its culmination—a futile house of cards, an expensive but beautiful dream that comes into existence but does not function, except symbolically. It did function briefly, at least, to show how well it could, for a few projects (and it is appropriate that those included Sol, Pat, Dick, and John). Maybe it is enough. The fact is, you may be too exhausted now to continue further. Is this true? (I guess it is, if I have to do it alone.)

So, if you take this option, and just stop, how would it work? Let Sol and Pat come back to finish, and Dick if he wants to finish the color one. At least print proofs of those. Print proofs of Clemente. Ask Alex if he wants to take over the production of his prints that Toda has going. Cancel all new scheduled projects and give all the employees notice except Valerie and Kyle. They would help sell what we can and organize finances and archive. By May first, everyone else could be gone.

I don't think I had ever before in Crown Point's history thought seriously about going out of business. Our normal situation is bootstrap mode. Our bank relationships have not included borrowing except, in affluent times, via a credit line requiring repayment once a year before possible renewal. I've used it mainly for artist commissions, keeping them current as a priority, and have managed the press on a cash basis. When sales have fallen unexpectedly below expenses, we have been able to sell proofs of older works that have become rare and are especially desirable. But the building had required me to dig deeply into those resources. And to complete the construction, I had borrowed at a high interest rate from a private individual. That loan was coming due and was the immediate problem.

Option One, Part One was the obvious place to begin. I had kept for my archive one print of each image we had published at Crown Point Press and also of the work I had done for Parasol. I also had a large number of unique working proofs that artists had allowed me to keep to become part of an archive. From the beginning, I had envisioned the archive in a museum that would exhibit the art and care for it, keeping it together so that in the future people could see what we'd done. I had thought I would eventually give it away to accomplish that. But now, unless I could find a museum to buy it, I would have to break it up and sell the high-value pieces separately. I talked with Karen and Valerie and discovered that if I took that approach, I would most likely realize at least double the amount of money I needed to pay the loan. But it would take time and I had a loan-payment deadline. And of course if I sold any of the art separately, the archive concept would be destroyed.

Years earlier I had met Ruth Fine, who was then curator of modern prints and drawings at the National Gallery in Washington, D.C. (She later became curator of special projects in modern art. In 2012 she—nominally—retired to live in Philadelphia.) Ruth had said that the gallery would be interested in a Crown Point Press archive whenever I might be ready to find a home for it. I called her and explained that I would need to sell the archive, not give it away. I asked for exactly what I needed to pay the loan. She said she would try her best to raise the money. Andrew Robison, the senior curator of prints and drawings, concurred.

Option Two, going out of business, fell out of focus as soon as I saw that Option One, Part One, selling the archive, was possible. The second part of Option One, reducing the staff, freeing space in the building so we could collect rent, and closing the New York gallery all would be necessary as well. But doing those things would not bring immediate cash.

We did already have a small start on renting space in our building. The Achenbach Foundation for Graphic Art, owned by the Fine Arts Museums of San Francisco, had taken over the lower level. They had needed temporary space while the Palace of the Legion of Honor, their home base, was being remodeled and retrofitted for earthquake safety.

Steven Nash, associate director of the Fine Arts Museums of San Francisco, stopped me in the downstairs hallway of our building. I had not said anything to the Achenbach Foundation about the archive because I had offered it to the National Gallery, but Steve asked me about it. "It would be great to keep it in San Francisco," he said. "How much money do you need and how long do we have to raise it?"

Karin Breuer, curator in charge at the Achenbach Foundation, was then a curator and was working in our lower level space. In writing this, I called her, hoping she would help me look back to 1991. "I'll never forget the day Steve first talked to you," she said. "It was a day that changed my life. Bob Johnson [then print curator in charge] was out of town. Steve walked into my office cubbyhole and said, 'Karin, I need you to write up this proposal right away. I am going to present it at the board meeting tomorrow.'" Karin has been taking care of our archive ever since. She vividly remembered the board meeting when Steve proposed our archive. "Phyllis Wattis [a famously generous trustee] stood up and pledged $100,000 right then and there, and she challenged everyone else. We raised a million dollars in one month. The museum has never done anything like that before or since."

On March 22, I noted this in my daybook: "Harry Parker [director of the Fine Arts Museums] called. 'The Board unanimously approved the purchase of the Crown Point Press archive . . . can deliver the cash immediately . . . excitement about an ongoing relationship . . . you are regarded so warmly by everyone. This is a treasure for the Bay Area.'" My first entry on the subject in my daybook had been February 11, and by March 22 our local museum had raised all the money I needed to pay off my construction loan.

I felt terrible about pulling away from the National Gallery at that time. Ruth had extended herself to present our material to the gallery, and also she had listened to me and buoyed me up as I was struggling with decisions about the long-range viability of the press. Nevertheless, in the end I thought it was a good thing to keep the archive at home in San Francisco, and I was glad to get my loan paid off without penalties or extensions.

To finish this train of thought, I'll jump forward five years. Ruth Fine and Andrew Robison kept their interest in Crown Point Press alive, rather than withdrawing it. I had one last complete set of prints published by Crown

Point (without the Parasol material), in the form of OK to Print proofs. The OK (some studios use the French expression *bon à tirer* or BAT) is the first print of an image finished by an artist. He or she signs it as a model against which each edition print is measured. The OK is always near the press while printing is going on.

In 1996 the National Gallery purchased my OK to Print proofs by Richard Diebenkorn. The gallery already held archives from Tamarind and Gemini, the print shops where he had done most of his (few) lithographs, so purchasing Diebenkorn's Crown Point prints made sense to its board; it now has a full-fledged study collection of Diebenkorn's print work. At the same time, I donated the OK to Print proofs from all our published editions up to that time, and will donate future OK to Print proofs as we produce them. Because we make an OK to Print for every edition we do, we could designate the set as an archive, and I am proud and pleased to have a Crown Point Press archive at the National Gallery of Art.

Archives are ongoing, and the San Francisco archive is also continuously enlarged; the Achenbach will receive an artist's proof of every image we produce so long as we are publishing. In addition—and this applies to both museums—I regularly donate working proofs and other educational material. I'm not obliged to do this, and of course the artists involved must give permission, but we generate many sheets of paper, printed, drawn on, or written on, that are beautiful and/or interesting without being marketable, and the museums are an excellent place for them. Crown Point Press has had a registrar on its staff from early in our history so that prints and proofs are sure to be cared for and documented. As I write this in 2012, Mari Andrews is about to celebrate her twentieth year in that job.

Only a few months after we opened our Crown Point Press building in San Francisco, Kyle had started making plans to dismantle one studio and move the gallery into its space upstairs. But since there was at first no opportunity for a tenant for the big gallery space, we didn't actually make the move until 1993. And we kept on doing artist projects, even though sales continued to be slow. We should do projects when the artists are ready to do them, I thought. We will sell the prints later if not now.

By that time, I was no longer thinking of going out of business, but I knew it wouldn't take much unexpected adversity to make my whole enterprise collapse. To be honest, since 1991 I have never been able to fully shake a worry about sales abruptly drying up and making it necessary for us to close. Right now, in 2012, forces resulting mostly from our country's adversarial politics are placing most small personally owned businesses in jeopardy, and Crown Point is not an exception.

As 1992 ended, with the construction loan paid, I wrote in my daybook that since the earthquake we had been "swept along by the river's current. Now we are in the reeds, paddling carefully, looking for a way out." (I'd just watched on VHS tape a forty-year-old Bogart/Hepburn movie, *The African Queen*.) I knew we wouldn't find the way out by continuing exactly what we had been doing. I did intend to find additional paying tenants, but also I thought we should use the studios we had built, especially the darkroom we had created in order to work with photogravure. Just as we were getting that nineteenth-century process going, however, a new way for artists to print photographs came along.

Francesco Clemente had showed me, in 1991, a print he had made called a digigraph. It was a reproduction of a self-portrait watercolor so perfect you couldn't tell it from the original. This was my first encounter with ink-jet printing. Fine art photography was then a second-class citizen in the art world, like fine art printmaking, but ink-jet printing would soon change photography's status. First in Germany, then quickly in the rest of the world, artists began using ink-jet to print enormous, powerful photographs that rivaled paintings, and two decades later, ink-jet prints have gained respect (and prices) on a par with paintings. If you had told me about that in 1991, I would not have believed you.

Tom and I made a trip to Manhattan Beach, near Los Angeles, to visit a workshop founded by rock musician Graham Nash and his associates, Mac Holbert and Jack Duganne, where Francesco's print had been made. Holbert and Duganne showed us the big ink-jet printer they had used. It looked like a stand-alone copier, only larger. The inks were dyes and were fugitive, but Duganne was silk-screening an ultraviolet-resistant coating over the finished prints to retard fading. Now, "archival" ink-jet prints are made with pigment inks, but the quantity of ink is still very thin and cannot be permanent in the way photogravure colors are; in photogravure the pigments are dense and embedded in the paper.

Photogravure is labor-intensive. Each individual print is created with the hands-on skill of a printer—a person, not a machine. The finished art, though it can be reasonably large, is limited in size to what a person can handle. As I write this in 2012, photogravure, despite its beauty, intensity, and longevity, cannot rival ink-jet in the fine art market. But I am hoping that the audience for photographs printed using this very old process will grow larger as time passes.

At Crown Point, for about twenty-five years artists could incorporate photographs into their work by using photoetching, less complex than photogravure and at that time dependent on Kodak materials. In 2012, several different forms of photoetching requiring proprietary materials are marketed by companies and are widely used in printmaking, especially in schools. Photogravure, on the other hand, uses gelatin, photosensitized by the user, as its basic ground.

In 1991, we produced and released Crown Point's first major work in photogravure: Christian Boltanski's *Gymnasium Chases*. Boltanski's given name is Christian Liberté. He was born in Paris on September 6, 1944, just two weeks after it was liberated from the Nazis. *Gymnasium Chases* is a portfolio of twenty-four photogravures that show every member of a group photograph of students in one class at Gymnasium Chases, a Jewish high school in Vienna just before World War Two. We had started Boltanski's project at Folsom Street, where we did not have a darkroom, and had asked Jon Goodman, the printer who pioneered the use of photogravure in our times, to make the plates; he lives in Massachusetts.

It turned out that a tremendous amount of trial and error was necessary for Boltanski's unusual images, and Goodman had work of his own to do. We put the project aside and picked it up again after we built our darkroom. Goodman generously allowed our printer Daria Sywulak to spend a week learning from him in his studio, and after we moved to the Hawthorne Street building he spent a week in San Francisco with us giving Daria and Lothar Osterburg a crash course. "There were many problems," Daria remembers, "but we managed, with Jon's help, to bring everything together. Now all we had to do was make the Boltanski plates! Lothar and I struggled through an assortment of frustrating failures that December."

In January 1991, we sent Christian three proofs, which he liked very much. After that it took Daria and Lothar three months to make the rest of the plates and proof them so he could sign OK to Print proofs. "He was very, very happy," Daria reported. "I felt great. Now, all that was left was to

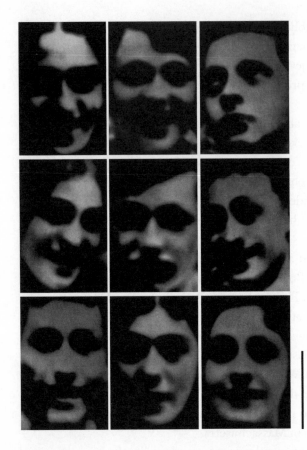

Christian Boltanski,
Gymnasium Chases, 1991.
Nine images from a portfolio
of 24 photogravures,
each 19 × 13¼ inches.

print twenty-five sets (fifteen in the edition and ten proofs), a total of six hundred prints." That year, besides the Boltanski project, we did two others in photogravure: Markus Raetz came from Switzerland, and John Baldessari from Los Angeles (see plate 33).

Anish Kapoor, who was born in 1954 in Bombay and lives in London, also worked in our new studio in 1991. This was his second project with us; the first was in 1988. Anish made intricate drawings on the plates, and a group of prints in which he hand-applied loose pigment to freshly inked and printed images made for this purpose. "My work has to do with coming to immateriality," he has said. "Apparently the concept of zero is an Indian invention. It implies vast emptiness and also it contains everything."

Judy Pfaff had worked with woodcut with us in Japan and then made very large woodcuts in our Folsom Street studio, but had resisted making etchings until she worked in our new building in 1991. She called her woodcut series *Six of One*, and the set of etchings is titled *Half a Dozen of the Other*. They are on very thin paper, and are subtle and beautiful. Valerie mounted a Judy Pfaff exhibition in our new gallery space to show the two sets of prints and also Judy's two woodcuts from Japan and an enormous sculpture that we borrowed.

In our gallery, in 1991 we also created a very large didactic show—without such a big space, we could not have done it. The exhibition was titled "Ink, Paper, Metal, Wood: How to Recognize Contemporary Artists' Prints." The following year we published, in association with the Trust for Museum Exhibitions, a handbook that I wrote explaining terms and concepts of printmaking. The Trust for Museum Exhibitions toured our show between 1993 and 1995, and it was exhibited in six small museums, including the Akron Art Museum, the David Winton Bell Gallery at Brown University in Rhode Island, and the University of Virginia Art Museum. I went on the road and gave talks at those three.

Anish Kapoor, *Untitled B*, 1991. Aquatint with hand-applied pigment, 36 × 29 inches. Anish with printers Daria Sywulak, Larry Hamlin, and Nancy Anello, 1991 (below).

An editor at Chronicle Books suggested to me that I expand my handbook *Ink Paper Metal Wood: How to Recognize Contemporary Prints*, into a book Chronicle would publish that would focus on identifying prints but also would be a picture book that would introduce our artists to a general audience. I wanted to do this, but I couldn't see how I could manage it. A year earlier when I had written my list of options, I said I might be too exhausted to continue our operations, especially if I had to do it alone. Of course, I did not have to do it alone; I had a dedicated and creative staff. But I was still exhausted. I thought it might have something to do with commuting every day across the bridge from Berkeley.

One morning on the way to work, stuck in traffic, standing still on an off-ramp to San Francisco, I looked out the car window at a factory-style building behind a big Hills Bros. Coffee sign, and said, "I want to live there." Tom and I talked about how, in the past, we had crossed the bridge and smelled the roasting coffee at that spot; we knew the coffee company had closed, and we hadn't noticed that particular building before. Later that day we rode our bicycles over there. The building we had seen from the freeway was newly constructed, designed to relate comfortably to the old coffee company's historic brick buildings clustered around a courtyard and fronting on the bay. The new building was built for mixed use, with stores below and condominiums above.

At Christmastime 1992, Tom and I moved into a small condominium at the Hills complex. Kevin's business was doing well enough that he was able to buy our Berkeley house so we could buy the condominium, which is an easy walk to the Crown Point Press building. I did become more productive after that, and the book for Chronicle was published in 1996 with the title *Ink Paper Metal Wood: Painters and Sculptors at Crown Point Press*. Chronicle Books was very good to me. My editor, Annie Barrows, told me to write as much as I could and we would edit it; my manuscript, when stacked up, was knee-high, and I learned something about editing after that. The book was beautifully designed by Laura Lovett, who—sixteen years later—has designed the book you are reading. Judith Dunham, who copyedited the Chronicle book, has edited all the books Crown Point has published since then.

The economy didn't improve until 1993 when Democrat Bill Clinton took office, and even then it was a guarded improvement, at least for Crown Point Press. As *New York Times* columnist Thomas Friedman pointed out in a column in June 2012, "We enjoyed a peace dividend, a dot-com dividend and a low-oil-price dividend, which combined to sharply reduce the Federal deficit." Clinton also cut spending and raised taxes. Our sales picked up at Crown Point, but not by enough to sustain our operation as it was then.

In 1993 I settled into a long-term strategy for the press, assuming ongoing economic stress in the world outside us. I already had laid off almost everyone with the title of "assistant," and Connie had gone back to the museum in Berkeley as a curator. "It is really the beginning of a new less-active era to lose Connie," I wrote in my daybook in June 1991. "Her arrival symbolized the busy time. I hired her in answer to it, and her presence fueled it, helping to put us in a position to get the building. But now, I have to face up to a real scaling down that is not temporary."

Until 1993 I hadn't been able to bring myself to lay off any printers, all so highly trained, but that year I narrowed our group down to three: Daria Sywulak, Larry Hamlin, and Renée Bott. Three is the correct number for the new world we are in; we continue to maintain that number nearly two decades later.

The four printers we lost in 1993 became independent forces in the print-making world. Pamela Paulson founded Paulson Press (now Paulson-Bott) in Berkeley. Lothar Osterburg founded Lothar Osterburg Photogravure in New York City and has also become a successful artist using the photogravure medium. Paul Mullowney started a press in Japan, then became director of Hui Press in Maui, Hawaii, a nonprofit where he instigated an ambitious and successful publishing program. In 2012 Paul moved back to San Francisco and started Mullowney Printing, a workshop with a publishing element. Brian Shure is teaching at the Rhode Island School of Design, where he has trained many serious printmakers, including several who have interned with us. He has written two books that we have published as part of our instructional series.

Kyle left in 1993 soon after the printers did. We had moved the gallery upstairs, as planned, and he didn't have enough to do after that. "You can't afford me," he said, "and Stacie can do the job." She is still doing it.

Finally, in 1994, Karen decided it was best to close the Crown Point Gallery in New York. Some years earlier she had married Jean-Yves Noblet, a silk-screen printer, and he had opened a workshop, Noblet Serigraphie, in the Chelsea district, destined to be "the new SoHo" but with little sign then of gallery

Karen McCready, 1995.

activity. "In the depths of the recession," I wrote later, "Karen created a professional gallery space within Jean-Yves's workshop, pioneering that part of town as a place to see art." She continued to represent Crown Point Press at Karen McCready Fine Art, and also she published prints that Jean-Yves printed.

About a year after Karen McCready Fine Art began, Karen was diagnosed with cancer. She died five years later in 2000 at the age of fifty-four. Karen formulated our Crown Point attitudes toward the public and made our work accessible; we weathered several storms in the business together and also traveled together, laughed together, had good times together.

Finally, I must mention one more death before I move on to happier aspects of the time. My mother died in 1997. She was eighty-nine and had had a long and productive life, but I thought she was indestructible and losing her was a blow to me.

Despite all the blows of the nineties, the decade ended well. To stay with the family for a moment, on December 4, 1999, just at the end of the twentieth century, my granddaughter, Tala Powis Parker, was born to my son, Kevin, and his companion, Camille Seaman. Crown Point Press also became full of promise in that I did begin to make some sense of what I was doing. In 1991, right after moving into the new building, I began to implement what would be an important part of a long-term strategy by restarting our workshops. Crown Point began with workshops, and when I designed our permanent space, I made sure we could accommodate them. We hold at least three workshops every summer, each a week long, and shorter ones on occasional weekends at other times of year. In each workshop, ten people can work, each at his or her own speed, in our studio with help from our printers.

We offer workshops, not classes. We don't have critiques because the workshops are not about the art; they are about the activity. On our website we have quotes from workshop participants. Here are a few, selected pretty much at random: "We all came in here with differing degrees of artistic and technical experience and different visions," wrote Kim Froshin, from San Francisco. "We were not compared to one another, but supported one another." Peter Kosowicz, from London, found the printers "extremely good at explaining the difficult processes in a manner that made it all seem straightforward and easy to cope with." "I loved this workshop," wrote Kelly Reemtsen, from Los Angeles. "I feel it made me a much better printer and somewhat of a better person." Carolyn Dodds, from Australia, said,

"Working here reassures me that art is a worthy pursuit."

Artists come to our workshops, and so do printers—we have had printers from many other presses, including Gemini, Pace, and Tandem, as well as small shops (my favorite is Slugfest, from Texas), joining in for a busman's holiday. Interested laypeople also come, sometimes print curators, sometimes people who collect prints and want to know firsthand how they are made. We have many participants from overseas. Essentially, our workshop audience resembles the make-up of the audience for the prints that we publish. Our most loyal customers are artists and nonprofit professionals—teachers, curators, people who care about art but don't necessarily have much money.

Valerie Wade officially became director of Crown Point after Karen set up her own business. Valerie has been closely involved with running the press since the early nineties. She and I together dreamed up the second step in our strategy for the future, after restarting the workshops. This is our Seasons Club. Club members in the summer can buy one editioned work at one-half the listed price if it is available in our regular inventory and is at least five years old—that is our definition of a club print.

The Seasons Club encourages people to look at our inventory, and also, because the best deal is available only in summer, it helps us get through a time when sales are usually slow. The secondary deal is that if a member wishes, he or she can buy another half-priced club print in each of the other seasons of the year if the purchase includes also a full-priced print—a new release, for example. We started the Seasons Club in the summer of 1991 and have continued it since then. Many of our artists are pleased that we're developing a younger, less affluent audience for their work than the one their primary dealers cultivate.

Writing and publishing books is also part of our long-term approach to business. That project began in the 1970s with our *Vision* magazine and continued with our artist-interview series called *View*. In the 1990s there were my two *Ink, Paper, Metal, Wood* versions. Then, under the direction of Sasha Baguskas, our publications director, who joined us in 1994, we went on to produce a series of "Magical Secrets" books about etching. You will hear about them in a future chapter. Because Amazon.com serves as a far-reaching distributor, book publishing has become profitable for Crown Point.

Our workshops, Seasons Club, and book publishing, however, remain satellites to our central purpose: publishing prints by artists. With fewer

Summer workshops at Crown Point, 2012.

printers, we do fewer projects than we did just prior to the nineties, but life at Crown Point Press continues to revolve around our artists. Whenever I give a public lecture, the question "How do you choose your artists?" is likely to be asked. It's a tough one to answer. We stake a lot on each project: our energy as well as our livelihood. We put the same kind of energy into our workshops, and when I get the question, usually I start by saying I would like to work with anyone who wants to use this time-consuming, ancient, hands-on way of art making, and in our workshops we do that. Publishing is something else.

We publish four to six artists a year, now that we have three printers. Valerie and I choose artists whose work we think is dealing with original ideas. We try to avoid being guided by personal taste—people mostly like what they know, and we hope to learn things we don't know. We look for artists with whom we, and our staff, will enjoy spending time, and we have an expectation that the work will last. I like to think the art of most of our artists will still be hanging in some homes and museums a hundred years from now. The artist must have some reputation already; we're not a discovery operation.

I'll tell you about our invitation to Per Kirkeby, a Danish artist we worked with in 1993, as an example. I had noticed a painting of his in a show at the Museum of Modern Art in New York in 1984, and in trying to describe it to Valerie, I resorted to the word *patchy*, which I thought of as an original quality. Nowadays it is likely that Valerie starts the conversation on an artist, but in Per's case I started it and she picked up the ball, keeping an eye out for his work as she traveled to various art fairs. We developed a clipping file on him. In 1992, when I read a review that described a painting of his as "like a load of laundry falling in super-slow motion," we asked him if he'd like to do a project at Crown Point. Per lives in Denmark, where he was born in 1938, and is a painter, sculptor, printmaker, geologist (his university degree is in geology), and writer (he has been elected a member of the Danish Literary Academy). He has said that painting is "the real reality" behind the "so-called reality" of our everyday experience. "We only see it in glimpses."

Per Kirkeby, *Inventory*, 1993. #3 and #4 from a portfolio of 18; image size varies.

I understand the notion of see-ing reality in glimpses, and I like the idea that Per Kirkeby (like John Cage and a few other artists we have pub-lished) has been successful in more than one line of work. But I am not

sure that any one reality is more real than any other. I like looking at art, and the realities I absorb from art influence the life that I, myself, live. For all my adult life, art has been for me not only a way of seeing and think-ing; it has also been the sole means of earning a living for myself and for others who both aid me and depend on me in that regard. In the 1990s, I exchanged a great deal of my art for a commercial building. Of course, after that, I did not give up making art and helping others make it. But, in addi-tion, I became a landlord.

In 1995 I signed a lease with an excellent tenant for the main floor of the building on Hawthorne Street. From the first moment Tom and I had started looking for a tenant, we had hoped for a restaurant, a good restaurant that would energize the building and be worthy of it, and that is what we eventually got. But by the time Anne and David Gingrass showed up, two well-known chefs, Paul Bertolli, formerly of Chez Panisse, and Joyce Goldstein, of Square One, had seriously considered our space and given up, mainly because of difficulties with the building code.

The Hawthorne Lane entrance; a ramp is invisible behind the vines (below). The bar area with Crown Point prints (opposite).

The problem would have been the same with any business, not just a restaurant. It is why we couldn't simply rent the space as soon as we realized we would need to. From the entrance, there are eight wide stair-steps down to the sidewalk on Howard Street, the well-traveled street connected to the convention center and the museum. The federally mandated Americans with Disabilities Act of 1990 had begun to be sporadically enforced as our plans were being made and the gallery space was being built—we had to install an elevator into the shipping area, for example. But our construction was completed before we discovered that the act specifies all front entrances to businesses must be wheelchair accessible. Our gallery had been given an occupancy permit, but no new business could get a permit for that space. (The Hawthorne Street entrance is accessible. It would have been a back way for wheelchairs into the rental space, but front-door access is required.)

David Gingrass solved the problem by making the third entrance to the building into a main entrance. This was a side door to Tom's Hawthorne Street studio at the time. By expanding that door further, David designed a grand restaurant entrance. It faces a small parking yard. David graded the yard so a gentle slope could take a wheelchair from it onto a ramp that he created inside the building's shell. Tom moved his studio to the Howard Street side.

David and Anne Gingrass left Postrio, Wolfgang Puck's restaurant in San Francisco, where David was manager and Anne was the head chef. They built their fine restaurant, Hawthorne Lane, in our building. It was large and welcoming with a bar facing Hawthorne Street. It was so successful that

our little street became quite famous; many people still think Hawthorne Street is named Hawthorne Lane. I had a food and drink credit earned from loaning our prints to the restaurant as part of its décor, and Tom and I, often with artists, spent a lot of time in the bar. We enjoyed Hawthorne Lane's presence in our building for fifteen years until its lease was up in 2010. It began in a recessionary period and also ended in one. We had some very good times there.

When I think of the good times we had at Hawthorne Lane, one of our artists in particular comes to mind: William Bailey. We published our first project with him in 1994 just as the restaurant was beginning its construction, and worked with him every other year or so through the end of the nineties and into the early 2000s. He enjoyed a drink at the end of the day, so every evening, before he made his way across the street to the hotel where our out-of-town artists usually stay, Tom, Bill, and I would hang out in the bar for a while. It was a curved bar, and the bartender and other customers sometimes joined in conversations. Bill drank Italian wine, Tom bourbon, and I would have a scotch—our friend the bartender poured us big ones—and we enjoyed the bar food of fried green beans and little crisp pieces of nori seaweed topped with chopped raw tuna.

Bill is good company and, having taught at Yale for many years, is used to varying points of view; he and Tom liked talking about art with one another though their approaches differ. Bill Bailey was born in 1930 in Iowa

William Bailey, *Viale*, 2002. Hard ground and soft ground etching with aquatint, 15 × 17¾ inches.

and studied at Yale before he taught there. He's often called a realist painter, but he steps back from that description. "Realism is about interpreting daily life in the world around us," he has said. "I'm painting a world that's *not* around us." Many of his paintings are of small pots laid out on tables; they are painted from memory. The pots are very lively. I wrote in our newsletter that I could imagine each of them as a small animal, poised for a look at me in that curiously contemplative way animals have. Bill, himself, has said he wants to bring to life "something with a presence, a silence, some sort of mystery." He works very slowly, building images in minuscule increments with hours of painstaking drawing.

Looking back on the nineties, I see the years as having moved like waves, falling into very deep depths when I lost four people close to me, but rising into crests as well. The highest crest for me (aside from my granddaughter's birth) was in 1997 when the National Gallery of Art, Washington, D.C., and the Fine Arts Museums of San Francisco celebrated the thirty-fifth anniversary of Crown Point Press and the archives each of them had acquired.

The National Gallery presented its exhibition first. It ran from June 8 to September 1. Ruth Fine installed it in a series of galleries just inside the main entrance to the soaring I. M. Pei–designed contemporary wing of the gallery. When I walked into the exhibition for the first time, I had a feeling that this couldn't be happening. My delight, my joy, was momentarily tempered by disbelief. It was like receiving a hard candy from Kokoschka (I only got one in

"Thirty-Five Years at Crown Point Press," National Gallery of Art, 1997.

the summer of studying with him), or like the slow smile of the refugee boy who pulled candies from the pocket of a donated coat. I was dazed.

At the entrance was a photomural of me, silhouetted against the windows of Crown Point's first workshop. And beyond it, the art my printers and I had produced for artists I knew so well, the work on the walls so familiar to me, so much loved by me, out there for great numbers of people to see, each work standing alone and together with the others. Ruth's installation was stunningly beautiful.

The National Gallery's trustees and its director Earl "Rusty" Powell hosted a cocktail party in the atrium, and many people connected with the museum complimented me. Several of our artists came down from New York, and most of our staff came from California. Karen was there, and Margarete. Suzanne Foley, who years earlier had been a curator at the San Francisco

Museum of Modern Art when it collected our prints, surprised me with a visit. I wish I could list here all the friends, artists, and supporters who were there. It was a truly touching tribute.

After the opening, there was a dinner party at the Cosmos Club, which is decorated with signed pictures of United States presidents and other celebrities. Tom and I didn't realize how formal it would be, and he dressed stylishly in a new black jacket (still his dress-up jacket fifteen years later) and collarless shirt. It turned out a tie was required. "But," Tom protested, "this is an Armani jacket. Doesn't that count for something?" "I'll have to seat you with your back to the room," the maître d' said. Tom loves to tell this story to demonstrate the difference between San Francisco and Washington, D.C.

We had a wonderful time in Washington. We went on a public tour of the White House; visited the Roosevelt Memorial, whose garden had been designed by an acquaintance from San Francisco; and walked up and down the Mall. We absorbed the splendid collection of the National Gallery and went to most of the other nearby museums. I remain grateful to Ruth and to all the people at the gallery for doing everything so graciously and well.

I am grateful also for the care and attention of Karin Breuer at the Fine Arts Museums of San Francisco. She mounted a different kind of exhibition. Of course, many of the prints were the same images as those shown in Washington, but Karin, having more space to work with, showed more prints in series and also a large group of working proofs by Wayne Thiebaud to demonstrate the making of his etching *Steep Street*. It was a complex and graceful installation, and was the featured exhibition at the California Palace of the Legion of Honor from October 4, 1997, through January 4, 1998.

The legion's spacious temporary exhibition galleries were new at the time. There are three, opening from a skylit space. After our exhibition, the skylight was covered—fear of light damage to artworks, I think, has caused it to be mostly unused. But for our show it provided an inviting and grand entrance gallery. The museum installed a small press under the skylight, and on the wall there were photo blowups of artists at work. Our printers gave demonstrations on weekends.

The opening was on a Friday evening; it was a grand event attended by a great many people. On Saturday the museum held a symposium. In the morning, Karin Breuer talked about the history of the press, I told some Crown Point Stories, and there were talks by two printers, Stephen Thomas and

Opening night of "Thirty-Five Years at Crown Point Press" at the Palace of the Legion of Honor, Fine Arts Museums of San Francisco, October 3, 1997.

Above: I am in the center with (left to right) Ruth Fine, Nathan Oliveira, Al Held, Tom Marioni, Bill Bailey, and Wayne Thiebaud. Below: One of the galleries in the exhibition.

Introducing the printers' panel. Hidekatsu Takada, Stephen Thomas, John Slivon, and Marcia Bartholme are on my right; Patrick Foy and Lilah Toland are behind me.

Daria Sywulak. In the afternoon Ruth Fine moderated a panel discussion with artists Pat Steir, Tim Rollins, Al Held, and Wayne Thiebaud.

Wayne, when asked about his large number of working proofs in the show, said something about how difficult it is to reconcile what you think you're doing with what the print thinks you should be doing. Some people describe hell, he said, as "a place where your elbows don't bend." But he added that "in the other place your elbows still don't bend, but you help feed each other. The wonder of working at Kathan's is that you are getting help, and that makes it a special kind of heaven." The talks and the panel were videotaped, and I used them as key parts of the *Ink, Paper, Metal, Wood* DVD that I later wrote and narrated.

At Crown Point Press on Saturday night, after the symposium, we held a printers' panel discussion, also taped. It meant a lot to me that many of our former printers came back "to the mother ship," as one of them put it, for the anniversary celebration. After the panel, there was a large dinner party for our staff and former staff, close friends, and longtime supporters. We held the dinner in our gallery; Hawthorne Lane catered it and Valerie coordinated. Afterward, we had a singer and a band for dancing.

At the dinner I gave out copies of a little book I had written called *Why Draw a Live Model?* Its subject is a replay of the Live Model Group that Crown Point held back in the 1960s. In redoing that workshop we had a model in the studio, and four local artists drew on plates. The book showed photos of them working and illustrated the etchings they made. In the text I talked about why each of them works from life. One of the artists, June Felter, had been in the original group almost thirty-five years earlier. I also included Fred Dalkey, a figurative artist from Sacramento; Enrique Chagoya, a young artist from San Francisco; and Nathan Oliveira, an old-timer, probably the Bay Area's most respected and loved artist at the time.

At the end of a tumultuous decade, the big wave that crested with Crown Point's two celebrations of its archive exhibitions in late 1997 settled down. My metaphorical ocean became full of rolling unbroken waves. We called them swells in my Florida childhood. I know that ocean well; it seems welcoming as the current carries you along. But I tell myself, Just remember: you'll need strength to return to shore, and even with strength you'll land a far distance up the beach from the place you think you're going.

At the opening with Karin Breuer (left) and Valerie.

Robert Bechtle in China, 1989.

18.

Do the Things You Want to Do

I met Robert Bechtle in the mid-1960s. The California Society of Etchers, to which I belonged, had merged with a lithography group, the Bay Printmakers, to which he belonged, and become the California Society of Printmakers. Bob and I were among a small group of printmaking society members who spent several days at the Legion of Honor museum working on a competitive print exhibition that was shown there. Hundreds of prints came by mail from all over the world. We opened the packages, organized the prints, and dragged them around for the juror, Gunter Troche, the director of the Achenbach Foundation for Graphic Art. Afterward, we packed up the rejects and sent them back to their respective artists. It was a time when jurors looked at actual art rather than at slides or computer files.

In 1967 I invited Bob to do a book in the *livres d'artistes* series I was publishing then. He proposed a title, *The Alameda Book*, and made four etchings, drawn with fine lines, of scenes in Alameda, the town across the bay from San Francisco, where he grew up. He is eighty years old in 2012 and has lived all his life in the San Francisco Bay Area. It is the subject matter of his art: suburban neighborhoods, automobiles, intersections with prominent street surfaces and stop signs.

Bob gave up *The Alameda Book* after making four plates. He said the images were "too ye-olde." I suggested he try another way of working, soft ground, that gives a crayonlike line, but he said he could do that in lithography—he had a lithography press set up in his garage. At the time, he was just beginning to find his mature style; it was the high time of pop art. "I guess

Robert Bechtle, *Alameda Camaro*, 1967.
Hard ground etching, 7½ × 9 inches.

back then," he said after we discovered the old *Alameda Book* plates in 2011, "we wanted everything to be brand new and terrific. Now I see a lot of connections to what I have done since. But in 1967, I suppose it seemed crazy to be so old-fashioned." We found the plates because in 2011 the cost of copper skyrocketed and we searched our basement for scrap copper that we could sell. Normally, after we have editioned a set of plates, we cut them up and sell them for scrap. But Bob's plates had not been editioned.   Carefully wrapped, they had survived forty-four years and the three times that Crown Point had moved from one studio to the next.

In 1982 Bob came back to Crown Point Press to make an ambitious three-panel color soft ground print titled *Sunset Intersection*. Between that year and 2011 he has done eleven soft ground prints with us, and a few monotypes, gravure prints, and woodcuts. His 2011 print, a soft ground etching of a San Francisco street titled *Three Houses on Pennsylvania Avenue*, is illustrated in plate 34.

Bob's world is the world we have learned to see in photographs. In looking at a photograph of a Bechtle painting, you could think it is a photograph of an actual scene. In the 1990s, philosophers often pointed out that everything we see—a landscape, a person, an object—is "mediated," separated from direct experience by our knowledge of how a camera lens sees things. Because Bob's scene is a camera's-eye view, it seems ordinary, not timeless. We sense that the light will be different in a few moments, the shadows stronger. A car will move. A person will appear. Nowadays some artist-photographers make models, build sets, or employ actors so they can set up their photographs to be unnerving by seeming to be timeless. Those artists are making photographs that imitate paintings. Robert Bechtle is making paintings that imitate photographs. To accomplish this, he builds them up one tiny mark at a time. Peter Schjeldahl, writing in the *Village Voice* in 1991, spoke of his "mysterious doggedness of depicting."

Robert Bechtle, *Sunset Intersection*, 1983.
Color soft ground etching in three panels
on one sheet of paper, 22 × 49¾ inches.

Bob in the Oakland
studio, 1983.

Bob has said that when he first began working from photographs, he
was "consciously trying to see how devoid of inherent interest" he could make
his paintings. "Photographs tend, of course, to be specific, so this was a challenge," he added. The world of commerce works hard to make its subjects
interesting and entice us with them. Pop artists use commercial methods to
make paintings that are as arresting as the ads on which they are based. Bob,
and other realists of the late twentieth century, made their art workmanlike
instead: "Just the facts, ma'am." They share this attitude with minimal and
early conceptual artists who developed at about the same time.

My subtitle for this chapter comes from Ed Ruscha, who said in a 1990
interview, "Just do the things you want to do, make the kind of pictures you
want to make." Ed's work looks very different from Bob's, but like Bob, Ed
takes a "just the facts" point of view. "I was trained and sort of programmed to

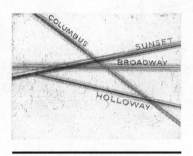

Ed Ruscha, *Motor City*, 2009. One from a portfolio of seven color hard ground etchings with aquatint, 7 × 6½ inches.

Ed Ruscha, *Columbus, Sunset*, 2001. From *Los Francisco San Angeles*, a portfolio of seven color soft ground etchings, each 4 × 5½ inches.

think like an abstract expressionist, and I was part of that for a while," he has said. "It became a question of either loading the brush with color and attacking a canvas—or something else, something preconceived. I took the second way."

The two artists who share this chapter are both from California and are both painters. Ed Ruscha, five years younger than Robert Bechtle, has lived in Los Angeles since 1956, when he arrived there from Oklahoma to attend art school. The subject matter of much of Ed's art reflects Los Angeles and its surroundings: gas stations, billboards, desert spaces, words isolated against sky. Ed, like Bob, is an active printmaker and has worked in lithography with at least two Los Angeles print shops as well as in etching with us. He came to Crown Point Press for the first time in 1982 and made a dark blue aquatint of the big dipper in a desert sky. He also made a set of three soft ground etchings of carefully lettered words. *Metro, Petro, Neuro, Psycho* (plate 35) is one of them. In his paintings Ed often uses words as subject matter. One of the etchings on this page is part of a series that mixes street names from Los Angeles and San Francisco.

When Ed works with photographs, they are generally snapshots he has taken himself and then presented in books. He produced the first of his books, *Twenty-six Gasoline Stations*, in 1962. When he published it in 1963 it

Ed Ruscha in the San Francisco Folsom Street studio, 1988.

had no precedent, but the idea of accumulating images of ordinary, ongoing things or actions was in the air. Andy Warhol, in New York, made the first of his famous films, called *Sleep*, that same year.

To Ed, *Twenty-six Gasoline Stations* was "a straightforward case of getting factual information and bringing it back." He talked about this with Patricia Failing, who quoted him in an article for *Art News* in 1982. "I had this idea for a book title—*Twenty-six Gasoline Stations*—and it became like a fantasy rule in my mind that I knew I had to follow. Then it was just a matter of being a good little art soldier and going out and finishing it."

Ed was a young artist, only twenty-five, in 1962. That year his work was shown in an exhibition called "New Painting of Common Objects" at the Pasadena Art Museum. The exhibition included Andy Warhol and Roy Lichtenstein, two artists from New York who were soon to be identified as key figures of pop art. Ed Ruscha's painting of the 20th Century Fox logo, *Large Trademark with Eight Spotlights*, 1962, is considered a pop art classic, as is his painting of a Standard station done a year earlier. But if you compare bodies of work by Ruscha, Warhol, and Lichtenstein, Ruscha doesn't fit the pop art category. "It is always too simple to reduce an activity to a category," he has said. "I have drawn from everything which is around me."

Stanley Grinstein, a partner in the Los Angeles fine art print press Gemini G.E.L., reported in an interview for the book *Rebels in Paradise* an interesting conversation he had with New York sculptor Richard Serra sometime in the 1970s:

> *Serra said, "I know the difference between California artists and New York artists." I said, "Really? What is it?" He said, "When New York artists make a work of art, they think how is it going to fit into the continuum, who is going to write about it, who is going to publish it and how many pictures. When L.A. artists make art, they just make art about how they feel."*

The book's author, Hunter Drohojowska-Philp says, "The remark was clearly meant to be insulting." I'm sure that's true—in the early days I heard remarks meant to be funny and insulting to California artists from some of the New York artists working with me.

When I read Grinstein's recollection, I thought that although advanced California artists at the time were not making art "about how they feel," they would not have found the accusation insulting. They would have been insulted, however, if someone had described them in the way Serra described himself. California artists, from both the north and the south, had then (and, I believe, in general, still have) what Ed Ruscha has said is an "almost priest-like commitment to working." He added that he, himself, "had to commit myself, in this way, to painting." The abstract expressionist painters in New York legendarily held this attitude; the pop artist Andy Warhol deliberately undermined it.

Los Angeles has a population of almost four million; San Francisco has less than one million. Los Angeles is seventy-five miles wide, San Francisco seven miles wide. Los Angeles has movie studios, warm weather, and beaches. San Francisco has complex wine and food, cool summers, warm winters, and a tradition of incubating cultural and creative movements from the beat poets to rock music to gay liberation to the dot-com revolution.

Los Angeles has developed more support for its artists than San Francisco,

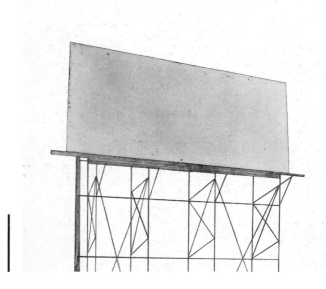

Ed Ruscha, *Your Space #1*, 2006. Sugar lift flat bite with hard ground etching, 19¾ × 23¾ inches.

but that may be a function of its size and the movie industry's appreciation of novelty—maybe, also, of L.A.'s relative youth as a city. Principally through its Hammer Museum (affiliated with the University of California, Los Angeles) and its Museum of Contemporary Art, it has demonstrated a healthy pride about the advancing edge of its culture. This may change, however, as museum personnel change.

San Franciscans support their city's museums well, and the museums, principally the San Francisco Museum of Modern Art, organize exciting shows by living artists from New York, Europe, and occasionally California. SFMOMA has given retrospectives to both Ed Ruscha (1982) and Robert Bechtle (2005). However, as a tradition, there is not much connection here between local museums and local artists or local galleries—the active art looking and art buying are done in New York or Los Angeles. Artists and art dealers are used to this, and they adjust. Richard Serra and some other New York artists, particularly of his generation, are so entrenched in New York that they may not realize that the creative people who are in California want to be here. "It was a badge of honor of that older group [from L.A.] that you didn't kowtow to the New York artists," Grinstein explained, remembering the early days of Gemini when the two groups mingled at his home.

I must add that the New York artists whom I know, along with the ones from California and around the world, are dedicated to art, and that the art dealers (in New York or otherwise) whom I most respect are like Gavin Brown as he has described himself: "with a sense of pride . . . that somehow you're in the orbit of something you believe will continue to have some positive effect on our ability to survive."

However, in 2012, we have a worldwide situation in which forces in the real world have connected with the Warhol side of the art world to create an out-of-kilter scene described by critic Jerry Saltz in the April 30, 2012, issue of *New York* magazine: "Art became news. Prices were equated with artistic value. The highest sellers were seen as the best artists. . . . Wherever money went, art followed (it should be the other way around)." Saltz's judgment is that "it remains to be seen whether high prices are the global warming of the art world, imperiling an entire ecosystem."

Most people in the United States have pulled back on spending during the decade that Saltz is describing, but a few have become richer and a few of them are spending wildly on art. Millions of dollars are paid for what Saltz describes as "boat-size paintings and sculptures, spotless installation extravaganzas, and other lobbylike spectacles produced by well-funded artists and teams of assistants." Saltz hopes that the museum directors and art dealers involved with

Ed Ruscha, *Big Dipper Over Desert*, 1982. Aquatint printed in blue, 24 × 36 inches.

Ed in the Oakland studio, 1982.

this work "may all thrive in Dubai," and adds that "the Establishment itself acknowledges that all the energy is on the romantic fringes."

The artists on the fringes, Saltz explains, are engaged in running galleries, organizing street performances, and coordinating Internet-advertised events. This kind of activity has been around in California at least as long as it has been in New York—the artist-run alternative art space movement began in San Francisco. So did *Artforum* magazine, but it quickly moved to Los Angeles and rented space above the Ferus Gallery, an influential gallery of the 1970s run by artists and a brilliant young director/curator named Walter Hopps. The best artists and art professionals, no matter where they live, do the things they want to do and promote the evolving world of art as best they can.

For Robert Bechtle in Northern California and Ed Ruscha in Southern California, doing what they want to do has meant making art by working hands-on, deadpan, with care and attention, "being a good little art soldier." They both have sustained the respect of other artists for decades, and both of them have gained a stardom that is likely to last.

My self-portrait on the way to the North Pole, 2002.

19.

KEEP SEARCHING FOR WHAT YOU NEED TO KNOW

Bill Clinton was finishing up his eight-year presidency when I decided to go to the North Pole. The economy had settled down, people were buying prints again, and the Crown Point Press house was in order, functioning well in its smaller size under Valerie's direction. I was eager for another of my own infrequent travel/book projects, and I told myself that this one would fit into the book publishing strategy we were following as part of a plan to somewhat diversify our business. Mostly, I needed a big, non-work-related trip.

When I planned my trip, I had no way of knowing that President Clinton had had a sexual engagement with a White House intern, and consequently the 2000 election would be so close that Supreme Court justices could appoint a Republican president by stopping a recount in Florida that likely would have tipped the vote to the Democratic side. George W. Bush put the country into an economic crisis that mimicked the one that changed the lives of my parents; in 2008 industrial production in the United States fell as much as it had in the early years of the Great Depression, and in 2012 it has only somewhat recovered. If this book were a novel, you might be saying, "Unbelievable," but you know those political events occurred. If I had known in 2002 what we all know now, I might not have spent money on a trip to the North Pole or time on writing a book about it. Looking back, however, I'm glad I didn't know.

Before I tell you about the trip, I'm going to pick up my narrative where I paused it in 1997 after the celebrations of Crown Point's thirty-fifth year. I'm thinking of this chapter as a tour through fifteen years beginning in 1997

Robert Colescott, *Pontchartrain*, 1997. Color sugar lift
and spit bite aquatints with etching and drypoint on
four sheets of paper, 41 × 117 inches overall.

and ending in 2012, Crown Point's fiftieth year, the year in which I am writing. The North Pole is a plateau, a resting place on the way.

The biggest artist project we did in 1997 was with Robert Colescott, an African American artist born in Oakland, California, in 1925; his father was a railroad Pullman porter and a jazz musician. Bob Colescott died in 2009. Roberta Smith, in her obituary about him in the *New York Times,* wrote that he "was well known for pitting the painterly against the political to create giddily joyful, destabilized compositions that satirized, and offended, without regard to race, creed, gender or political leaning. . . . He said he wanted his surface to 'squirm.'" The print Bob made with us is nearly ten feet long (in four panels). He titled it *Pontchartrain* after a New Orleans district where he once lived. Even in the small reproduction on this page, you can see that in this print the surface squirms.

Etchings by two artists, Nathan Oliveira, from the San Francisco Bay Area, and Richard Tuttle, from New York, are threads running through the decade of Crown Point history from the mid-nineties to the mid-2000s. In that period, we worked regularly with both. Nathan Oliveira, who taught at Stanford University near San Francisco for most of his adult life, died in 2010 at the age of eighty-one. He did seven projects with us between 1994 and 2007. Richard Tuttle, born in 1941, had his first show at the Betty Parsons

Gallery in New York in 1965. He spent a week with us in the etching studio every summer from 1998 through 2005.

Nathan Oliveira and Richard Tuttle are artists at opposite ends of the contemporary art spectrum. They both created/create their work in a tactile way, sensually, from the inside out, without much concern for "the continuum," the ongoing flow of art ideas in history. Nathan was a painter, working traditionally, often from a live model. Richard is a sculptor, subverting tradition, working from a world inside his own consciousness.

"Given all the technology that we're in the middle of," Nathan said to me, "I would be so pleased if someone would look at one of these prints and say, 'You know, sometimes I feel like that.'" Consider an image from his final project with us, 2007. It is printed in warm brown against red ochre. The model has one foot solidly on the ground, the other braced against her calf. She stands straight and very still, her arms so inactive as to have become invisible; she stretches upward, elongating herself. Inside your own body, have you not felt, at times, the way this figure looks? I have.

Nathan in the studio (above). Nathan Oliveira, *Standing Figure*, 2007. Color sugar lift and spit bite aquatints with hard ground etching, 45 × 36 inches.

"In our culture," Richard has said, "there is a job for art, because we can't experience reality anywhere else." The San Francisco Museum of Modern Art organized a retrospective of his work in 2005 and traveled it to several museums around the country, including the Whitney Museum of American

Richard working on *Deep, in the Snow*.

Richard Tuttle, *Deep, in the Snow*, 2005. A wall construction of a large intaglio print with wooden supporting slat and a copper wire basket containing 12 smaller prints, 32 × 28 × 3¾ inches overall.

Art in New York. *Time* magazine called Richard a "man of small things" and "a genuine, if highly idiosyncratic, American master."

Richard's art seems simple at a glance but becomes oddly complex as you give it attention. If you are willing to go along with it, it opens up after a while and takes you somewhere else, a hopeful place. "I just think that people who have art in their lives have better lives," he said in an easily grasped remark. His wife, the poet Mei-Mei Berssenbrugge, once told me, "You can only use forty percent of what he says." At Crown Point, the printers and I loved Richard's logic, sometimes revelatory, sometimes mystifying. The first day he walked into the Crown Point studio, for example, he said, "A printing plate is material that is immaterial. The print has complete integrity right from the start."

In the spectrum of art being made during the time in which we are living, there are a lot of wavelengths, and one of art's pleasures, to me, is getting on one of those wavelengths with an artist. Suspend judgment. See where it leads. It's almost like a carnival ride, except that I keep trying to make sense of it. One way of making sense (the most useful one, I think) is to look at the approach the artist is taking.

In 1999, just before the new century appeared, I looked at landscape, an old-fashioned approach to art, and broke it down into specific sub-approaches taken by eleven different artists. I explored the approaches using an old-fashioned form: a book, sold as a book and also as a companion to a portfolio of original prints. I asked each of the artists to talk with me about the subject and to create a small print. We produced the prints in editions of fifty, with twenty reserved for the portfolios. Here, I'll describe three examples from the eleven in the book, *Why Draw a Landscape?*

Sylvia Plimack Mangold, *Pin Oak Detail,* 1999. Color drypoint with spit bite aquatint, 11 × 9 inches.

Sylvia Plimack Mangold, a painter who is the subject of the chapter on *investigation,* is on the cover of the book, standing at an easel in a field, painting a portrait of a tree on a large canvas. She always works "firsthand," she says, outside or looking out a window. "My body sees it," she adds. "I'm standing in the landscape or a few feet away. And I want you to have a physical sense of the space. If you were a bird, you could fly through it." Sylvia was born in 1938 and lives on a farm in Washingtonville, New York, with her husband, artist Robert Mangold.

David Nash, who represents *illustration* in the book, is an English sculptor born in 1945. He uses trees to make his work. He often carves, in place, trees that have died, and frequently those works stay where he made them. His major ongoing work is a dome of living ash trees on the property where he lives in the Ffestiniog Valley in Wales. Since he planted the trees in 1977, he has been mulching, pruning, and grafting them to encourage the dome shape. David's print for our portfolio is an illustration that he drew of the actual work of art, the ash dome. Conceptual artists often make art with unusual materials in unusual places, and sometimes they illustrate it with photos, drawings, or texts that function in art collections as stand-ins for the actual works.

Bryan Hunt, born in 1947, is a sculptor who in my landscape book represents *exploration*. He experimented with earth works when he was a student. "So much was going on about materials," he remembers, naming some unusual ones: lead, rubber, latex, string, wire. "Bronze had such a bad name." In his mature work he is exploring energy, trapping it in weighty bronze sculptures or heavily worked prints of the moving changing forms of water or other unstable entities—his print for our portfolio is inspired by the forms of cairns, heaps of stones hikers use to mark a trail.

Valerie put together many one-person shows at Crown Point in this period, in addition to our normal group exhibitions. In 1998 Bryan Hunt had a one-person show in our gallery; we borrowed sculpture to exhibit along with prints from the

Cairn 1, a sculpture by Bryan Hunt, with his prints *Cairn 1* and *Cairn 2* in his exhibition in the Crown Point gallery, 1998.

five projects he had done with us. In 1997 it was exciting to see two big paintings of Robert Colescott's, along with his new print. Colescott represented the United States in the Venice Biennale that year.

In 2000 Chris Burden shipped from Los Angeles a bridge he had made entirely of Erector Set pieces. It took up almost half the gallery's floor space, and a big drawing took up half the wall space. That year we had published three large color photogravures in which Burden developed the Erector Set theme, and we showed those as well. In 2001 we had an exhibition of the prints and sculpture of Markus Raetz, and in 2005 when Richard Tuttle's retrospective was on view at the San Francisco Museum of Modern Art, around the corner from us, we mounted a print retrospective for him, borrowing his print works from other publishers to add to our own projects.

In 2000, one year after *Why Draw a Landscape?*, I wrote and Crown Point published *John Cage Visual Art: To Sober and Quiet the Mind*. Karin Breuer, of the Achenbach Foundation, exhibited at the Palace of the Legion of Honor the entire set of prints in John's series called *Dereau*, 1982. One of the images is illustrated here; another is in color in plate 3. The title is a contraction of *décor* and *Thoreau*. In the prints, there is a stable framework of images from Thoreau's journals. Those images stay the same, except for color changes; they provide the décor. Other elements (circles, lines, rectangles) move around, and appear and disappear throughout the series. A horizon line changes position in each print.

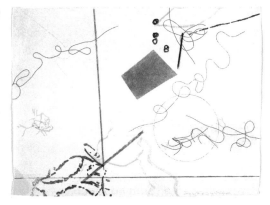

John Cage, *Dereau #10*, 1982. One in a series of 38 color etchings with aquatint, engraving, photoetching, and drypoint, 18½ × 24½ inches.

We had printed two sets of the *Dereau* etchings, one set to be kept together, the other to be dispersed, the prints sold separately. I gave the Achenbach Foundation (as part of our archive) the set of thirty-eight prints that John said should be kept together. In the book I talk about how he used maps and scores to create the prints, and I illustrate all the works in the series. I also illustrate and discuss *HV2*, 1992, John's last work in which he kept one set together, and a sampling of his other etchings, watercolors, and drawings. Ever since John died, I had been thinking about writing something about his visual art, and Karin's show was the impetus for me to do that. In our Crown Point Gallery, parallel to the exhibition at the Legion of Honor, we had a John Cage exhibition, showing his art's development over the years.

Valerie and I, by 2000, had enough confidence in our—and our country's—economic recovery that Valerie made a trip to Switzerland to meet with the organizers of the Basel Art Fair to see if we could revive our connection with the fair. Crown Point's first expedition into the international world of art commerce had been at the Basel fair in 1977, and we had a booth there again in 1978. After that, the fair limited its booths for editions, then moved them to a separate floor. Karen oversaw a Crown Point booth there in 1984,

With Valerie in the Crown Point booth at Basel, 2004.

1985, and 1986. Margarete showed our prints in her booth in 1987. We then were absent from Basel for more than a decade, although we were participating regularly in the International Fine Print Dealers Association (IFPDA) fair in New York and other fairs in the United States. The fair in Basel is the most prestigious in the world of art fairs. It is difficult to secure booth space, and once you are accepted there is no guarantee you will be accepted in subsequent years. When our application was accepted for 2001, we were pleased, and continue to be pleased to have exhibited at the Basel Art Fair every summer from 2001 through 2012. In 2001, back at Basel, I felt as if Crown Point had found its way back to the yellow brick road after having strayed from it.

My North Pole trip was the following summer, 2002. I flew to Oslo, then to Spitsbergen in the archipelago of Svalbard. Spitsbergen is a little town mainly occupied by scientists (there is a Norwegian university). It is the nearest inhabited place to the North Pole. Many serious dogsled expeditions have started there. I took an easier way, a tourist trip on a Russian icebreaker named *Yamal*; the name translates from Russian to mean "end of the earth."

Yamal is nuclear powered. It is a working ship, launched in 1992 as part of a fleet that breaks ice for freighters traveling the Russian coast and through the Bering Strait to routes in the Pacific Ocean. The North Pole (unlike the South Pole, which is on land) is surrounded by an expanse of frozen ocean. The spot cannot be marked; the ice above is always moving. There is truly nothing there. When I went to the North Pole, no ship had ever been able to reach it without the force of nuclear power to break its surrounding ice. But as I write this only ten years later, the ice sheet has melted to such an extent that diesel-powered ships can make the trip.

Yamal is solitary in summertime. In the week we were aboard, after we left Spitsbergen we saw one group of walruses and one polar bear. There were no other animals, and only occasional birds. There were no ships. There were no planes. The sun never set. There was a line at the horizon but often no difference above or below it. *Yamal* was alone in an expanse of white, but she was not quiet. There was no meditation. She would ram against the ice sheet with a great shuddering, then back up with a sustained grinding noise, then ram again, over and over until a great glistening pale blue prism the size of an SUV appeared, followed by another and another, water dripping and freezing immediately into icicles. The grinding and banging were punctuated by the sharp cracking sound of splitting ice as dark blue fissures more than twelve feet deep opened at our sides. Some of these split delicately with an almost tuneful sound, and others opened quickly with a sound like a rifle shot.

In my cabin, I climbed onto a narrow ledge with my camera and pushed my head and arms out the open window, pulling in after each photo to warm myself and keep the camera from freezing. Hours passed. Days passed, some of them relatively quiet as we moved through leads, nudging ice interlaced with blue pools. When we stopped for the polar bear, we were in a place not permanently frozen, but as soon as we stopped, ice formed close around us. The bear was confident and unhurried. He walked completely around the ship and halted at the spot where I was standing at the rail. Suddenly his spine unfolded upward from his hind legs like a jointed doll's, each vertebra rising effortlessly above the last. A white unfolding, enormous, ten feet high, and the head only a short distance below me. The steady eyes looked up and met mine. If I had not been safely out of reach, it would have been different, but since I had no reason to

The polar bear, 2002.

fear, I held his gaze. The bear, his curiosity satisfied, folded himself down and stood watching us as we started our engines and pulled away.

I put 120 photographs into my book titled *The North Pole*, published in 1994. It is a long, inquiring collage of pictures, stories, and information. For my text I interviewed fellow travelers, scientists, and experts in the history of the exploration of the Far North. I interleaved the interviews with a narrative of my trip and excerpts from a journal by Fridtjof Nansen, who a hundred years ago traveled by dogsled on part of the route we took. Nansen, incredibly, made it home alive. On July 24, 1895, the day he realized he and his companion would survive, he wrote:

> *At last the marvel has come to pass—land, land, and after we had almost given up our belief in it! After nearly two years, we again see something rising above that never-ending white line on the horizon yonder—a white line which for countless ages has stretched over this lonely sea, and which for millenniums to come shall stretch in the same way.*

Nansen, oh Nansen, how I wish that were the case! As I write, it is only a century since you were on the lonely sea, and not even a decade more is possible for an unchanging Arctic.

My next book, *Magical Secrets about Thinking Creatively: The Art of Etching and the Truth of Life*, published in 2006, is short and to the point. The *Magical Secrets* series, which my "thinking creatively" book introduced, became a set of four how-to books accompanied by DVDs. After my introductory volume, Crown Point master printers wrote the other three: Catherine Brooks, who was with us from 2002 to 2006, wrote one about line; Brian Shure wrote about chine collé; and Emily York, who in 2012 has been at Crown Point seven years and is our senior master printer, wrote about aquatint. I edited the texts before sending them to our regular editor. All the books Crown Point Press has published since 1997—there are nine counting the one you are reading— have been produced on a computer in-house by Sasha Baguskas, who in 2012 is in her eighteenth year at Crown Point Press. We send the books to Hong Kong to be printed.

Our *Magical Secrets* books include instructional DVDs that Javier Briones made with the authors and edited in-house. Javier, born in Guatemala, joined us in 2005 as a student in the Antioch College job program and continued on with us after he graduated. I have been shooting video footage of most of our Crown Point artist projects since the late seventies, and have accumulated a lot of tapes; Javier edited some of them and also shot, edited, and put on our website many new ones. Since Javier left us, I've been trying to learn video editing myself and have added some new short video pieces to our site.

Crown Point Press has had a website, www.crownpoint.com, since 1997,

The Crown Point staff, 2011. I am at far left. Standing, from left to right: Tiffany Harker, Asa Muir-Harmony, Mari Andrews, Ianne Kjorlie, and Emily York. Kneeling: Sasha Baguskas, Stacie Scammell, and Valerie Wade.

earlier than most other businesses in our field, thanks to a young gallery assistant named Bao Vo, who was with us from 1996 through 2003. The website was his idea, and we let him run with it and gave him time to learn on the job. With publication of the first *Magical Secrets* book we started a second website, www.magical-secrets.com, to emphasize the process of printmaking, and we continue to maintain both sites. They are both highly trafficked.

Our staff is small again in 2012. In the photo on this page we are holding our "instruments," connecting, as we frequently do, with Peter Drucker's analogy of the orchestra, a collection of skilled specialists working cooperatively. We are nine people, including three printers. In 2008, with two of our local artists, Gay Outlaw and Susan Middleton, and with Griff Williams, a colleague in the print business, our staff organized a debate party at Crown Point to raise money to help elect Barack Obama president of the United States. We had a big crowd, laughing and cheering. Our downstairs restaurant, Hawthorne Lane, provided food, and we raffled one of our prints. We raised $10,000. We had enthusiasm then; we had hope.

Four years later, with another election imminent, we hope to avert bringing the "trickle-down" economy back in full swing. I cover my ears so as not to hear the bitter epithets that fill the airwaves—just the other day the Republican presidential candidate, playing to crazy "birthers," who question Obama's citizenship, called the president's politics "foreign." The *New York Times* reports that "powerful undercurrents of identity, wealth, race, and religion are shaping this election," undercurrents stirred up by advertising brought on by the Supreme Court's invalidation of long-standing campaign contribution laws. Millions of dollars are being spent to cement tightly into place the loss of confidence in our government that began with the assassination of President Kennedy long ago. Reading this, you know (as, writing it, I cannot know) whether that loss of confidence translated into a Republican victory in November 2012.

Did you notice in the Crown Point staff photo that we are all women? Never before, in fifty years, have we been for any lengthy period without men in our "orchestra." Also, it is possibly a coincidence, but the members of one of our workshops this summer were all women; men traditionally dominate the printmaking field and usually provide about half of our workshop attendance. Finally, on this subject: In the dozen years since 2000, Crown Point Press has published thirteen women artists new to us, and nine men. In our history overall, we have published fewer women than men because until now it has been much more difficult to sell the work of women than of men. Now that no longer seems to be true. I don't think it matters to the market today whether a young artist is a woman or a man.

Who are the artists of the new century, the young artists new to Crown Point Press in the years roughly between 2000 and 2012? Are there generalizations that can be made about them? With that question in mind, I marked up an article in the *New York Times Sunday Book Review*, July 22, 2012. It concerns a new novel by Dave Eggers and contains some ideas that seem to fit, in a loose and general way, the artists who have worked at Crown Point lately.

The review of Eggers's book is by nonfiction writer Pico Iyer. He compares Eggers to Norman Mailer and says Eggers, who was born in 1970, is from "a much more sober, humbled, craft-loving time." Iyer sees Eggers's novel *A Hologram for the King* as "almost a nostalgic lament for a time when life had stakes and people worked with their hands, knew struggle." He writes, "A sense of impermanence and possible disaster is always very close in Eggers's work . . . and that is what makes his good nature and hopefulness so rending, and so necessary."

Our artists, in their own studios and ours, struggle and work with their hands, so they don't have the nostalgia Iyer describes (though perhaps our customers do). And a sense of impermanence is recognizable throughout our society. Iyer's third point, however, strongly applies to the group of artists I am styling as members of the new century. They all show good nature and hopefulness.

Mary Heilmann, whose aquatint *21st Century Fox* is in plate 36, worked with us earlier and is older than the others in this group. I put her here, however, because she fits so well. Mary was born in 1940 in San Francisco, grew up in Southern California, and lives in New York. Critic Dave Hickey sees her as part of "the last generation for whom being an American seemed an intriguing and exciting proposition." The apparent nonchalance of her images is built with careful work that begins with making drawings using a computer.

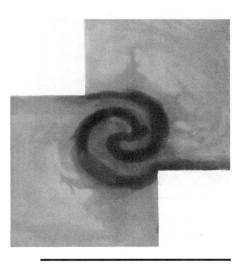

Mary Heilmann, *Undertow*, 2006. Color aquatint printed on gampi paper chine collé, 12 × 12 inches.

Anne Appleby, born in 1954, grew up in Pennsylvania and at seventeen moved to Montana, where she still mainly lives; she also has a studio in San Francisco. Anne's biggest influence is an apprenticeship she served with an Ojibwe elder in Montana. She gained a habit of patient and continuing observation, and her paintings, though they appear to be abstract, are in most cases portraits of plants. Her portrait of sage is in plate 37. Each panel in a painting represents a different part of the plant—a leaf, the fruit or seed, the bud or flower—or the plant in a different season or stage of growth. Anne paints nature changing. "I'm fascinated by the cusp of things," she has said.

Laurie Reid, Gay Outlaw, and Brad Brown all live in the San Francisco Bay Area. Laurie Reid has made a reputation for delicate, large, abstract watercolors, but in printmaking she chose to work relatively small. "Printmaking is imposing in itself," she said. "When I put the prints on the wall, they stood

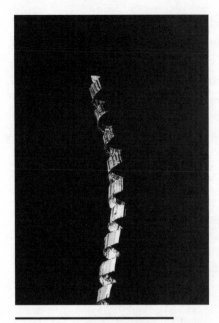

Gay Outlaw, *Tailing*, 1995.
Photogravure, 13¾ × 9½ inches.

up and stared right back at me." Reid was born in 1964. Gay Outlaw's unusual name is the one she was born with, in Alabama in 1959. She is a sculptor who trained as a pastry chef and began her art career creating a work of sculpture from fruitcake and another from caramel. She also studied photography. To make the photogravure illustrated here, *Tailing*, she first fashioned a small temporary form out of aluminum foil.

Brad Brown, born in 1964, studied in the mid-eighties at Virginia Commonwealth University, moved to New York in 1986, and then to San Francisco in 1989. As a student, he told me, he was "surrounded by nihilistic painting, coming out of punk. You were supposed to develop attitude. Everyone was posing. Everyone wanted to get rich and famous, but of course we hadn't done any work to get rich and famous with." He hopes now to make art that is "socially responsible, transformative, and magical," art that "changes daily life." He handles his art casually, allowing stains and accidental marks to accumulate along with the marks he draws, and he often tears large sheets of drawings into smaller pieces that he groups together in random order.

None of these artists seem very concerned about "the continuum," I thought. Then I remembered that Brad once said to me, "John Cage is always in my mind. But so is de Kooning." I told him Cage's story of an argument he once had with de Kooning in a restaurant. There were bread crumbs on the paper-covered table and, drawing a line around them, de Kooning said, "That isn't art."

"But," John explained to us, long ago at Crown Point Press, "I would say that it was." In his eyes, de Kooning had made the bread crumbs art by selecting them and framing them, but in de Kooning's eyes he had made a point, not art. I said to Brad that to me Cage and de Kooning are essentially incompatible. Brad said he hoped to adapt both of them to his own ends. This is different from how my generation learned to pursue knowledge. Ideas come now in bits and pieces, not in a continuum where one idea leads to another or is necessarily compatible with another.

Looking at a list of Crown Point "new century" artists, I am surprised at how few of them are living in New York. Kiki Smith, born in 1954, lives there, is deeply embedded there, but her art is eccentric, not part of a movement with a name. Kiki has made a good deal of art about the body: its makeup, its functions, its fluids, and what inhabiting it feels like. She is also interested in puppets, fairy tales, and animals, and these have made their way into some of her work. A retrospective exhibition, "Kiki Smith: a Gathering," organized by the Walker Art Center, Minneapolis, was at the San Francisco Museum of Modern Art in 2005 and traveled to the Whitney Museum of American Art in New York the following year.

Four more artists on my list live in New York: Shahzia Sikander, Fred Wilson, Julie Mehretu, and Amy Sillman. With Kiki Smith, they bring the number of New Yorkers to five out of the eighteen artists who are new to Crown Point in this century. But even the artists living in New York are less New York–centric than those we have worked with in the past. They are so different from one another, it's hard to find connections.

Shahzia Sikander was born in Pakistan in 1969. She has lived in this country, mainly in New York, about twenty years. "I think of myself as an American," she says, "but I also feel that I have a privileged place from which to express things through art." That position carries a strong undercurrent of possible disaster but, in general, remains hopeful; notice in the illustration on this page that the guns are tied in knots. In Shahzia's

Shahzia Sikander, *Entangled*, 2001. Color photogravure with soap ground and spit bite aquatints and soft ground etching printed on gampi paper chine collé, 10 × 7½ inches.

studies in Pakistan before coming to the United States, she learned "respect for tradition and respect for patience." She draws precisely, often using a computer to change and reuse an image she has drawn. She employs layers of drawings, frequently juxtaposing loosely painted shadowy figures with images that are uncannily detailed.

Fred Wilson was born in the Bronx, New York, in 1954 and grew up there. His mother was a schoolteacher. "I thought all kids knew about art from their moms," he has said. He describes his heritage as "African, Euro-American, Cherokee, and Caribbean." Shortly after graduating from the State University of New York at Purchase he worked in the education departments of the Metropolitan Museum of Art and the American Museum of Natural History. Later he was an installer at the Museum of Modern Art.

In his art Fred specializes in rearranging museum collections to create his own exhibitions. In an exhibition called "Speaking in Tongues" at the de Young Museum in San Francisco, he displayed art from the collection using the exhibition style of the museum's ethnographic section. He placed a sculpture so close to a painting as to partly obscure it and labeled a painting as "painted fabric," for example. "The museum is a microcosm of the society to which it belongs," he says, "and it is impossible to see cultural biases if you are deeply embedded in the culture." He adds that "the story is shifting rapidly. When I was growing up, images of black people were singular and negative. Now they are multi-focal." The prints Fred made with us in 2004 are literally ink spots, patiently and deliberately created.

Julie Mehretu was born in Ethiopia in 1970; her father is Ethiopian, her mother American. She grew up largely in the Detroit area and still spends a lot of time there. She also spends time in Berlin, though New York is her home base. In a lecture she gave at the San Francisco Art Institute in 2008 during her second project with us (her first was in 2006), Julie spoke, almost as an aside, of "the thing that I'm chasing." I think all good artists are chasing something in their work, and this group of artists also is unselfconsciously chasing something in life. You could call it "values." (It is not money, though that—for some of them—has come.) A student asked Julie if she was "an activist," and she answered, "I think of myself as a person engaged in the world and trying to make sense of it."

Julie uses both architectural drawing and intuitive marks as structure for her enormous complex paintings. "As marks collide they create other marks,

Julie Mehretu with a big
copper plate, 2008.

and a community develops in my mind," she says. Drawing and printmaking are tools that help her think about her paintings. One of her prints is illustrated in color in plate 41; after her first project with us she told me "a painting came directly out of the prints." In her second project, she did a lot of scraping, erasing, and changing of images she had drawn on plates. "Everything becomes specks or smudges and has to be developed again," she said, and added, "in New Orleans, Detroit, Berlin, you see that type of erasure happening."

Amy Sillman, whose work you can see in plate 39, was born in 1955 in Detroit, grew up in Chicago, lives in New York and teaches part-time at Bard College, about ninety miles from New York City. She calls teaching "a kind of real politics" and adds that it is "about giving something back." When Amy worked at Crown Point in 2007, she used aquatint, a transparent medium, in a physical way, punctuating layered washy see-through marks with concentrated deeply bitten passages. She said working this way was like making an experimental film, "the kind that you don't necessarily storyboard. You go out and just shoot, and then you make sense of the footage in the editing room." The editing room was the Crown Point studio; Sillman's etchings went through permutation after permutation before she settled on their final forms.

In 1999 when I put together my *Why Draw a Landscape?* project, I had wanted to ask British painter Peter Doig (born in Scotland in 1959) to be a part of it. But locating him and acquainting him with what we do seemed daunting. A year later, however, there he was at the Berkeley Art Museum having an exhibition! Peter visited Crown Point, and agreed to come back in May 2002 to work with us. He made five color etchings, for him a big project (he releases very few paintings, often working on a single one for a year). During our project he talked about the Caribbean island of Trinidad; he had lived there as a child with his family for a few years and had visited several times since then. Three of the images in the etchings (including the one shown in plate 38) are from photographs he took there.

When Peter came back to San Francisco in November that same year to sign the prints and attend a reception in our gallery, he told us he had moved to Trinidad with his wife and four children. He is still there in 2012. Every week he shows a film in his studio, free and open to everyone in his commu-

Peter Doig, 2002.

Peter Doig, *Grand Riviere*, 2002.
Color spit bite and sugar lift aquatints,
14½ × 16¾ inches.

nity. He usually starts his paintings with an image from a film or photograph, something that seems telling or poignant to him. It's "like a map," he says, "a way of giving me a foot into a kind of reality I want." He has spoken about "collective reality" and about a particular painting as "a memory, a flashback, or a dream." His work has a narrative feeling but is not linear. Peter's art is strikingly original and influential, and his move to Trinidad has not diminished those qualities.

The year we worked with Peter at Crown Point, I went to the North Pole, and on that trip I had a layover in London. At the Victoria Miro Gallery, Peter introduced me to Chris Ofili. Chris was born in England in 1968. In his exhibition, "The Upper Room," were thirteen paintings of monkeys in deep colors, each one spotlighted and supported by two pedestals of elephant dung. (After a trip to Africa, Chris had begun to use the dung in his work—the mayor of

New York in 1999, Rudy Giuliani, had a public angry fit over a painting of Chris's shown in Brooklyn. It was a painting of a black Virgin Mary with one bare breast made of elephant dung.)

When I walked into "The Upper Room," I stood there for a moment and I was suddenly happy. Simple as that, and just for a few moments, but it was a memorable and distinct feeling. Of course you were happy then, I tell myself. You'd just been to the North Pole. And that's true. But the odd quick happy feeling came to me again six years later when I walked into our Crown

Chris Ofili working on *Rainbow*, 2008.

Point Gallery and saw, unexpectedly, a wall of newly hung images from a series of small etchings Chris had made called *Rainbow* (plate 45). I stood absorbed in them, feeling happy. "It's just like the 'The Upper Room,' " I said to Valerie.

"But I thought that was an installation work," she said. "Big paintings, bright colors."

"Elephant dung, glitter," I continued her thought. "We have none of that. It's the strangest thing. He's trapped the same feeling using none of the same means, comparatively no means at all."

Chris's project at Crown Point was in November 2008. A few artist friends, including Chris with his wife and two-year-old daughter, gathered in Tom's and my living room on the night Barack Obama was elected president of the United States. When the count went over the top, we all cheered, the child jumping, clapping, and laughing. Chris moved solemnly around the room shaking hands formally. "Congratulations," he said to each one of us individually. "Congratulations."

Tomma Abts, who—like Chris Ofili—had won the prestigious Turner Prize, given by the Tate Gallery in London, worked with us in 2009. Tomma was born in Germany and lives in London. In an interview for our newsletter, Valerie asked her if her prints are a synthesis of painting and drawing. She replied that they are not. "I think they occupy their own place," she said.

Laura Owens, *Untitled (LO 271)*, 2004 (left). Color spit bite aquatint with aquatint and soft ground etching, 24 × 20 inches. Laura in the studio (below).

"The imagery evolved from the etching technique. In the drawings the empty space is the background; it's just the paper. In my etchings the background has a more material quality. It is, of course, not as material as in the paintings, where there is always an ambiguous relationship between background and foreground." You can see the complexity of this thought in her print *Untitled (Brushstroke),* illustrated in plate 40. Tomma's prints, drawings, and paintings are restrained in size and thoughtful in character.

The biggest print illustrated in our color plate section (plate 44) is by Laura Owens, done in 2010 in her second project with us (the first was in 2004). The three-panel aquatint, presented in three frames, extends across almost eight feet on a wall. It is an ocean scene with rolling waves, blue sky tinged with pink, dark clouds rolling in and then withdrawing. The space is deep, pulling you into it with a strong physicality. There are little pink stars in the dark clouds. Laura has no embarrassment about "girlie" pictures, and her work in general has what she has called "an aura of acceptance of whatever has happened."

On the Internet I found a photo of a painting of Laura's using the ocean subject. It fills a very large wall; a person in the photo is dwarfed by it. Sometimes people call prints "poor man's paintings," and that's OK, but it's more important to me that prints are nearly always human in scale. Laura's print hangs on my office wall, and—large as it is—I hold my own.

The print and the painting, by the way, are related, but they are not the same image. "Anything I start with is just a framework to get going," Laura told an audience at the San Francisco Museum of Modern Art—she and I were on a panel discussion there while she was working on the ocean print in 2010. "Once you pull the first proof off the plate, you have to take the plate into account. You can still try to guide the print by using your working drawing, but etching is so specific. It's more important to be doing etching than to be following a particular work."

Edgar Bryan, *The Surrealist*, 2008. Color spit bite aquatint and aquatint with soft ground etching, 15 × 15½ inches.

An audience member wondered what "doing etching" means. "You come with a lot of intentions," Laura answered. "And then you get working and you start to see what can be done. The more I think I understand etching, the more I see there is a real connection to my painting, mainly because of the layering. But it's really crazy. It's really hard. I want things to be very immediate on the plate. So I have to concentrate. What you are drawing on the left is going to be on the right in the picture. You have to take your brain and make it do that with your hand. And then there's, like, five or six plates!" She laughs, and the audience laughs with her. Laura Owens was born in Ohio in 1970. She lives in Los Angeles, with her husband, artist Edgar Bryan, and their two children.

Edgar Bryan was born in Alabama in 1970. The project at Crown Point in which he did the self-portrait on this page was in 2008. That same year, Roberta Smith wrote of his "sweet, sharp meditations" in her *New York Times* review of his first show in New York. Edgar spent five years in the Air Force before attending the Art Institute of Chicago, where he received his BFA in 1998. In his self-portrait he is at a toy easel, happy, working, keeping busy. I think it's about life, not art.

Mamma Andersson and Jockum Nordström, *Hunter*, 2010. Color spit bite and sugar lift aquatints with aquatint and soft ground etching, 15½ × 22 inches.

Jockum painting on a plate, 2008.

Our Crown Point Press artists of the new century include another couple with a life together: Jockum Nordström and Karin "Mamma" Andersson. (*Karin* combined with *Andersson* is a common name in Sweden, so Karin shows her art under the name *Mamma Andersson*.) Karin and the couple's two sons, aged seventeen and twenty-one, visited during Jockum's project with us in 2008 — Karin came back for a project of her own later that year. Jockum was born in a suburb of Stockholm in 1963, Karin in northern Sweden, near the Arctic Circle, in 1962. Both have distinguished exhibition records including one-person surveys at Stockholm's Moderna Museet. Both are represented by a major New York gallery, David Zwirner. As well as doing an etching project with each of them separately, we also did one in which they collaborated with one another, working together on the same plates. That project was their idea and is surprising because the two of them work from different approaches, as you can see by looking at their individual prints in plates 42 and 43. One of the jointly made images is on this page.

In Jockum's approach everything is flat. He came to Crown Point with a suitcase full of cut-out paper figures of people, houses, sticks, bugs, trees, furniture, all of them painted with watercolor. He spread them on a table and selected images from that abundance of material, ordering and reordering them, laying out the figures and their props on a sheet of copper, then tracing, redrawing, and aquatinting each one onto the metal. "Images are flat things," he said. "Collage is a flat way to see the world."

Karin's world, on the other hand, is dimensional, inspired by theater and film. We can see that the image shown in plate 43, *Room Under the Influence*, is a stage set—there are curtains at the edges. To her, film and theater register as captured stills—she is unlike Peter Doig, who sees them as moving. Karin's work has a dreamlike edge despite its apparent solidity; she usually works from photographs, often old ones. "One hundred years ago or a few years ago, it doesn't matter," she says. She speaks of a photograph, film still, or theater set as "a small story in a small space. To make a concentrated feeling for something, I have to reduce it to the few small things that can tell a story."

The story of how we met Jockum and Karin is one of serendipity. Anders Krüger, curator at Grafikens Hus, a printmaking workshop and gallery located in a small town near Stockholm, proposed finding a Swedish artist for us; he would approach anyone we chose. His organization had received a grant to help Swedish artists do projects overseas and would pay the travel expenses. We asked if Jockum Nordström might be available—Bob Bechtle had suggested him to us, but we had not yet acted on that recommendation.

By coincidence, the grant to Grafikens Hus originated in San Francisco with the Barbro Osher Pro Suecia Foundation, and Barbro Osher has become a frequent visitor to Crown Point. The grant helped us indirectly by opening the door to our projects with Jockum and Karin. It helped the artists indirectly by providing their introduction to us. It helped Grafikens Hus directly: its gallery sold some prints and received commissions, and the gallery held exhibitions of two famous Swedish artists and of Crown Point work by other artists. Grafikens Hus also sent a printer/teacher, Jenny Olsson, to Crown Point for training through our workshop and intern programs. Overall, it seems to me, the project demonstrates a foundation functioning effectively. The foundation gave the curator latitude; the curator gave Crown Point latitude. He started out by asking what would work for us.

In 2005, we brought an artist from China to work with us. Contemporary Chinese art was at a high point of popularity in the Western world—a handful of artist millionaires were created in China at the end of the twentieth century. But underneath radical (for China) subject matter that often mocks the state, the broad brushstroke figure painting of many of the newly famous

Wilson Shieh, *Baby*, 2005. Color direct gravure with aquatint and spit bite aquatint printed on gampi paper chine collé, 15½ × 16 inches.

Wilson working on an aquatint plate for *Baby*.

Chinese painters looks like Russian-style social realist art. It was being taught in art schools when we were going to China in the 1980s, and to me, the art based on it doesn't seem very original.

Wilson Shieh is different. He is young, born in 1970 in Hong Kong. His haunting images are so finely and intently tuned that they seem new despite the fact that his technical approach is hundreds of years old. "Before I learned the fine-brush technique, I considered this style as just a kind of antique craftsmanship," he has said. "But, after all, as you can see, I have adopted the fine-brush manner in my work. The ancient sense of beauty looks fresh to contemporary eyes."

At the edge of the Taklamakan Desert in northern China near the oasis town of Dunhuang are the Mogao Caves, decorated over the course of a thousand years, from the fourth century to the fourteenth, by the best artists in China. I have visited these caves and seen there many beautifully preserved paintings in the fine-brush tradition that Wilson Shieh is using. In the fourteenth century as Mongol warriors approached, the caves were sealed. They remained sealed, the paintings protected in the dry air, for the following six hundred years.

The fine-brush technique depends on swelling and thinning lines fluidly and precisely drawn. Many of the caves' paintings are of colorful flying dancers, musicians, and holy men with halos. They guard (as our guide explained) the different territories of people's lives: compassion, knowledge, the future. The Diamond Sutra, the world's oldest printed book, was found in a cave at Dunhuang. It was printed in 868. Here is a stanza from it:

This fleeting world is like a star at dawn, a bubble in a stream,
a flash of lightning in a summer cloud, a flickering lamp, a phantom,
and a dream.

Jiaohe is a ruined city not far from Dunhuang. It grew and thrived for fifteen hundred years from the second century BC until the Mongols destroyed it at the time the Mogao Caves were sealed. Jiaohe today sits in the windswept desert as a vast network of dun-colored mounds, most of them with windows and doors, some with towers, some with niches for storage or for statues. The city is bleak and deserted, but its heart still beats in the Mogao Caves and in the British Museum, which owns the printed Diamond Sutra and also the Lotus Sutra, a manuscript dated 722, found in the ruins of Jiaohe. Life is short. Art is long. Not only do human beings protect works of art and perpetuate them, but also new art is always being made. If an art style or technique has been set aside, put away, it can be picked up again at any moment, as Wilson Shieh has picked up the fine-brush technique in the twenty-first century and applied it to his way of seeing the world.

Is it possible to imagine an art approach being used today that is even older than the one that Shieh has adopted? Yes! A cave drawing in Australia has been carbon dated as 28,000 years old, and it is similar in style to paintings being done by Aboriginal artists living and working in Australia today. Similar doesn't mean the same, however. Jennifer Isaacs, who has organized shows and written a good deal about this art, makes clear that its forms are not "primordial" but are the "changing and highly responsive art forms of modern non-Western peoples."

In 2004 Crown Point Press published nine prints by Dorothy Napangardi, an indigenous Warlpiri artist originally from the Tanami Desert region of Central Australia. The Warlpiri tradition is loosely called "dreaming"—*jukurrpa* in Dorothy's language—and it describes the origins and

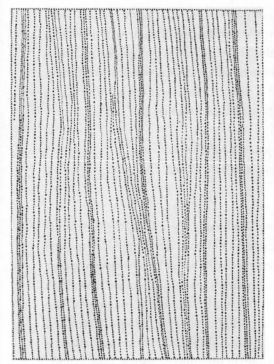

Clockwise from above: Dorothy Napangardi, *Salt on Mina Mina*, 2004. Sugar lift aquatint printed on gampi paper chine collé, 23¾ × 17¾ inches. Dorothy with printer Dena Schuckit. Dorothy dotting a plate.

journeys of ancestral beings in the land. The art is maplike, identifying sacred spots, places in which the spirits presently reside. Dorothy settled into her style in 1998 when she put aside references to animals and plants and began constructing her paintings entirely of dots.

Dorothy's home area of Mina Mina is significant to Warlpiri speakers as the place where legendary digging sticks emerged from the ground and were taken up by women ancestors who danced with them, creating life forms and features of the land as they went. In her art, she sees the paths of the women from above and creates flowing interconnecting lines by patiently and precisely accumulating dots. Dorothy has had success in the art world; a painting of hers sold for more than $130,000 at auction in 2004, and she won the prestigious first prize in the Telstra Art Awards in Australia in 2001. She has been able to provide several Toyotas and other useful items for her relatives in the desert, but even more than that she values the high regard in which she is held by her community because of her wider recognition as an artist.

Our Crown Point Press project with Dorothy came about because of our workshops. In the summer of 2003, Belinda Fox, who was then chief printer and studio manager of Port Jackson Press, Melbourne, joined us for a workshop. She showed me some catalogs of Dorothy's work and suggested the project to me. I contacted Dorothy through Roslyn Premont and Lotte Waters of Gallery Gondwana in Sydney, which represents her, and Dorothy liked the idea. But she did not think she could make art far away from her homeland. We ended up sending our senior master printer at the time, Dena Schuckit, to Australia.

Dena kept a diary of her trip—we published it in our newsletter, *Overview*. Her Australian hosts took her into the indigenous area around Darwin, where, surprisingly, there is a lot of printmaking activity. She met Basil Hall, who runs Basil Hall Editions in Darwin, and also printers from Northern Editions, affiliated with Charles Darwin University. Basil Hall had taken our workshop nine years earlier in San Francisco. "He pulls out a picture of a large-haired me from 1995, my first summer at Crown Point," Dena wrote. "Basil, and the printers from Northern Editions, often work out in the bush," she continued. "If they can drag a press and material into such remote areas to make good prints, then certainly Belinda and I can make a success with Dorothy here in this well-equipped space!"

The well-equipped space was the etching studio of the National Art School in Sydney, which our Crown Point group used thanks to the generosity of Simon Cooper, the head of the printmaking department there. Dena brought the finished plates and OK to Print proofs back to San Francisco to edition, and later Dorothy made the trip here with Roslyn and Lotte. Dorothy signed the prints and we had a reception for the three of them. Dorothy doesn't talk much, but she seemed very happy about the experience. The prints are a revelation to me and to many people who see them.

To wind up this chapter, I'm going to talk about four artists who have worked at Crown Point Press in the new century using the old process of photogravure. Because my father taught me about photography in my childhood,

Pia working on a soap
ground plate.

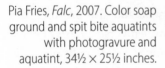

Pia Fries, *Falc*, 2007. Color soap
ground and spit bite aquatints
with photogravure and
aquatint, 34½ × 25½ inches.

I've always thought of photographs as an integral part of life (which now, with cell phone cameras and e-mail, they have inarguably become). From the early days of Crown Point's history, if an artist has wanted a photograph in an etching, we've put it in, with improving accuracy over the years—as you can see by comparing the photoetching of mine (1972) on page 17 to Chuck Close's unpublished color photogravure (2011) in plate 8. In making art, as in living lives, we use the tools we have and improve them as we can.

In the Crown Point studio, Pia Fries combined photogravure with invented hand-drawn elements; John Chiara taped a sheet of film the actual size of his print into the back of an enormous box camera that he transported to an outdoor scene; Susan Middleton made portraits of a plant, a bird, an octopus, and a frog; and Darren Almond captured experiences in Africa and Japan in moonlight and at dawn.

Pia Fries was born in Switzerland in 1955; she lives in Düsseldorf. She is a painter, and in her paintings she often uses flat, silk-screened photo images of paint alongside physical piles of troweled, caked, painted, or smeared actual paint, everything set off against a white background. "I build forms from lumps of oil paint," she has said, "and they do not relate to or mimic forms found in nature." The forms in her prints, she says, came from manipulating the materials of printmaking. "They are not at the service of formal painting issues, or representation, reference, or reproduction."

John Chiara, a photographer, lives and works in San Francisco, where he was born in 1971. A review in the *New Yorker* of his 2008 show in New York began this way: "Long exposures and their inevitable accidents give Chiara's Bay Area landscapes a fogged, dreamy look. The camera is drunk or drugged and can't quite focus." His camera, which he invented and built, is the

John Chiara, *24th at Carolina (Left)*, 2007. Color photogravure printed on gampi paper chine collé, 23½ × 19¾ inches.

size of a large closet. He drives it on the back of a pick-up truck to a landscape and usually shoots only a single large-size image directly on photographic paper (there is no negative). He develops the image inside the camera. "There's a noise in the process that I think is revealing and meaningful," he has said. "It's like the failure of memory."

Susan Middleton is a photographer who is also an author, certified diver, film producer, and (with David Liittschwager) the subject of an Emmy Award–winning National Geographic television special, *America's Endangered Species: Don't Say Goodbye*, 1997. Susan was born in Seattle in 1948 and lives in San Francisco. "I consider myself a portrait photographer," she has said. "My subjects are plants and animals, and I hope to evoke an emotional response." To photograph a live wild animal like the frog shown in this chapter she constructs a "mini-studio" with a plain backdrop, then with patience lures the

Susan Middleton, *Plain Rain Frog*, 2008. Photogravure printed on gampi paper chine collé, 8 × 11¾ inches.

Susan, with camera, and printers Ianne Kjorlie and Asa Muir-Harmony, 2008.

animal temporarily into it. Her animal portraits are unusual in isolating her subjects; this, she says, lets us perceive them as individuals. She has also worked in museums, and two of the photogravures she made with us at Crown Point are poignant images (one in color) of museum specimens of the extinct passenger pigeon, once the most abundant bird in North America.

Darren Almond is a conceptual sculptor, photographer, and filmmaker who lives in London and was born in Wigan, England, in 1971. He is best known for his *Fullmoon* photographs, time exposures taken by moonlight. A color photogravure of one of those images is in plate 46. He photographed it after hiking to the headwaters of the White Nile in Uganda (a "seriously difficult landscape to get through," he said). Darren made his first *Fullmoon* photograph, he told me, in 1998 at Lacock Abbey in Wiltshire, England, where Henry Fox Talbot made the first paper photographic negative in 1841. Soon after that invention, Talbot invented rudimentary photogravure as a way in which his photographs could be permanent and printed repeatedly.

Darren Almond made two series of photogravure prints in 2010 while he was with us at Crown Point Press. The first was a set of four *Fullmoon* images in color, the second a portfolio of five black and white images called *Civil Dawn*. Over the course of three years, Darren made several visits to a group of monks who live on Mount Hiei near Kyoto. The monks use running

Darren Almond,
Civil Dawn 1, 2010.
From a portfolio of five
photogravures printed on
gampi paper chine collé,
each 10 × 10 inches.

as their meditation. Darren ran with them, often with a camera on his shoulder, and created a six-screen video work titled *Sometimes Still*. His *Civil Dawn* photogravures also came out of those running experiences.

Civil dawn is the fleeting space of time just before dawn when there is light but the sun has not yet appeared. It is a moment when the monks, standing in the mist rising from the mountain, pause to offer a blessing over the city of Kyoto stretching below them and to put out the lanterns that they have carried through the night.

In 2012 we are only slightly into our new century. What does each of us need to know in order to survive as long as possible, however tenuously? Is there a common denominator that artists are searching for? If so, could it be, as Laura Owens has said, "an aura of acceptance of whatever has happened"? Could it be hopefulness?

Sol LeWitt in the Crown Point studio, 1997.

20.

SOL LEWITT

LEAP TO CONCLUSIONS THAT LOGIC CANNOT REACH

"Why does everybody love Sol LeWitt?" asked Peter Schjeldahl in the *New York* when a LeWitt retrospective opened at the San Francisco Museum of Modern Art in 2000. In the course of the article, Schjeldahl answered the question. LeWitt's work, he said, is "clear, accessible, and generous. . . . He structures large understandings of perception and thought. . . . His wall drawings belong in a hall of fame for parsimonious, incredibly potent inventions, like the lever and the wheel. . . . His art belongs directly to the viewer." At Sol LeWitt's death at age seventy-nine in 2007, Michael Kimmelman called him, in the *New York Times*, "a lodestar of modern American art."

Looking through old photographs, thinking about Sol, I came across my dogs, Yo Yo and Rufus, walking in front of my Berkeley house/studio. My extravagant Volvo P1800 (dented) that I had traveled to Sweden to buy in 1966 is in the driveway. The photo is from such a long time ago! Yo Yo and Rufus, escaping from the house, almost knocked Sol down the steps in 1971, the first time he arrived to make prints with me. My son, Kevin (then ten years old), and I had a cat and turtles in addition to the dogs. Sol told us about his cat, Puss.

There is a photo of Puss in Sol's book titled *Autobiography,* a bookstore book published in 1980; later that year, Sol used photoetchings for a similar book called *CrownPoint*. The pictures in both books are in individual squares laid out in grids, and in

Autobiography Puss is between a television screen shot of artist John Baldessari and a newspaper with Ted Kennedy's picture under a headline about his possible run for the presidency. Eighteen pictures are on each set of facing pages. There are no words. The spread where Puss appears is mostly made up of people in snapshots or clippings push-pinned on a wall. One snapshot is of Carol Androccio, whom I knew as Bob Feldman's assistant and whom Sol later married. If Sol had made the book a decade or so later, his and Carol's two daughters, Sofia and Eva, would have been prominent.

Notes and clippings from friends, and postcards he had received from them, are also push-pinned on the wall. Sol had circles and circles of friends, and he sent out a lot of postcards himself, usually with little drawings on them, on holidays and otherwise to keep in touch. Despite his multitude of friends, however, most of the subjects of the photos in *Autobiography* are not people, but things: lamps, dishes, pots and pans, hand-labeled music tapes, books— page after page of things. His mother and father are shown, in frames, but there is no picture of Sol. He is represented in his *Autobiography* by all the other pictures, pictures of everything in his apartment at the time.

CrownPoint, 1980, which I will talk about as we move on, was the first project Crown Point Press published of Sol's. Before that, beginning in 1971, we did about half a dozen projects with him for Parasol Press, including the monumental *Color Grids* and a complicated project called *The Location of Six Geometric Figures.* Each print in the set of six involved using commercial printing for a complex text description of how to find a particular location of a triangle, square, or other figure. Hand-printed on the same page is an etching of the figure with its locating guidelines. The texts are much more complex than the etchings.

From the beginning of his career, Sol was a sculptor. He called his sculpture works "structures," and they were usually fabricated and/or built by technicians; some are monumental and made of concrete blocks. He began doing his wall drawings, the work for which he is best known, in 1968, and when I first met him in 1971, they were becoming a primary focus for him. He would lay out a plan, maybe as complicated as *The Location of Six Geometric Figures* that I described above, maybe as simple as *Lines Not Long, Not Short, and Not Touching.* Other people would execute the plan by drawing on a wall.

A wall drawing of Sol's can be painted out later by an owner as desired and redrawn at any time by following the signed plan that Sol provided when a work was sold. He started out by allowing almost anyone to execute a work of his, sometimes unsupervised, and I remember during his first print project (we were in my basement) he received some photos of a wall drawing executed by students at an art school. His instructions had been followed to the letter, but deliberately subverted so the figure that resulted was convoluted, not straightforward. "Whoever draws it has to have good intentions," he said. It's something I have always remembered.

Eventually Sol had on his own payroll long-term a skilled and trusted person, Jo Watanabe, to draw (and oversee the drawing of) his wall drawings, and Jo also worked with him in making prints in New York. Sol loved making prints. "Whatever you see, whatever enters your understanding, comes out somehow," he said in an interview about his working methods in general. "Sometimes just doing something in a different medium or different space sets things off and makes for a change."

Sol did all the drawing in his prints himself—and, eventually, he did none of the drawing in his "major works." He made a lot of prints over the years. After 1980, when it became clear to me that Parasol Press was out of the publishing picture for Sol, Crown Point published a project with him every few years, eight all together before his death. Our last project with him was in 2002 and

Sol LeWitt, *Black Loops and Curves No. 4*, 1999. Sugar lift aquatint, 35¾ × 35¾ inches.

included a portfolio called *Not Straight Lines*: six small black and white line etchings reminiscent of the very first prints he made with me back in 1971.

Each time Sol would come for a project in the etching studio, he would spend about a week with us. He liked to start working early in the morning and take off in midafternoon. He would have a swim at the hotel then, he said, and read or watch television. This was a good system for us because it gave our printers a chance to catch up with him in etching his plates. I always gave him at least three printers, and they worked very hard; there was not much waiting, talking, or hanging out.

Sol would come with an idea, a few scribbles on paper usually, then give the printers the dimensions of the plates he wanted and tell them the processes he wanted to use. He liked to have a number of plates ready, laid out on the table. He would draw rapidly, relaxed but concentrated, one plate after another, and leave the plates on the table for the printers to etch and proof. The next day, if the work was to be in color, he added new plates. He did not make changes and corrections except to get the correct color densities. The studio wall would fill up with finished images. He would set out his project's parameters and then do as many variations as existed, if possible, or—more likely—as many as there was time to do.

Arcs From Four Corners, 1986, the print Tadashi Toda made for Sol in Japan, was different. For all the prints we did in Japan, we sent drawings ahead to Toda. Then either Connie or I would spend a week or ten days there with the artist so the artist could work with Toda to make adjustments. Sol prepared his drawing and pointed out that most of his work was executed by others, usually without his presence. But he agreed to go, mostly to humor me, I think. Carol planned to come with him, and Tom would join us as well. But, at the last minute his daughter Sofia became ill and Carol could not make the trip. Sol didn't want to go. "If the print seems to require it, I'll go at another time," he promised. "Just send me the proof by overnight mail and I'll call you right back."

Sol LeWitt, *Arcs From Four Corners*, 1986. Color woodcut, 18½ × 28½ inches.

Sol in the Crown Point studio, 1997 (opposite).

In my notebook I wrote this in Kyoto on May 26, 1986:

Sol called. He got the proofs today and he loves them. He says the print exceeds his expectations and he can't imagine it could be any better. He likes the proof with the slightly whiter white because he likes the idea of the white as a color rather than just the paper. He wants to keep the colors on the deep side—don't go lighter in the edition. Anyway, Sol is delighted and wants to include the print in a show he's having at the Tate in September.

It turned out that the exhibition at the Tate Gallery in London was a major retrospective of Sol's prints with an illustrated catalog with *Arcs From Four Corners* on its cover. As I studied the catalog, with all the prints inside that Sol had drawn directly on plates, starting in my basement in 1971, I felt a pang of distress about the prominence of *Arcs From Four Corners,* which had been done by remote control. I said to Sol that I was afraid we had let the cat out of the bag with this print. "You never really can keep cats in bags, you know," he replied.

The only other project that we did with Sol in which he didn't draw directly on plates was the one made up of photo images, *CrownPoint,* 1980. It had immediately followed his *Autobiography.* Our book resembles *Autobiography* in its approach, but not in its material form. *CrownPoint* is a

Sol LeWitt,
CrownPoint, 1980.
Page from a book
of photoetchings,
11 × 11 inches.

book of photoetchings hand-printed and hand-bound. Kevin, age eighteen and with a bookbinding business going on in the basement of our house, did the binding, and he also took the photographs, following Sol's directions. Sol arranged the photos on the pages. There are 640 two-by-two-inch images, thirty-two on each of twenty sets of facing pages.

CrownPoint shows the Crown Point Press Oakland studio in detail. The section you see here includes a desk lamp, a heat lamp, a magnifying lamp, and an odd wrought-iron lamp—my grandmother designed it and had it made in the Philippines. The page also shows our hot water heater, a ventilating hood for acid baths, and several views out of windows. No one, even me, could attach meanings to all the things in the book, but all the things are there, one after another, arranged in an orderly way without aesthetic manipulation. Besides demonstrating the way in which Sol understood the world, *CrownPoint* is also a lasting manifestation of the overriding approach to life that I have used: put one foot in front of the other.

Back in 1972, in my own book of photoetchings, *Album,* I had written that my grandfather "knew he understood the world. He did not doubt himself, his human rightness, his (and others') ability to manipulate the world into rightness." Even the Depression didn't shake his confidence, I wrote, and added that people in my parents' generation, "like me, have seen this change in the world, this lack of confidence in the rightness of humans that my grandparents, sure of themselves, never saw."

I didn't know anything about politics or economics when I wrote that; I can't imagine where the observation came from, but it seems to be correct. As I write this I am reading a book published in 2012 titled *Land of Promise,* by Michael Lind, and I am beginning to see that the business heights and depths of Crown Point Press were, in the big picture, a predictable consequence of what Lind calls "the great dismantling" of Roosevelt's New Deal. Lind briefly mentions my grandfather's name. In 1937 when the country dived back into Depression after three years of recovery, Owen Young was part of a committee of business and union leaders (John L. Lewis among them) who tried to persuade Roosevelt not to give up on his New Deal programs. As William O. Douglas said, speaking for the committee, "Mr. President, the market is going down because you cut spending."

In 1940 economist John Maynard Keynes wrote of the political impossibility of conducting "the grand experiment which would prove my case—except in war conditions." A year later, war conditions took hold and his case was proved: government stimulus pulls an economy out of Depression, and cutting spending sinks it deeper. Fiscal prudence is necessary for a nation, but not at a time when foxes have already been allowed to eat most of the hens. I wish that at the beginning of the 2008 economic crash we could have proved Keynes's theory again, as we did during World War Two—but this time without war.

Both George W. Bush, on whose watch the 2008 crash came, and President Obama, who followed him, used some stimulus measures and apparently warded off the worst that could happen, although the national recovery from what did happen has been slow. On the Charlie Rose television interview program in the week in which I am writing, Timothy Geithner, the secretary of the treasury said, "It will take years, still, and not just to repair direct damage—there is a huge erosion in people's confidence."

I've been keeping Crown Point Press alive for fifty years, and there have been crises, serious ones, as you have seen in the stories in this book. But I

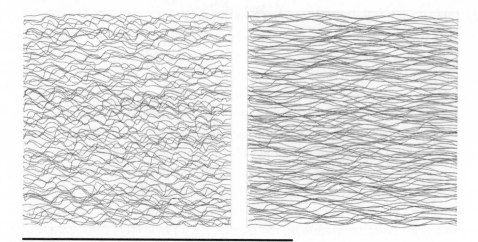

Sol LeWitt, *Not Straight Lines*, 2003. Two from a portfolio
of six hard ground etching, each 6 × 6 inches.

have never felt unsure of its staying alive for any extended period, and I am
not unsure of that now. But I have no confidence in the rightness of humans,
especially when they are banded together as corporations for which making
money is the stated purpose above all other purposes.

Looking back to the 1970s, when Crown Point was mostly working for
Parasol, I see that Michael Lind speaks of a "decade of crisis." He starts with
Peter Drucker (my business guru) saying, "Companies do not make money;
companies make shoes." But soon the concept of conglomerates took hold
and "it did not necessarily matter what a company made as long as it made
money."

Lind quotes an executive at a 1974 conference who worried that in
the aftermath of President Lyndon Johnson's Great Society "the have-
nots are gaining steadily more political power to distribute the wealth
downward." Since President Ronald Reagan's "supply-side" economics
took hold, however, the have-nots have not had political power. Little by
little, the voting public has been swallowing Reagan's catchy notion that
government is the problem, not the solution, and with that attitude, there
are in government few possibilities for solutions that can protect the rest of
us from money-oriented corporations. If Mitt Romney, the head of one of
those corporations, wins the presidential election upcoming as I write this,

we will be (to extend the fable I referred to earlier) putting a fox in charge of all the henhouses in the nation.

As our country navigated the eighties and the nineties, Michael Lind explains, financial regulations were cut away by administrations of both the Republican and Democratic parties; industry was deregulated, unions decimated. A crisis in the savings and loan industry, bankruptcies of airlines, and banking/financial manipulation scams by Enron and others ensued. A "bubble economy" blew itself up and down in bubble fashion until the bubble burst dramatically in 2008.

Lind talks about "too much money going to the rich, who use it to gamble on assets, rather than the middle class and the poor, who would have spent the money on goods and services generated in the productive economy." Of course, art is one of the assets the rich have been gambling on. Many of the artists I have written about in this book have become rich since I have known them—but they have done it by making "shoes," not by making money.

In helping artists in their work, Crown Point has prospered by selling some of the "shoes" and holding others for a rainy day. Then, after an earthquake destroyed my second investment in physical space (my first was a New York gallery), I exchanged many "shoes" for ownership of a commercial

building. It provides a home for Crown Point Press and also real estate that we can rent for income. Our first major tenant, the restaurant Hawthorne Lane, was in our building for fifteen years but succumbed to the 2008 crash and moved out in the first weeks of 2010.

In early fall that same year, Corey Lee, after redesigning and rebuilding the space with the 22 Hawthorne Street address, opened his restaurant Benu there. A little less than a year later, the *Michelin Guide* awarded Benu two stars. The Huffington Post asked, "Is Benu just a flash in the pan, or is it really the next big restaurant in the

Chef Corey Lee in Benu's kitchen, 2012.

Sol LeWitt, *Irregular, Angular Brushstrokes*,
1997. Color sugar lift aquatint,
39½ × 29¾ inches.

Proofing for Sol in the
Crown Point studio, 1997.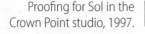

world?" The *Wall Street Journal* wrote about a revitalization of San Francisco as a "culinary capital." It reported that "Celebrity chef David Chang hailed chef Corey Lee's South of Market–district restaurant Benu the best in the country." I hear that foodies from around the world, especially Asia, are arranging trips to San Francisco around reservations at Benu. Corey Lee was born in Korea in 1977 and grew up in New York. He creates food at Benu that is surprising and delicious. I think I'm beginning to believe something I learned in China: favorable forces escape from the earth in places of beauty. Our Crown Point Press building, the building that luck provided us, is such a place.

In 2012 the Crown Point Press building, with its three addresses, is fully occupied. Crown Point Press, of course, is still at 20 Hawthorne Street, upstairs, and Adrienne Fish's bookstore and gallery, 871 Fine Arts, is on the lower level. At the 657 Howard Street address we have an Internet company called Pocket Change. From the corridor into our studio we can look down through our light well to see young people tap-tapping all day long on their computers.

In a video interview taped in 1999 by the San Francisco Museum of Modern Art when Sol LeWitt had a retrospective there, Sol talked about a time before our Internet people were born, the 1960s, when he and his friends were young artists in New York. "Everyone was really interested in starting with square one, getting rid of previous art influences and trying to find new ways of doing things," he said. "The abstract expressionists made great works, but the great work had already been done. Only ripples were coming off at that time." Sol and his friends looked back to constructivism and futurism, which were essentially optimistic movements, and rejected dada and surrealism, which were in many ways pessimistic. Abstract expressionism, which came out of surrealism, was about the individual artist, tortured, self-possessed, and alone in his studio.

Sol and his friends took an opposite approach. Because Sol famously wrote that "the idea becomes a machine that makes the art," he is sometimes described as a rationalist. But that was never the case. At the beginning of this chapter when I talked about Sol's book *Autobiography,* I described a photo in it of the Los Angeles artist John Baldessari. It is a still from a video called *Baldessari Sings LeWitt.*

Baldessari has a mustache; his shoulder-length hair hangs straight down, partly over one eye. His singing is dutiful and not very tuneful. He is mostly looking at the paper he is holding. In the video he sings the entire set of Sol's thirty-five *Sentences on Conceptual Art.* (They were published in 1969 in two small artist-run journals: *0-9* in New York and *Art-Language* in London.)

> *1. Conceptual artists are mystics rather than rationalists. They leap*
>   *to conclusions that logic cannot reach.*
> *2. Rational judgments repeat rational judgments.*
> *3. Irrational judgments lead to new experience.*
> *4. Formal art is essentially rational.*
> *5. Irrational thought should be followed absolutely and logically.*

And so on, for thirty-five sentences. Baldessari's performance is humorous, but also it is an homage. Sol LeWitt didn't apply his thinking to achieve desired ends. He stood rationalism on its head and used its procedures in the service of something beyond reason and beyond the self. By following through on irrational judgments in a rational way, he subverted his own taste and the subjectivity that he knew is almost inescapable.

Sol was comfortable and quietly natural in relating to others and to the world, both personally and in his art, in ways that are absolutely honest. He is one of the few artists of our times whose place in history is assured; no one I know who is acquainted with contemporary art would argue otherwise. This is encouraging, because in the greatest art, we see what's coming, not what's past. I hope the future holds for all of us what Sol's art demonstrates: beauty, simplicity, optimism, and a surprising range of ideas.

Sol LeWitt, *Stars–Light Center–9 Pointed*, 1983. One from a set of seven aquatints, 16½ × 16½ inches.

PLATE I **Markus Raetz**

Flourish, 2001
Photogravure printed in black and
red on gampi paper chine collé,
21½ × 18¼ inch image on 31 × 27½
inch sheet, edition 60. Printed by
Case Hudson.

PLATE 2 **John Cage**

Changes and Disappearances #31, 1979–82
One in a series of 35 color etchings with
photoetching, engraving, and drypoint in
two impressions each, 11 × 22 inches.
Printed by Lilah Toland

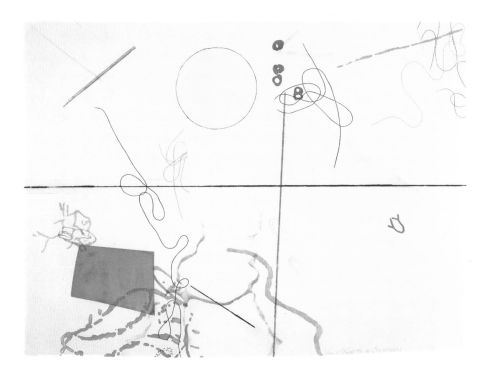

PLATE 3 **John Cage**

Dereau #37, 1982
One in a series of 38 color etchings with
aquatint, engraving, photoetching, and
drypoint, 18½ × 24½ inches. Printed by
Lilah Toland.

PLATE 4 **Wayne Thiebaud**

Park Place, 1995
Color hard ground etching with drypoint,
spit bite aquatint, and aquatint, 29¼ ×
20½ inch image on 39½ × 29¾ inch sheet,
edition 50. Printed by Daria Sywulak.

PLATE 5   **Wayne Thiebaud**

Big Suckers, 1971
Color aquatint, 17½ × 22 inch image on
22 × 30 inch sheet, edition 50. Printed
by Kathan Brown at Crown Point Press.
Published by Parasol Press.

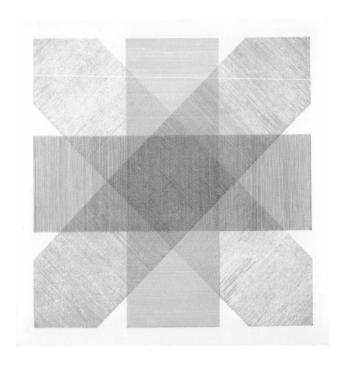

PLATE 6   **Sol LeWitt**

*Bands of Color in Four Directions
& All Combinations,* 1971
From a set of 16 color hard ground
etchings, 21 × 21 inches, edition 25.
Printed by Kathan Brown at Crown Point
Press. Published by Parasol Press.

PLATE 7 **Kathan Brown**

Ponape, 1982
Color photoetching from the bound
book *Paradise,* 6¾ × 9½ inch image
on 13 × 15½ inch sheet, edition 10.
Printed by Lilah Toland.

PLATE 8 **Chuck Close**

Untitled self-portrait, 2010
Color photogravure, 28½ × 23½
inch image on 35¼ × 30 inch
sheet, unpublished.

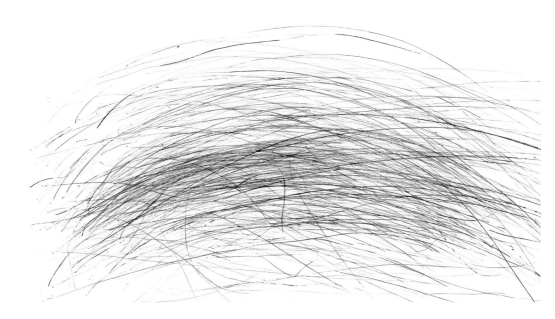

PLATE 9 **Tom Marioni**

Flying with Friends (Drypoint), 2000
Color drypoint, 33¼ × 59¾ inches,
edition 15. Printed by Dena Schuckit.

PLATE 10 **Pat Steir**

When I Think of Venice, 1980
Color spit bite and sugar lift aquatints with
aquatint, drypoint, and hard ground and
soft ground etching, 36 × 48 inch image on
42 × 55¼ inch sheet, edition 35. Printed by
Hidekatsu Takada.

Vito Acconci

*3 Flags For 1 Space and 6 Regions,*1979–81
Color photoetching on six sheets of paper
72 × 64 inches, edition 25. Printed by
Nancy Anello.

PLATE 12 **Wayne Thiebaud**

Dark Cake, 1983
Color woodcut, 15 × 17½ inch
image on 20¼ × 22¼ inch sheet,
edition 200. Printed by Tadashi Toda
at Shi Un Do Studio, Kyoto, Japan.
Published by Crown Point Press.

PLATE 13   **Chuck Close**

Leslie, 1986
Color woodcut, 24¾ × 21¼ inch image
on 31¼ × 25¼ inch sheet, edition 150.
Printed by Tadashi Toda at Shi Un Do
Studio, Kyoto, Japan. Published by
Crown Point Press.

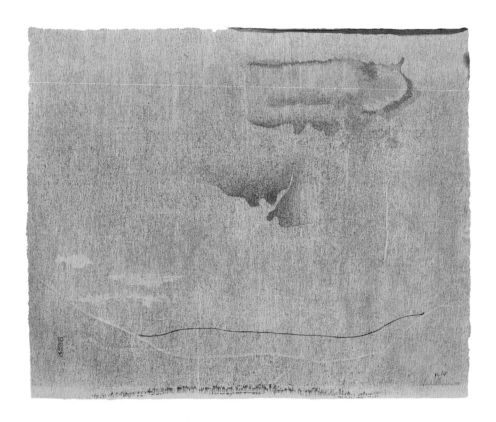

PLATE 14 **Helen Frankenthaler**

Cedar Hill, 1983
Color woodcut, 20¼ × 24¾ inches,
edition 75. Printed by Tadashi Toda
at Shi Un Do Studio, Kyoto, Japan.
Published by Crown Point Press.

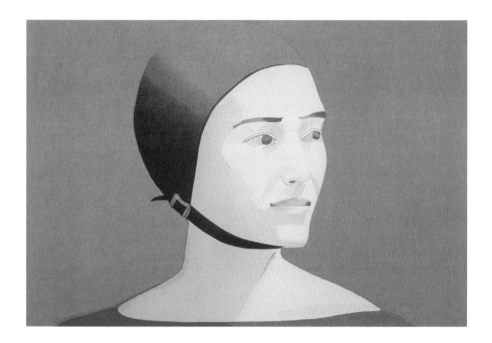

PLATE 15 **Alex Katz**

The Green Cap, 1985
Color woodcut, 12¼ × 18 inch image
on 17½ × 24 inch sheet, edition 200.
Printed by Tadashi Toda at Shi Un Do
Studio, Kyoto, Japan. Published by
Crown Point Press.

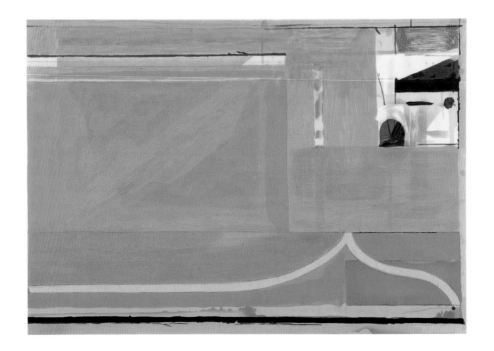

PLATE 16 **Richard Diebenkorn**

Ochre, 1983
Color woodcut, 25 × 35¾ inch
image on 27½ × 38¼ inch sheet,
edition 200. Printed by Tadashi Toda
at Shi Un Do Studio, Kyoto, Japan.
Published by Crown Point Press.

PLATE 17 **Richard Diebenkorn**

Blue, 1984
Color woodcut, 40 × 25 inch image
on 42¼ × 27 inch sheet, edition 200.
Printed by Tadashi Toda at Shi Un Do
Studio, Kyoto, Japan. Published by
Crown Point Press.

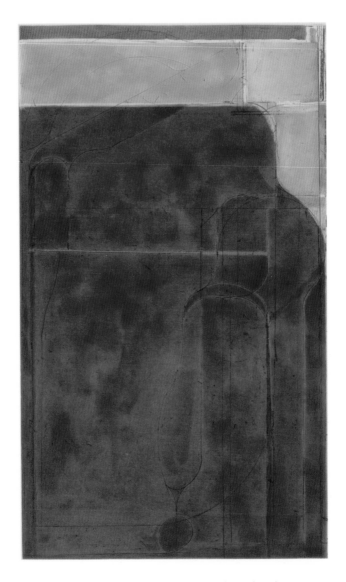

PLATE 18 **Richard Diebenkorn**

Large Bright Blue, 1980
Color spit bite aquatint with aquatint
and soft ground etching, 24 × 14½ inch
image on 40 × 26 inch sheet, edition 35.
Printed by Lilah Toland.

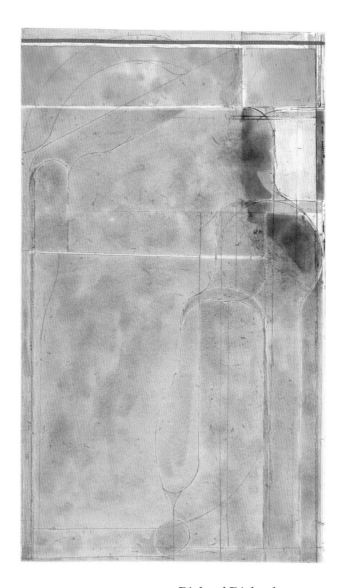

PLATE 19 **Richard Diebenkorn**
Large Light Blue, 1980
Color spit bite aquatint with aquatint
and soft ground etching, 24 × 14½ inch
image on 40 × 26 inch sheet, edition 35.
Printed by Lilah Toland.

PLATE 20 **Richard Diebenkorn**

Green, 1986
Color spit bite aquatint with soap
ground aquatint and drypoint, 45 × 35¼
inch image on 53¾ × 41½ inch sheet,
edition 60. Printed by Marcia Bartholme.

PLATE 21 **Francesco Clemente**

Untitled, 1984
Color woodcut, 14 × 20 inch image on
16¾ × 22½ inch sheet, edition 200.
Printed by Tadashi Toda at Shi Un Do
Studio, Kyoto, Japan. Published by
Crown Point Press.

PLATE 22 **William T. Wiley**

Eerie Grotto? Okini, 1982
Color woodcut, 21 × 27 inch image
on 22½ × 29½ inch sheet, edition 200.
Printed by Tadashi Toda at Shi Un Do
Studio, Kyoto, Japan. Published by
Crown Point Press.

PLATE 23 **Al Held**

Liv, 1992
Color hard ground etching with aquatint,
35½ × 44¾ inch image on 40½ × 54¼ inch
sheet, edition 30. Printed by Renée Bott.

PLATE 24 **Bertrand Lavier**

Untitled Modern Painting 1, 1987
Color aquatint with spit bite aquatint
and soft ground etching, 34 × 34
inch image on 44¾ × 40½ inch sheet,
edition 25. Printed by Mark Callen.

PLATE 25 **Alex Katz**

Reclining Figure, 1987
Color aquatint, 36 × 43 inches, edition 60.
Printed by Doris Simmelink.

PLATE 26　**Robert Bechtle**

Potrero Houses—Pennsylvania Avenue, 1989
Color woodcut printed on silk, mounted on
rag paper, 11 × 16 inch image on 27 × 26¼
inch sheet, edition 38. Printing supervised by
Sun Shumei at Rong Bao Zhai Studio, Beijing,
China. Published by Crown Point Press.

PLATE 27 **Robert Bechtle**

Albany Monte Carlo, 1990
Color woodcut printed on silk mounted
on rag paper,10 × 14½ inch image on
26 × 25¾ inch sheet, edition 50. Printed
by Zhi Jin Gu and Zhu Di Wang at Tao
Hua Wu Studio, Suzhou, China. Published
by Crown Point Press.

PLATE 28 **Li Lin Lee**

Lucky Life, 1989
Color woodcut on silk mounted on rag
paper, 23¼ × 23¼ inch image on 30¼
× 29¼ inch sheet, edition 35. Printed by
Wang Shi Juin and Wang Yun Shao at
Rong Bao Zhai Studio, Beijing, China.
Published by Crown Point Press.

PLATE 29 **Robert Kushner**

White Anemone, State 2, 1989
Color woodcut on silk mounted on rag
paper, 11 × 15 inch image on 20½ × 23
inch sheet, edition 21. Printed by Fong Jin
Da at Tao Hua Wu Studio, Suzhou, China.
Published by Crown Point Press.

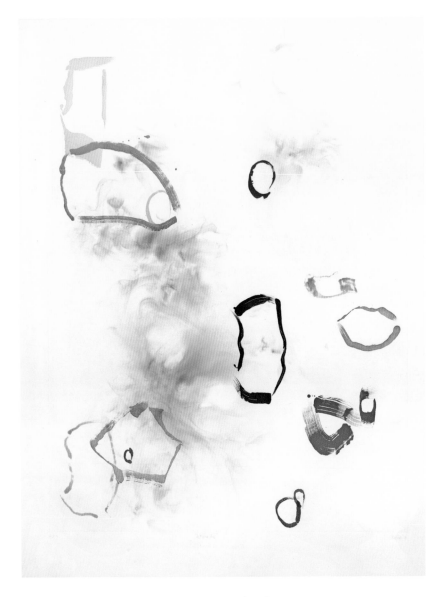

PLATE 30   **John Cage**

The Missing Stone, 1989
Color spit bite aquatint with sugar lift
aquatint on smoked paper, 45 × 36 inch
image on 54 × 41 inch sheet, edition 25.
Printed by Pamela Paulson.

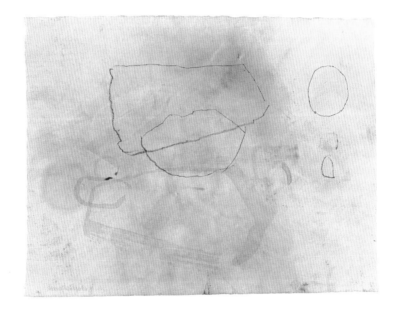

PLATE 31 **John Cage**

Smoke Weather Stone Weather #14, 1991
One from a series of 37 unique color spit
bite and sugar lift aquatints with soft
ground etching on smoked paper,
15½ × 20 inches. Printed by Paul
Mullowney.

PLATE 32 **Richard Diebenkorn**

Touched Red, 1991
Color aquatint with spit bite aquatint,
soft ground etching, and drypoint, 24 ×
16 inch image on 35¾ × 26½ inch sheet,
edition 85. Printed by Renée Bott.

PLATE 33   **John Baldessari**

To Insert: Person and Ladder (Red)/Hose/ Smoke, 1991
Photogravure with color aquatint and spit bite aquatint, 27¼ × 19 inch image on 36¼ × 27 inch sheet, edition 25. Printed by Lothar Osterburg.

PLATE 34 **Robert Bechtle**

Three Houses on Pennsylvania Avenue, 2011
Color soft ground etching with aquatint,
21½ × 31 inch image on 30½ × 39 inch
sheet, edition 40. Printed by Ianne Kjorlie.

PLATE 35 **Ed Ruscha**

Metro, Petro, Neuro, Psycho, 1982
Color soft ground etching, 15½ × 14½
inch image on 24 × 22½ inch sheet,
edition 25. Printed by Peter Pettengill.

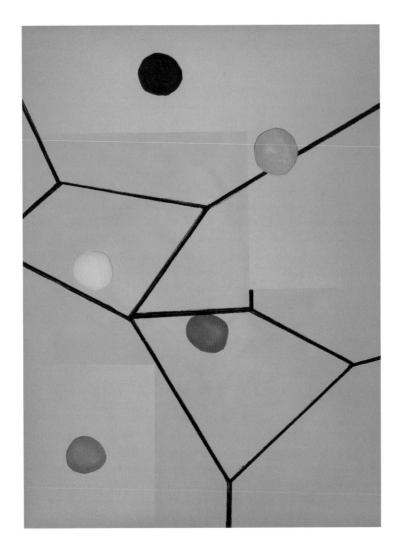

PLATE 36 **Mary Heilmann**

21st Century Fox, 1998
Color spit bite aquatint with soft ground
etching and aquatint, 29½ × 21½ inch
image on 41 × 30½ inch sheet, edition 40.
Printed by Daria Sywulak.

PLATE 37   **Anne Appleby**

Sage, 1997
Color aquatint,18½ × 18½ inch image
on 31 × 29½ inch sheet, edition 30.
Printed by Dena Schuckit.

PLATE 38 **Peter Doig**

Carrera, 2002
Color spit bite aquatint with aquatint
and hard ground and soft ground
etching, 9½ × 14½ inch image on
18½ × 22 inch sheet, edition 25.
Printed by Daria Sywulak.

PLATE 39 **Amy Sillman**

O & N, 2007
Color sugar lift and spit bite aquatints
with soft ground etching, 26 × 20 inch
image on 35 × 28 inch sheet, edition 20.
Printed by Catherine Brooks.

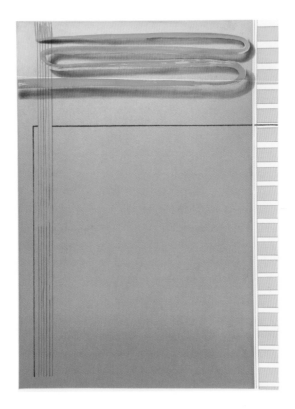

PLATE 40 **Tomma Abts**

Untitled (brushstroke), 2009
Color water bite aquatint with aquatint,
hard ground etching, and drypoint,
17⅝ × 12⅞ inch image on 23 × 17⅝ inch
sheet, edition 20. Printed by Ianne Kjorlie.

PLATE 41 **Julie Mehretu**

Diffraction, 2005
Color sugar lift aquatint with aquatint, spit
bite aquatint, and hard ground etching on
gampi paper chine collé, 27¾ × 39¾ inch
image on 35½ × 46¾ inch sheet, edition 35.
Printed by Dena Schuckit.

PLATE 42   **Jockum Nordström**

Back to the Land, 2008
Color spit bite and sugar lift aquatints with
aquatint and soft ground etching, 26 × 48½
inches, edition 50. Printed by Emily York.

PLATE 43   **Mamma Andersson**

Room Under the Influence, 2008
Color spit bite aquatint with aquatint
and soft ground etching, 20¾ × 35¾
inch image on 29¾ × 43¾ inch sheet,
edition 40. Printed by Emily York.

PLATE 44 **Laura Owens**

Untitled (LO 426), 2010
Color sugar lift, spit bite and soap
ground aquatints on three sheets of
paper, each 31 × 23¼ inch image on
36½ × 28¼ inch sheet, edition 25.
Printed by Asa Muir-Harmony.

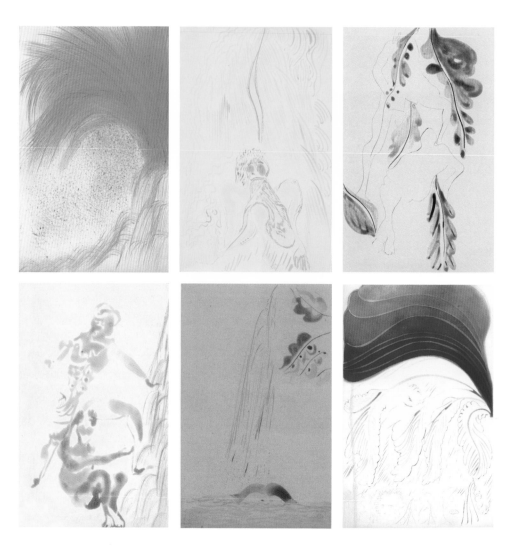

PLATE 45 **Chris Ofili**

Rainbow, 2008
Six color etchings from a series of twelve,
each 11 × 7 inch image on 20 × 15 inch
sheet, edition 10. Printed by Catherine
Brooks.

PLATE 46 **Darren Almond**

*Fullmoon@Rwenzori:
Mountains of the Moon*, 2010
Color photogravure, 20 × 20 inch image
on 29¼ × 28½ inch sheet, edition 10.
Printed by Asa Muir-Harmony.

PLATE 47 **Sol LeWitt**

Curvy Brushstrokes I, 1997
Color sugar lift aquatint, 39¾ × 14¾
inch image on 52½ × 26 inch sheet,
edition 25. Printed by Daria Sywulak.

ACKNOWLEDGMENTS

A memoir is a special kind of book, and this one is unusually special in that only seven people, besides myself (and its printers in Hong Kong), have been directly involved in making it, and I have known six of them a very long time.

Sasha Baguskas, as the book goes to press, is in her eighteenth year at Crown Point. She started as an intern in 1994 and soon gained desktop publishing skills. *Know That You Are Lucky* sits at the top of a tower of nine books she has produced in-house. In addition to doing most of the computer work, Sasha has selected many of the pictures and situated them into the layout, organized and coordinated everything (and everybody), and remained unfailingly cheerful. It is impossible to acknowledge her contribution strongly enough.

Laura Lovett designed *Know That You Are Lucky,* and I am feeling so very lucky that she was available to do that. Eighteen years ago, when she was working for Chronicle Books, she designed *Ink, Paper, Metal, Wood,* and I have always thought that a good part of the success of that early book of mine was due to its beautiful design. Working with her again has brought one revelation after another and has been a pleasure. Laura introduced me to Laurie Frankel, the photographer who took the openhearted cover and front-matter pictures. I am grateful for the pictures and for the opportunity to get to know Laurie.

Judith Dunham has edited all the books Crown Point Press has published, including this one, and I can't imagine what we would do without her. She combines subtlety of thought with precision of expression and a good nature; this is a rare and priceless mix. Valerie Wade, my anchor here at Crown Point, read the manuscript, gave me good advice, and buoyed my confidence. Ruth Fine generously contributed the comments on the book's jacket flap and also read the developing book as I was writing it and helped me enormously with discussions and with encouragement.

Finally, I publicly offer love and gratitude to my encourager-in-chief, my husband, Tom Marioni. Many of his good ideas are at work here.

PHOTO CREDITS

Text photography by *Kathan Brown* with the exceptions listed below, by page number:
Ben Blackwell: 231 (all). *Mildred Bowman:* 36, 37 (right). *Bradford Brown:* 55. *Stanley Brown:* 12, 14, 16, 17. *Richard Diebenkorn:* 161 (top). *Patrick Dullanty:* 37 (left), 46, 54 (bottom), 190. *Chris Felver:* 238. *Laurie Frankel:* 1, 2, 4. *Thomas John Gibbons:* 233, 263 (top), 265. *Marion Gray:* 263 (bottom), 264. *Denise Hall:* 145. *Leo Holub:* 163, 168, 169. *Anders Kruger:* 298. *Tom Marioni:* 19, 170, 222, 223, 287, 317. *Colin C. McRae:* 28, 39, 65 (left), 70, 132, 138, 140 (top), 140 (bottom), 156, 188, 191, 212, 243 (bottom), 269. *Kevin Parker:* 86, 105 (left), 108, 115 (right), 124, 126 (all). *Museum of Modern Art,* New York: 196. *National Gallery of Art,* Washington, D.C.: 261 (bottom). *Don Saff:* 107. *Brian Shure:* 205, 209. *Unknown:* 15, 32, 38, 52, 54 (top), 64, 71, 88, 93, 94, 100, 129, 132, 143, 144, 147 (left), 172, 184, 196 (right), 213, 228, 230, 253, 302, 304.

NOTES

I have woven into this book passages from my earlier writings, including *Ink, Paper, Metal, Wood* (Chronicle Books, 1996) and issues of the Crown Point Press newsletter, *Overview*. Direct quotes from artists, unless otherwise attributed, are from the Crown Point Press interview series, *View*, interviews by Robin White or Constance Lewallen.

1. INTRODUCTION

The copy of *Tristram Shandy* we used is the 1995 Modern Library Edition. The drawing Markus Raetz imitated is on page 643, as is the quote about freedom. The full title is *The Life and Opinions of Tristram Shandy, Gentleman.* It was initially published in installments between 1759 and 1767.

2. THE FAMILY STORY

My mother's saying that starts "Go as far as you can see" is attributed on the Internet to both Thomas Carlyle and J. P. Morgan.

My quote from Marjorie Kinnan Rawlings is on page 485 of *The Private Marjorie: The Love Letters of Marjorie Kinnan Rawlings to Norton S. Baskin,* edited by Rodger L. Tar (University Press of Florida, 2004).

I quote from *Lords of Finance: The Bankers Who Broke the World* by Liaquat Ahamed (Penguin Books, paperback, 2009). The quote about Owen D. Young is on page 331, and the quote from John Maynard Keynes about the Young Plan is on page 336.

I mention John Cage's "Diary: How to Improve the World (You Will Only Make Matters Worse)." The essay was written in 1968 and published in *M: Writings '67–'72* (Wesleyan University Press, 1973).

I write about some awards and accomplishments of Owen D. Young and Elwood S. Brown. I found that information on the Internet: Young's in Wikipedia and Brown's in the *Journal of Olympic History,* fall 1998.

3. JOHN CAGE

The mesostic by John Cage is from "Composition in Retrospect." It was published for the first time in *John Cage Etchings 1978–1982* (Crown Point Press, 1982).

Montaigne's quote is from *Essays 1.25,* first published in 1580.

Edward Rothstein's comment on John Cage in the *New York Times* was in a column called Classical View. It is titled "Cage Plays His Anarchy by the Rules" and was published September 20, 1992. Bernard Holland's "John Cage's Music: Room for Nearly Anything" was in Critic's Notebook, *New York Times,* August 27, 1992.

Ina Blom, a professor of art history at the University of Oslo, wrote "Signal to Noise" in *Artforum,* February 2010.

4. THE FIFTIES AND SIXTIES

I mention a study of higher education by Richard Arum and Josipa Roksa. It was reported in the *New York Times Magazine,* September 18, 2011.

I quote Robert Skidelsky from his book, *Keynes: The Return of the Master* (Public Affairs, Perseus Books Group, 2009). The quote about the "golden age" is on page 24, and the one about "the long run" is on page 80.

5. WAYNE THIEBAUD

Thiebaud's admonition to students is from a 1972 lecture in Carmel, California, sponsored by the Friends of Photography and published in its journal, *Untitled 7/8,* in 1974.

Matisse and Picasso: The Story of Their Rivalry and Friendship was published in 2003 by Icon Editions, Westwood Press, Perseus Books Group.

6. THE EARLY SEVENTIES

I quote part of a lyric from *Easter Parade,* a song written by Irving Berlin. Judy Garland sang it in the 1948 movie of that name.

I quote Sidney Felsen, a partner in Gemini G.E.L., the Los Angeles print workshop, and also John Coplans, former editor of *Artforum.* The quote from Felsen is on page 171 in *Rebels in Paradise: The Los Angeles Art Scene and the 1960s* by Hunter Dohojowska-Philp (Henry Holt, 2011). It is footnoted to Ruth Fine in an online catalog from the National Gallery of Art. The Coplans quote is on page 172.

The curator I mention from the Tate Gallery is Jeremy Lewison. He published the Brice Marden quote in *Brice Marden Prints 1961–1991* (Tate Gallery, London, 1992).

7. Pat Steir and Agnes Martin

The interview with Pat Steir in the *Brooklyn Rail* is by Phong Gui, published April 1, 2011. Pat Steir's remark about the self was made to Juliane Willi in 1988, published in *Pat Steir, Gravures, Prints 1976–1988*, Cabinet des Estampes, Geneva, and the Tate Gallery, London.

The quotes from Jeff Koons, Damien Hirst, and Matthew Barney are from Calvin Tomkins's *Lives of the Artists* (Henry Holt, 2008). In the book, Tomkins writes, "The profiles were all published in the *New Yorker* in the last decade." I quote Damien Hirst in an interview with Charlie Rose on January 12, 2012, on PBS.

The quote from Pat Steir about John Cage is from Kay Larson's essay for *Winter Paintings* (Cheim and Read, New York, 2011). Barbara Pollack's review of Steir's 2011 show at Cheim and Read is in the May 2011 *Art News*.

9. The Middle Seventies

Fareed Zakaria's television program on CNN is called *GPS* (Global Public Square). His interview with David McCullough was on December 25, 2011.

I talk about Malcolm Gladwell's *Outliers*, published in 2008 by Little, Brown and Company, and about *Thinking Fast and Slow* by Daniel Kahneman, published in 2011 by Farrar, Straus and Giroux. Mihaly Csikszentmihalyi's *Creativity: Flow and the Psychology of Discovery and Invention* was published in 1996 by HarperCollins.

Richard Field's exhibition catalog, *Recent American Etching*, from which I quote at length, was published by the Smithsonian Institution and Wesleyan University in 1975.

I mention a review in *Art News* of Dorothea Rockburne's work. It is in the September 2011 issue and is by Lilly Wei.

11. Crossing into the Eighties

Grace Glueck's article in the *New York Times* about our Ponape trip appeared on February 24, 1980.

The article on Daniel Buren in *Modern Painters* is by Coline Milliard and was published in the November 2011 issue.

The quote from Robert Atkins is from *California Magazine*, September 1982. The quote from Günter Brus is in *Günter Brus* by Arnulf Meifert (Whitechapel Gallery, London, 1980). I quote

Michel Poniatowski in *Representing Reality: Fragments from the Image Field*, the exhibition catalog from Crown Point Press. Poniatowski's comment was originally in *Pourquoi Pas?*, June 3, 1982, reprinted in *World Press Review*, October 1982, vol. 29, no. 10.

12. The Early Eighties

The quote from Karen McCready about me was the catalog for Crown Point's thirty-fifth anniversary exhibition at the California Palace of the Legion of Honor. Karen was interviewed by Ruth Fine.

The account of the discussion of the Crown Point woodcut program in Japan in the *Print Collector's Newsletter* is from the article "Collaboration East and West" in the January/February 1986 issue.

13. Richard Diebenkorn

The interview I mention with Diebenkorn was for a film in 1977 by the Los Angeles County Museum of Art in conjunction with an exhibition there. The film was remastered as a video in 2012 and shown in conjunction with the exhibition *Richard Diebenkorn: The Ocean Park Series*, curated by Sarah C. Bancroft, organized and presented by the Orange County Museum of Art and the Modern Art Museum of Fort Worth.

I quote several times from Sebastian Smee's "Richard Diebenkorn, a West Coast Painter, at His Best," a review of the above exhibition. Smee's review appeared in the April 1, 2012, *Boston Globe*.

I quote several passages from Dan Hofstadter's profile of Diebenkorn, "Almost Free of the Mirror," in the June 1, 1987, *New Yorker*.

The article by Richard B. Woodward, "When Bad Is Good," was in the April 2012 *Art News*. The information about Damien Hirst's platinum skull and its plastic siblings is in *Time* magazine, April 5, 2012, "Damien Hirst Exhibit Gift Shop Sells $58,000 Plastic Skulls," by Katherine Cooney. The quote from Paul Schimmel is in the blog Blouin Artinfo, November 19, 2007.

The quote from Andy Warhol is from page 7 of Hal Foster's *The First Pop Age* (Princeton University Press, 2012). The quote from David Brooks about Sam Spade was on the op-ed page of the April 13, 2012, *New York Times*.

14. The Middle Eighties

The quote about portraits is from *Elaine and Bill: Portrait of a Marriage* by Lee Hall (HarperCollins,

1993). The *Art in America* interview is by Rose Slivka and is in the December 1988 issue.

My quote about the work of Charline von Heyl comes from the March 2006 *Brooklyn Rail*. The author is Roger White.

The interview with Hans Haacke is from *Flash Art,* February–March 1986, and is by Paul Taylor. The quote from Tony Judt in the *New York Review of Books* appeared in the March 22, 2012, issue and is from an excerpt of "On Intellectuals and Democracy" in *Thinking the Twentieth Century*.

The article on Rammellzee was in the February 26, 2012, *New York Times*.

15. THE EARTHQUAKE

The song "Lucky, Lucky, Lucky Me" was written by Milton Berle and Buddy Arnold, circa 1950.

I quote a remark made by Al Held in the panel discussion at the California Palace of the Legion of Honor during the Crown Point exhibition there in 1998. Parts of the discussion are on the DVD called *Ink, Paper, Metal, Wood*.

The quote from Bertrand Lavier is from the website of the Museum of Modern and Contemporary Art in Geneva, Switzerland, and concerns an exhibition there in 2001.

17. THE NINETIES

My quotes from Per Kirkeby are from an interview with Eddy Devolder published in 1994 by Philippe Guimiot in Brussels.

18. ROBERT BECHTLE AND ED RUSCHA

Peter Schjeldahl spoke of Robert Bechtle's "doggedness of depiction" in the May 28, 1991, *Village Voice*.

Ruscha's quote that starts "Just do the things you want to do" is from an interview with him by Bernard Blistène in 1990 for an exhibition catalog published by the Museum Boijmans van Beuningen, Rotterdam, and the Centre Georges Pompidou, Paris. Another quote from the same interview is about not reducing things to categories. I quote Blistène's interview a third time when Ruscha speaks of his commitment to working.

Patricia Failing's article in *Art News*, April 1982, in which she quotes Ruscha about being "a good little art soldier" is titled "Edward Ruscha, Young Artist: Dead Serious About Being Nonsensical."

In Hunter Drohojowska-Phip's *Rebels in Paradise* (Henry Holt 2011), she reports the remark I quote by Richard Serra. It was related to her by Stanley Grinstein when she interviewed him. Another remark from the same interview appears a bit later.

The quote from New York art dealer Gavin Brown comes from an article by Amy Larocca in *New York* magazine, April 30, 2012. In the same issue, in an article titled "Reject the Market. Embrace the Market," Jerry Saltz discusses an out-of-kilter art scene focused on money. I quote three times from his article.

19. THE NEW CENTURY

Roberta Smith's obituary of Robert Colescott was in the *New York Times,* June 9, 2009. The quote from Fridtjof Nansen is from the first edition in English of Nansen's *Farthest North,* published by Archibald Constable and Co., London, 1897.

The quote from the *New York Times* about "powerful undercurrents" appeared on July 26, 2012. Pico Iyer wrote in the *New York Times Sunday Book Review,* July 22, 2012. Jennifer Isaacs is the author of *Spirit Country: Contemporary Australian Aboriginal Art* (Fine Arts Museums of San Francisco).

20. SOL LEWITT

The Peter Schjeldahl article in the *New Yorker* about Sol LeWitt's retrospective was published on July 15, 2002. The obituary by Michael Kimmelman was in the *New York Times* on April 9, 2007. LeWitt's book *Autobiography* was published by Multiples, Inc., New York City, and Lois and Michael K. Torf, Boston, in 1980.

In *Land of Promise* by Michael Lind (HarperCollins 2012), Owen Young's connection to Roosevelt is on page 302, John Maynard Keynes is quoted on page 307, and Peter Drucker is quoted on page 367. Lind's quote about the "have-nots" is on page 377, and about the rich on page 470.

The television interview with Treasury Secretary Timothy Geithner was with Charlie Rose on PBS, July 23, 2012. The Huffington Post blog wrote about the restaurant Benu on October 5, 2011. The *Wall Street Journal* talked about Benu on May 24, 2012.

Sol LeWitt's quote on page 319 is from his "Paragraphs on Conceptual Art," first published in the June 1967 *Artforum*.

INDEX